55 ADVANCED COMPUTER PROGRAMS IN BASIC

BY WM. SCOTT WATSON

TAB BOOKS Inc.

BLUE RIDGE SUMMIT. PA. 17214

FIRST EDITION

FIFTH PRINTING

Printed in the United States of America

Library of Congress Cataloging in Publication Data

Watson, William Scott.
    55 advanced computer programs in BASIC.

    Includes index.
    1. Basic (Computer program language) 2. Computer
programs. I. Title.
QA76.73.B3W37   001.64'24   81-9181
ISBN 0-8306-0012-4   AACR2
ISBN 0-8306-1295-5 (pbk.)

Contents

Preface

This book presents 55 useful programs in BASIC. The programs represent many different uses of the microcomputer; no matter how specialized your tastes or needs, you will most likely find a few programs herein which will be useful to you.

A valuable aspect of these programs is that they represent not only an inexpensive software library but they can be used as a means to improve your understanding of programming techniques. How? Easy! Written in skeletal form, the programs are easy to understand and easier to change. Suggested variations accompany each program description. You will doubtless think of your own variations.

So, get ready to have fun with and learn from your microcomputer.

I would like to take this opportunity to thank the following people for their help:

To *John White* of COMPUTER ANALYSTS, Rochester, PA: for his many tips and help above and beyond the call of friendship.

To *John Watson*, Chippewa, PA: for many of the business programs, and other help above and beyond the call of blood relatives (thanks, Unc!).

To *my family and friends:* for their tolerance of my folly.

To *me:* for sticking with this darn thing.

Wm. Scott Watson

5

Chapter 1
Introduction

I can remember seeing one of the first magazine advertisements for a handheld, four-function, LED readout calculator. The manufacturer's name escapes me, but I vividly recall two things about the calculator. First, it was rather large and bulky looking (compared to calculators today); and secondly, the price tag was well over $150. Five short years later, calculators the size of credit cards were flooding the market, and the now-primitive four-function calculator could be had for under 10 bucks. Perhaps this is not so shocking to the generation which witnessed both Kitty Hawk and the first man on the moon, but I am continually amazed at the hidden implications.

For many years, the very idea of even getting physically close to a computer was intimidating to the general population of this country. Those few men and women who chose to work with computers as a career were considered oddballs, stereotyped as long-haired Einsteins who chain smoked and developed ulcers early in life. The public was simply not ready for the computer to become an intimate companion, and science fiction writers had a heyday taking advantage of the public's fear of these mysterious machines. In their work, these writers created computers that devoured man in order to preserve its own "life". There were computers that teamed up to start World War III, computers that went haywire and killed astronauts, and, as a final insult, even a computer that raped a housewife on her kitchen table.

Jumping on the bandwagon, newspapers and magazines published articles regularly on computers that made mistakes and printed one thousand dollar paychecks as one million dollars. Errors on our bills were nearly always blamed on the computer, and street prophets screeched about the day when people would lose their identities and exist only as faceless numbers in some obscure computer's memory bank.

Today, you can go down to your local electronics store and buy a computer for the same price you would expect to pay for a console color television. Hundreds of thousands of microcomputers have been sold to lawyers, doctors, teachers, scientists . . . and laymen.

Once again, an extraordinary metamorphosis had taken place in the world of electronics. The computer had been made available to the common man. The once feared machine was now a cherished work-saver. Instead of walking away with egg on their faces, the newspapers and magazines which had dedicated themselves to disclaiming computers now published articles extolling the virtues of the machines and fantasized about future developments. The common man could now communicate with a computer.

Much of this success is certainly due to the creation of near-English computer languages which greatly simplified the chore of communication between man and machine. One of these languages, BASIC, has been chosen as a standard for microcomputers. BASIC is a strong computer language, is easy to learn, and in many applications is more than fast enough when it comes to execution speeds. BASIC computer language has been taught regularly in adult education courses, colleges and high schools across the country, and even in a few progressive elementary schools. The reason for this widespread interest in computer education is simple. Just as the handheld calculators have become an essential part of our society in a few short years, the true value of microcomputers will actualize in the near future. Our students must be suitably prepared to inhabit a society where the computer is as common and necessary as the telephone. If for no other reason, people must learn to understand computers out of self defense.

It is no great secret anymore that there exist huge data banks containing various types of confidential information. Chances are that if you have done any type of business on a credit arrangement, your name has found a place in one of these data banks. Over the years, this confidential data has been bought and sold (sometimes illegally) by various businesses and agencies that wish to know more about a person. It has been only recently that legislation concerning such distribution of confidential information has become a reality. However, it is the computer programmer's chief goal to overcome obstacles by alternate routes, and I must wonder how long this legislation will remain viable.

On the other side of the coin, computer theft has also become a serious threat to the business computer. I have been told by a systems analyst of a large corporation that given forty-five minutes or less with a microcomputer, he could have the darn thing spitting out as many paychecks in his name as he wished, with no record left behind in the computer. After seeing the BASIC coding of a few PAYROLL programs intended for microcomputers, any doubt of his bragging disappeared. The programmers of business oriented programs never seem to consider computer theft, and therefore do very little to prevent it. I sincerely hope that, in the near future, something is done to rectify this threat to the small businessman.

Even in the agriculture industry the microcomputer is taking its place among other farm implements. With the increasing threat of huge automated "factory" farms, many farmers are recognizing that they have no other alternative than to automate some of their operations or go broke. The microcomputer can take such time consuming chores as record keeping, animal selection and culling index operations, and leave the farmer with more time for other necessary chores. Of course this is only in the experimental stage at present, but I am convinced that in the near future, a microcomputer will be nearly as important as a tractor.

For teachers, the microcomputer has become a medium to provide the best mixture of personalized instruction and student interaction. The computer presents information to the student, quizzes the student for comprehension and retention of the information, and reinforces the information that the student did not learn sufficiently. A teacher is always on hand to help out when the computer simply cannot get its point across to the student. It is important to note that the computer does not replace the human teacher, but supplements her. Here again, computer-assisted instruction (CAI) is in its infant stage, and I expect to hear a great deal more of it in the near future.

Probably the most exciting news I have heard concerning hardware development is mass storage memory. Scientists are predicting that in the near future they will perfect a memory chip capable of containing every piece of information in the entire

Library of Congress. It will become interesting to see just how the microcomputer itself will change to accommodate an advance of this sort. Many observers predict that instead of having separate microcomputers in each home, terminals will be installed and will connect to a large computer network over the telephone. In my opinion, both systems have their advantages and disadvantages, and I would much rather see an inexpensive hybrid system.

What all of this points to is the necessity of extensive hardware and software development. From the hardware standpoint, I would certainly feel silly now had I gone out and bought one of the first handheld calculators for a hundred and fifty bucks, but it would seem just as silly to me to wait for the price of a calculator to go down from $8.95 to three bucks.

Clearly, it is the software development that will allow the use of microcomputers to increase in potential. Software is needed desperately for many different areas such as those mentioned before (teaching, agriculture, etc.), and these industries are willing to pay big bucks to the person who pioneers that field. The only way I can see this happening is to get the people in these areas involved in computers, and not to wait for the computer people to get involved in their field. This is, indeed, slowly beginning to happen as more people from different walks of life get involved with computers and realize what a computer can do for them. If there was ever an industry begging for entrepreneurs, here it is!

This book is meant for people who have learned the rudiments of programming a computer using the BASIC language. The fifty-five programs in this book represent many different uses of the microcomputer, and even the most specialized reader should find a few that will interest him or her.

I have written these programs with two primary goals in mind. First, when a person buys a computer, he or she will have an immediate need for compatible software. There are a number of sources available. There is the professional programmer, but unfortunately not many of us can afford them. There is the "canned" or storebought program market, but accumulating any number of these programs can quickly eat away your checkbook. Finally, the owner can choose to write all of the software. Although this is the cheapest method, it is also the most time consuming. This book is meant to serve as an inexpensive software library.

The other goal is to provide a forum to improve the user's understanding of advanced programming techniques, and provide the easiest environment for the user to exercise these techniques.

The programs in this book have purposely been written in skeletal form. It is left to the user to upgrade or improve these programs to personal needs or tastes. The suggested variations provided with each program should serve as a starting point for the user. The user is urged to dissect the programs and see how they work. In many cases, the user will find that the most efficient coding was not used. This was deliberately done in order to allow the concepts involved to stand out and be recognized to the experimenter.

ABOUT THE PROGRAMS IN THIS BOOK

All of the programs in this book were written and tested on a TRS-80 16K Level II computer. This does not exclude the users of other microcomputers. Check the command definition guide in Chapter 2 in order to make the necessary conversions in commands and syntax. Each program (with the exception of utility program GAM-MEM) has been written in the following format:

REMARKS - This section gives an introduction to the program and defines the purpose. The user is advised to skim through the REMARKS sections of various programs in order to decide which programs are of interest. The *REMARKS* section will also list any restrictions or important instructions necessary to use the programs effectively.

VARIABLES - Although these lists are rarely comprehensive (by nature of the program), they should provide the user with all of the neccessary information to dissect and reconstruct the programs. Also, the variable lists can be an invaluable tool for debugging. Each main variable is listed and its purpose defined in these lists.

SUGGESTED VARIATIONS - This section is designed to give the user a few ideas to improve or change the programs. The user is strongly advised not to take the programs for granted, but to take them apart and personalize them. If a change is found to be desirable, the user should save this version on cassette along with the original version, instead of making changes every time the program is used.

SAMPLE RUN - This is how the program should look when it has been entered correctly into the computer. While many of the SAMPLE RUNs do not give a complete run from start to finish of the program, enough information is given to determine whether the program is working correctly or not. The user is advised to use the same input as the sample run, and then compare the output with that of the sample run for similarities.

PROGRAM LISTING - This is the actual program listing that the user will type into the computer. *The user should note that the up arrow appears as a left bracket in the program listings.* Also, the user should realize that some lines longer than 64 characters will be continued on the next line. Do not confuse these with separate lines.

Chapter 2
Programming Hints
And Mechanical Magic

Every hard-core keyboard hacker knows that the name of the game is getting the most out of their computer, even if it means cheating a bit! Many users will be surprised (to put it mildly) to find that some of the most useful little routines were never even discussed in their operator's manual. So, it has been left up to the general population of computer owners to dig through the guts of their machines and find these routines on their own. Here is a forum of these routines, collected diligently from the many frustrated users I have come in contact with. If you are able to use even one of these routines, it may very well justify the entire cost of this book.

RECOVERING A KILLED PROGRAM

The Scenario: After spending three tedious and nerve-racking hours typing in a program listing you got from a buddy, your faithful hound Fido suddenly alarms you with his insistent demands to be let out. Groggy-eyed and hunchbacked, you obediently bid Fido *adieu* and return to your throne in front of the computer. In order to recover your concentration, you attempt to type LIST. However, your well conditioned fingers have been bushwacked by your fatigue and instead type the command NEW. Even as you realize your error, it is too late to react as your over-anxious little finger stabs the ENTER key. Oh noooooooooo! Horror of horrors! Three hours of digital turmoil thrown to the electronic cesspool. As horrendous thoughts of an early retirement for Fido cross your mind, a cool smile suddenly sweeps your face from ear to ear. "Ah!", you say, "my good buddy Scott Watson has provided me an alternative to otherwise abhorrent behavior!". You proceed to type:

☐ *POKE 17130,1*
☐ *SYSTEM*

and then answer the prompt with

☐ */11395*
☐ and finally *LIST*

It is important to CSAVE the program immediately, because any further fooling around will lose your program for good.

FOOLING AROUND WITH THE PORT

If your system does not have an expansion interface, there is only one input/output of any use to you: port 255. Even so, a variety of interesting effects can be created using this single port.

FOR I=1 TO 500: OUT 255,4: OUT 255,25: NEXT I

This little statement can really spice up a program. It causes a wavy screen effect and rattles the cassette relay. Very impressive to the unexposed!

When used inside a program, the statement OUT 255,8 will change your output to 32 characters per line format, and using OUT 255,32 will return you to the normal 64 character format. If you want to add a little sound to your programs, try the following: FOR I=1 TO 500: OUT 255,1: OUT 255,2: NEXT I In order to hear the sound, do the following:

☐ Remove any cassette in your recorder.
☐ Find the small metal lever in the rear left corner of the tape compartment of your recorder.
☐ While pressing the lever towards the back of the recorder, simultaneously press the *PLAY* and *RECORD* keys on the recorder.
☐ Disconnect the earphone and remote motor control cables from the recorder. Leave the auxiliary cable connected.
☐ Plug in an eight ohm speaker (any old thing will do) to the earphone jack.
☐ Keep all cassettes away from the speaker. The magnet can erase them (and I don't have a cure for that!).

Who says that your computer is equipped for sound?

DISABLING THE BREAK KEY

Have you ever had your computer on display somewhere and had to put up a sign saying PRESSING THE BREAK KEY WILL CAUSE IMMEDIATE ELECTROCUTION or something equally intimidating? Although typing the command CONT will cause the program to resume execution at the point it was interrupted, it will also ruin any graphics or display you had on the screen before the mishap. One alternative is running the program again, but then you lose all of your variables! This can be very depressing if it happens in the middle of the business day while running a cash register program. To make matters worse, the BREAK key is located right up next to the backspace key. In some applications, it would be much better if we could just do away with the BREAK key altogether. Hold on to your hats, folks, because this is a lot easier than you think.

Typing *POKE 16396,23* will disable the BREAK key.

Typing *POKE 16396,201* will place it back in normal function. This can be used in command mode or inside a program. Remember, the break key will stay disabled until you re-enable it. This is true even after a program has completed execution.

USE OF THE INKEY$ FUNCTION

For those of us who graduated from a primitive low-level BASIC computer, when we found that we could process direct data without the use of the ENTER key and without stopping program execution to await a user's input we felt as if we finally had the ability to run those fantastic real-time arcade games. Well, as those of us who have fooled around with the INKEY$ function have found, we were partially right and partially wrong. Though the INKEY$ does have its usefulness and deserves its place in high level BASIC, it is probably the most misused command in its various capacities. For those not yet familiar with this command, the INKEY$ function simply scans the keyboard for an instant and assigns the alphanumeric value of the key pressed during the scan into a string variable we earlier assigned to the INKEY$ command. For example, if a line in our program read 10   A$=INKEY$:IF A$=" " GOTO 10 the program, when it encountered this line, would continually scan the keyboard until a key was pressed. When a key has been pressed (assuming it was an alphanumeric key) the alphanumeric value of the key would be assigned to the string variable A$. Add the following two lines and try this short program:

```
20   PRINT "LAST KEY PRESSED— ";A$
30   GOTO 10
```

Whenever you press a key while this program is running, the key symbol will be printed out (in line #20), and the program will go back to scanning the keyboard again. Say . . . I bet the old brain gears are turning now! To put this command into practical use, let's try the following menu program:

```
10   PRINT " PRESS 'R' TO MOVE ROCKET RIGHT"
20   PRINT " PRESS 'L' TO MOVE ROCKET LEFT"
30   PRINT " PRESS 'U' TO MOVE ROCKET UP"
40   PRINT " PRESS 'D' TO MOVE ROCKET DOWN"
50   PRINT " PRESS 'P' TO FIRE PHASERS"
60   A$=INKEY$:IF A$=" " GOTO 60
70   IF A$="R" OR A$="L" OR A$="U" OR A$="D" OR
     A$="P" GOTO 80 ELSE GOTO 60
80   IF A$="R" THEN C=1
90   IF A$="L" THEN C=2
100  IF A$="U" THEN C=3
110  IF A$="D" THEN C=4
120  IF A$="P" THEN C=5
130  ON C GOTO 500,1000,1500,2000,2500
140  CLS:GOTO 10
```

By inserting the appropriate graphic routines into the line numbers specified in line #130, you could have the beginning to a fast action space game. While I won't kid you and tell you that the possibilities are endless, there are many variations of this program that can be of immense help to you. You might even find that it could replace the old "PRESS ENTER TO CONTINUE" message with the following:

```
10   PRINT "PRESS ANY KEY TO CONTINUE"
20   A$=INKEY$:IF A$=" " THEN 20
30   CLS:REM ***GAME INSTRUCTIONS START HERE***
```

One advantage to this type of routine is that the INKEY$ function does not cause an automatic linefeed like pressing the ENTER key does. Therefore, it can preserve any graphic or chart displays you have on the screen while still accepting input from the user. If you need numeric input from the user, just change the string variable to a numeric variable using a VAL(A$) statement.

You will notice that I used the U, D, R, and L keys to designate up, down, right, and left respectively. Actually, in many of the programs in this book using the above routine, I instead chose the Q, A, ;, and L keys simply because they felt more comfortable to me. You can change these with ease as you become more comfortable with the INKEY$ command. Also, we can actually use the four arrow keys to designate the appropriate directions (what would be simpler?). Try the routine below:

```
10  A$=INKEY$:IF A$="" GOTO 10
20  I=ASC(A$)
30  IF I=9 THEN PRINT "RIGHT ARROW":GOTO 10
40  IF I=8 THEN PRINT "LEFT ARROW":GOTO 10
50  IF I=10 THEN PRINT "DOWN ARROW":GOTO 10
60  IF I=91 THEN PRINT "UP ARROW":GOTO 10
```

Consult the ASCII appendix to see why these keys are read as these numbers.

YOU PEEKED!

O.K., so you've mastered the INKEY$ function and are aware of its limitations, eh? The main problem with INKEY$ lies in the fact that it can collect only one key at a time, and it automatically resets itself so that the key must be constantly stabbed like a jackhammer in order for a command to be continually read. In the INKEY$ rocket example, the 'move right' key must be pressed some sixty times to move the rocket from the left hand side of the screen to the right. Also, if you are playing a two player game, you will notice that only one player's command can be read at a time, resulting in a gross loss of precision in a fast paced game. Here we will discuss using the PEEK command to directly read the keyboard.

If you examine the computer's memory map, you will see that the keyboard is scanned in a block of ROM located between decimal memory addresses 14336 and 15359. The keyboard itself is nothing more than an eight-by-eight matrix of normally open switches. These switches are monitored within the above memory locations in the following way. Certain addresses within the keyboard memory block monitor a certain row of switches. When a key is depressed, a value corresponding to the key appears in its memory address. Consult Table 2-1 for these memory addresses, the keys monitored by these addresses, and the values representing these keys.

Back with us again? Type in the following program:

```
10  A=PEEK(14400)
20  PRINT@500,A
30  GOTO 10
```

RUN this program and start by typing the left arrow key. Does the value 32 appear at print location 500? If it doesn't, you've done something wrong (or else you're not looking at the right place). Press the other arrow keys and check their values against Fig. 1. Now let's try something really daring. Press the space bar. Now the ENTER key. Whoopee! Notice that the value remains on the screen only as long as you continue to press the key.

Now press the left and right arrows simultaneously. What? This value doesn't even appear on our chart! Well then, where the heck did this value of 96 come from? If we add the value of the left arrow (32) and the value of the right arrow (64) we come up with 96. You will also notice that, by the way the values are assigned, no combination of keys will ever equal the value of any one key. Therefore, we can actually process more than one key at a time. As a matter of fact, any keys on the keyboard can be read directly by the PEEK statement except for the BREAK key. This is because the computer gives high priority over the BREAK key, and will automatically process it before anything else. However, if you use the BREAK disable routine described in hint #3, you will find that you can now even utilize the BREAK key (it will return a value of four).

Another useful function of the PEEK statement is actually looking through your program memory. Load in any program of your choice, and before running it type in the following statement:

FOR X=17219 TO 32767:PRINT CHR$(PEEK(X));:NEXT X

Since this statement is executed in the command mode, there is no need for a line number. After typing this statement, press the ENTER key and the statement will be automatically executed. Use the SHIFT keys to pause the display when something interesting pops up. You may be surprised at how your program and variables are actually stored in memory. I have tried this on a particular adventure-type program and found all of its secrets. The addresses you will be PEEKing at start at address 17219 (the start of program memory) and end at address 32767 (the top of memory for a 16K machine). If you wish, you can change the address 17219 to address 0, and you will then be looking through your computer's ROM.

POKEING AROUND

Another very useful statement is the POKE command. With it, we can place any value we wish into any RAM location. You might recognize this from the method we used to disable the

Table 2-1. Addresses Within Keyboard Monitor Switches.

KEY PRESSED								PEEK ADDRESS FOR ROW	
@ A B C D E F G								14337	EN - ENTER CL - CLEAR
H I J K L M N O								14338	BR - BREAK UA - UP ARROW
P Q R S T U V W								14340	DA - DOWN ARROW LA - LEFT ARROW
X Y Z - - - -								14344	RA - RIGHT ARROW SP - SPACE BAR
0 ! " # $ % & '								14352	SK - SHIFT KEYS (left and right)
1 2 3 4 5 6 7								14368	
( ) * + < = > ?									
8 9 : ; , - . /									
EN CL BR UA DA LA RA SP								14400	Example: When the H key is pressed, PEEK (14338) will return a value of 1. When the right arrow is pressed, PEEK (14400) returns a value of 64.
SK								14464	

DATA VALUE PLACE AT PEEK LOCATION WHEN KEY IN THIS COLUMN IS PRESSED

1	2	4	8	16	32	64	128

BREAK key. However, the most useful function of POKE besides this is its ability to also access any PRINT @ position of the CRT directly through memory. Consult the computer's memory map again and you will see that the CRT video memory lies between addresses 15360 and 16383 (decimal). There is no coincidence that this block of memory contains 1024 addresses (the same number of PRINT @ positions). While in the command mode, type the following line:

FORX=15360 TO 16383:POKE X,88:NEXT X

When you press the ENTER key, you will see the entire screen fill up with the character 'X'. But why 'X', you ask? Look at the ASCII table and you will see that the ASCII code for the character 'X' is 88, the value we POKEd into each of our video memory addresses. Getting the picture? If we changed the value 88 in the above statement to 191, the screen would fill with solid graphic characters. Using POKE graphics in our programs can speed things along tremendously! While we're on the subject, don't forget that you can also PEEK any of the video memory addresses to see what is in there. If PRINT @ position 100 contained a '5', then PEEK(15460), which is 15360 plus 100, would return the value 53–, the ASCII equivalent of '5'. Using a combination of PEEK and POKE in your programs can result in some very powerful routines.

Don't be afraid to POKE around and find out what various addresses are used for. One little chuckle I found is in location 16445. Poke a value of 8 into this location and your screen is converted to a 32 characters-per-line mode. Poke a 0 into this location and you are returned to the 64 characters-per-line mode. I'm sure there are many more quirks like this just waiting for you to discover, so: POKE away!

SPEEDING THINGS UP A BIT

I wish I had a nickel for every real-time game I have spent hours writing, coding, and debugging only to find in the final analysis that it was too darn slow to be of any good. It stands to reason that the fancier your programming gets, the longer it will take to process the increased number of instructions. Outside of shucking BASIC altogether for assembler, there are a few good ways to improve the execution time of your programs: Some of these are good common sense, and others seem to be ignored frequently.

☐ *Use as few arrays and strings as possible*. Not only do these eat up a lot of memory, they can also slow you down if you use them unnecessarily.

☐ *Stay away from subroutines*. Too many GOSUBS can slow you down considerably.

☐ *Structure your programming*. While for many of us it is downright impractical to try and totally exclude any branches and subroutines completely, try to keep your programming in a block style. Jumping from place to place in the program takes time.

☐ *Delete any REM statements*. It is wise to keep two copies of a program. One that has all REM statements intact for use in debugging and examination, and another copy that is used for fast execution time.

☐ *Combine statements when possible*. If you have the capability to put more than one statement on a line, use it!

☐ *Always use variables rather than constants*. If a constant is going to be frequently used throughout a program, assign it to a variable. This saves quite a bit of time since the computer will not have to continually convert the constant to its floating point representation.

☐ *Always use integer variables in FOR-NEXT loops*. This alone can save you more time than all other suggestions combined. Of course, this will not apply when you are using a fractional STEP size in your loop for a specific purpose.

CUTTING DOWN MEMORY REQUIREMENTS

Although none of the programs in this book (with the possible exception of GAMETES) should pose any problem for a computer with 16K of memory, as the user personalizes and adds to a program the memory requirements will obviously increase. There are also many programs in this book that can be operated as is on as little as 4K of memory. Other programs will require a little fixing in order to get them below the 4K ceiling. Here are a few tips to help you cut down on memory when necessary.

☐ *Delete all REM statements*. All statements that have no actual operation in the program should be deleted. Of course, a separate documentation should be kept to aid in reference and debugging.

☐ *Delete all unnecessary spaces* from your program lines. Don't try to delete the space between the line number and the beginning of the statement.

☐ *Use low memory variables*. Integer variables use only one third as much memory as single precision variables, and only one fifth as much as double precision variables.

☐ *Use subroutines* instead of repeating statements.

☐ *Use all reserved array variables first*. Eleven subscript addresses for each array are automatically reserved by the computer. Don't forget that you can use the zero subscript too.

☐ *Keep operations simple*. Complex expressions using many levels of parentheses can really eat up your memory.

☐ *Use multiple statements*. Each new line takes a minimum of five bytes: two bytes for the line number, and one byte each for line pointer and carriage return.

Chapter 3
BASIC Statements

Although the programs in this book were constructed on a TRS-80 microcomputer using Level II BASIC, users of other brands of computers or differing dialects of BASIC are by no means excluded. All the statements used in the programs in this book will be listed and defined in this chapter. Users of other BASICs and newcomers to Level II BASIC are advised to read through this guide to determine any dissimilarities between Level II BASIC and the dialect of BASIC used by their own computer. Once these dissimilarities have been noted, it should be easy for the user to provide alternate commands or the necessary changes in syntax to convert these programs to a form compatible with the particular brand of computer and BASIC they are using.

A WORKING KNOWLEDGE

It is assumed that the reader has a working knowledge of their computer's BASIC dialect, since it is beyond the scope of this book to serve as a comprehensive guide to the BASIC language. The reader should therefore consult their computer operator's manual to discern the commands available to them, as well as the necessary syntax required by their machine.

LEVEL II COMMANDS IN THIS BOOK

Here is a definitive list of the Level II commands utilized by the programs in this book:

Input/Output Statements

PRINT—This command is used to output an expression to the output device (CRT screen in this case). If no expression is specified, the computer will print a blank line and execute a

23

carriage return. Two PRINT modifiers are addressable: the semi-colon and the comma. The comma advances the cursor to the next PRINT zone on the screen, and the semi-colon prints one space after a numeric expression (but none after a string expression) and suppresses the carriage return.

PRINT @—This statement causes the expression to be printed starting at the screen position specified after the PRINT@. The CRT is divided into 1024 PRINT@ positions starting with position zero at the upper left corner of the screen, and ending with position one thousand twenty four at the bottom right corner of the screen.

PRINT TAB—Causes expression to be printed after moving cursor the specified number of spaces from the left margin.

INPUT—Stops program execution and waits for keyboard input from the user. In this version of BASIC, a message can be contained within the INPUT statement.

PRINT#-1—This outputs the expression (numeric or string) to cassette recorder number one. It is used for creating cassette data files.

INPUT #-1—This statement retrieves an expression (numeric or string) from cassette recorder number one. It is used to retrieve cassette data files.

DATA—Used to create a permanent data file within a program. The DATA statement may contain either numeric or string data, or a mixture of both. The DATA statement can be placed anywhere in the program, but all DATA statements must be placed in the sequential order for which the data is to be read.

READ—Reads the next piece of data from the DATA statement, and assigns it to the variable specified by the READ statement. The variable specified by the READ statement must be the same type as the data element to be read (numeric or string).

RESTORE—Causes the data pointer to be reset to the beginning of the DATA list. In other words, after a RESTORE, the next READ statement will read the first data element in the first DATA statement.

Program Statements

DEFINT—Defines all specified variables as integer variables. Variables can be specified as single variables, or a range of variables as in DEFINT A-Z would define all variables in the program as integer type.

CLEAR—When used without an expression, erases value and type for all variables. When used with an expression, sets aside number of bytes of memory specified by the expression for use by string variables.

DIM—Allocates specified types of memory for arrays specified in the DIM statement. One, two, or three dimensional arrays can be specified. The DIM statement must be followed by a list of arrays separated by commas, Eleven elements are allocated automatically for each array not specified in the DIM statement. The zero subscript is allowed as an element for all arrays.

LET—Assigns an expression to a variable. This version of BASIC will accept and process a LET statement, but it is optional. Both statements: LET A=10 and A=10 can be processed by Level II BASIC. Some dialects of BASIC require use of LET.

Execution Sequence Modifying Statements

END—Ends execution of the program and returns computer to Command mode. Not necessary if execution is meant to end on the last sequential statement in the program.

STOP—Halts execution of program and prints BREAK AT message. Execution can be continued by typing, CONT, and variable values will not be reset.

GOTO—Unconditional branch to specified line number.

GOSUB—Unconditional branch to subroutine starting at specified line number.

RETURN—Unconditional branch from subroutine to statement immediately following GOSUB last encountered.

ON-GOTO—Evaluates expression and branches to line number specified in list.

ON-GOSUB—Evaluates expression and branches to subroutine starting at line number specified in list.

FOR-TO—Opens a loop and increments loop counter by one until counter reaches end value specified.

STEP—Changes the loop counter increment to amount specified. STEP is optional.

NEXT—Returns to beginning of current loop and increments loop counter. If loop counter exceeds the end value specified in the FOR-TO loop, execution starts with the immediate statement following the NEXT statement.

ON ERROR GOTO—When an error is encountered in a program, this statement causes the program to branch to the line number specified by this statement. When this statement is used, the computer will not halt execution and print an error message as it normally would.

RESUME—After an error has occurred and program is branched by ON ERROR GOTO statement, this statement causes the program to resume execution at the specified line number.

RANDOM—This statement causes the pseudo-random number generator to be reseeded. This is an optional statement and is not required when the pseudo-random number generator is used.

REM—Allows user to place remarks within the program text. The computer will immediately branch to the next line number when a REM is encountered.

Conditional Statements

IF-THEN—If expression specified is true then execute statement specified after THEN. Otherwise branch to next line number (unless an ELSE is specified).

ELSE—If expression in IF-THEN statement is not true, the computer will execute the statement following the ELSE statement.

Graphics Statements

The CRT is divided into a grid as a 128 x 48 graph. There are 48 vertical positions (0 to 47) and 128 horizontal positions (0 to 127). Position 0,0 is at the upper left corner of the screen, and position 127,47 is at the bottom right corner of the screen. Each alpha-numeric (or PRINT @) position on the screen contains six graphics positions.

SET—Lights a graphic position at specified X, Y position. An error will occur if the X or Y positions exceed the parameter listed above, or are smaller than zero.

RESET—Turns off a graphic position at specific X, Y position. An error will occur if the X or Y positions exceed the parameters listed above, or are smaller than zero.

CLS—Clears the CRT screen. Removes all alpha-numeric and graphics characters on the screen and returns the cursor to the home position (upper left corner of the screen).

String Functions

ACS—Returns the ASCII code of the first character in a string variable.

CHR$—Returns a one character string that is an equivalent of the specified ASCII code. If the specified code specifies a control function rather than a character, the control function is automatically performed.

INKEY$—Strobes the keyboard and returns a one character string equivalent to the key pressed during the strobe. The null string results if no key is pressed during the strobe.

LEFT$—Returns a string representing the first X (specified) number of characters from a specified string.

LEN—Returns a numeric expression equal to the number of characters contained in a string variable.

MID$—Returns a substring of a specified string variable consisting of X characters starting at position Y in the string (both X and Y are specified).

RIGHT$—Returns a string expression consisting of the last X (specified) characters in a specified string variable.

STR$—Converts a numeric expression to a string expression.

STRING$—Returns a sequence of a specified number of a specified character. STRING$(25, "*") would return a string of 25 asterisks.

VAL—Returns a numeric value equal to a string expression containing numeric characters.

Arithmetic Functions

ABS—Returns the absolute value of an expression.

ATN—Returns the arctangent of an expression. It is expressed in radians.

COS—Returns the cosine of an expression. The expression must be submitted in radians.

EXP—Returns the natural exponential of an expression.

INT—Returns the largest integer not greater than the specified numeric expression.

LOG—Returns the natural logarithm of a numeric expression. The expression must be positive.

RND(0)—Returns a pseudo random number between 1×10^{-6} and 9.99999×10^{-1} inclusive.

RND(X)—Returns a pseudo random number between 1 and X inclusive.

SGN—Evaluates sign of numeric expression. Returns a -1 if expression is negative, zero if expression is zero, or 1 if expression is positive.

SIN—Returns the sine of an expression. The expression must be submitted in radians.

SQR—Returns the square root of an expression. Expression must be non-negative.

TAN—Returns the tangent of an expression. The expression must be submitted in radians.

Special Functions

POKE—Loads a decimal value into a specified memory location. Value must be greater than a – 1 and less than 256.

OUT—Outputs a value to a specified port. Both the value and the port must be between zero and 255 inclusive.

PEEK—Returns the decimal value stored in a specified memory location. The specified memory location must be a valid address and be in decimal form.

POINT—Evaluates the condition of a specified graphics location. Returns a zero if location is unlit, and a negative one if location is lit. Specified graphic location must be within the parameters stated in *GRAPHICS STATEMENTS* or an error will occur.

Variable Type Declaration Characters

$ String
% Integer
! Single precision
Double precision
D Double precision (exponential notation)
E Single Precision (exponential notation)

Arithmetic Operators

+	Addition
–	Subtraction
*	Multiplication
/	Division
Up-Arrow	Exponentiate

String Operator

+	Concatenate

Relational Operators

<	Is less than
>	Is greater than
=	Is equal to
<=	Is less than or equal to
>=	Is greater than or equal to
<>	Does not equal

String Expression Relational Operators

<	Precedes alphabetically
>	Follows alphabetically
=	Is alphabetically equivalent to
<=	Precedes or is alphabetically equivalent to
>=	Follows or is alphabetically equivalent to
<>	Is not alphabetically equivalent to

Order of Operations

1) Exponentiation
2) Negation
3) Multiplication and division
4) Addition and subtraction
5) Relational operators
6) NOT
7) AND
8) OR

Procedence of operations is always from left to right for operators on the same level (such as addition and subtraction).

If the user needs additional information concerning Level II BASIC, consult the *LEVEL II BASIC REFERENCE MANUAL* (Cat. No. 26-2101) available from Radio Shack.

Chapter 4
Miscellaneous and
Specialized Programs

TRIGONOMETRIC FUNCTIONS - NATURAL AND DERIVED
Remarks

Here is a handy little program for the math teacher or those who use trigonometry frequently in their work or studies. Nearly all of the functions used in common trigonometry are included in this program, and a routine to change degrees to radians is included to simplify its use. The derived functions (those not included intrinsically in your computer's ROM) are constructed using the natural functions as well as other intrinsic functions. All trigonometric functions use *only* values expressed in radians. An error trapping routine is used for non-defined operations.

Variables

A$(Z) — Name of Function choice #Z in menu
X — Value to be inserted to chosen function
Y — Output of processed X
D — Value in degrees
R — Value in radians

Suggested Variations

1) This program has been constructed to allow you to insert any additional operations you need. Don't forget to redimension the string array to hold the new titles.

2) These functions can only be as accurate as your computer. You might wish to add double precision variables and a significant digit rounding routine to increase the accuracy of these functions.

Sample Run

TRIG FUNCTIONS - NATURAL AND DERIVED
ALL VALUES OF X MUST BE IN RADIANS FOR THIS PROGRAM
DO YOU NEED A CONVERSION:
1) FROM DEGREES TO RADIANS
2) FROM RADIANS TO DEGREES
3) NEITHER—CONTINUE PROGRAM
4) NEITHER—TERMINATE PROGRAM
ENTER YOUR CHOICE (1, 2, 3, OR 4) ?3
THE FUNCTIONS AVAILABLE ARE:
1 : TANGENT OF X
2 : COSINE OF X
3 : SINE OF X
4 : SECANT OF X
5 : COSECANT OF X
6 : CONTANGENT OF X
7 : INVERSE SINE OF X
8 : INVERSE COSINE OF X
9 : INVERSE TANGENT OF X
10 : INVERSE SECANT OF X
PRESS ENTER TO CONTINUE?
11 : INVERSE COSECANT OF X
12 : INVERSE COTANGENT OF X
13 : HYPERBOLIC SINE OF X
14 : HYPERBOLIC COSINE OF X
15 : HYPERBOLIC TANGENT OF X
16 : HYPERBOLIC SECANT OF X
17 : HYPERBOLIC COSECANT OF X
18 : HYPERBOLIC COTANGENT OF X
19 : INVERSE HYPERBOLIC SINE OF X
20 : INVERSE HYPERBOLIC COSINE OF X
21 : INVERSE HYPERBOLIC TANGENT OF X
22 : INVERSE HYPERBOLIC SECANT OF X
23 : INVERSE HYPERBOLIC COSECANT OF X
24 : INVERSE HYPERBOLIC COTANGENT OF X
ENTER YOUR CHOICE (1-23) OR 24 TO REVIEW LIST? 19
ENTER X ? .5

INVERSE HYPERBOLIC SINE OF .5 IS EQUAL TO .481212
ALL VALUES OF X MUST BE IN RADIANS FOR THIS
PROGRAM
DO YOU NEED A CONVERSION:
1) FROM DEGREES TO RADIANS
2) FROM RADIANS TO DEGREES
3) NEITHER—CONTINUE PROGRAM
4) NEITHER—TERMINATE PROGRAM
ENTER YOUR CHOICE (1, 2, 3, OR 4) ? <u>4</u>

Program for Trig Functions: Natural and Derived

```
10 ON ERROR GOTO 850
20 DIM A$(24):FOR X=1 TO 24:READ A$(
X):NEXT X
30 CLS:PRINT "TRIG FUNCTIONS- NATURA
L AND DERIVED":PRINT
40 GOTO 710
50 PRINT "THE FUNCTIONS AVAILABLE AR
E:"
60 FOR X=1 TO 10:PRINT X;": ";A$(X);
" OF X":NEXT X
70 PRINT:INPUT "PRESS ENTER TO CONTI
NUE";A$:CLS
80 FOR X=11 TO 24:PRINT X;": ";A$(X)
;" OF X":NEXT X
90 PRINT:INPUT "ENTER YOUR CHOICE (1
-23) OR 24 TO REVIEW LIST";C
100 IF C>=24 OR C<=0 THEN CLS:GOTO 5
0
110 INPUT "ENTER X ";X
120 ON C GOSUB 150,170,190,210,230,2
50,270,290,310,330,350,370,390,410,4
30,450,470,490,510,530,550,570,590,6
10
130 CLS:PRINT A$(C);" OF";X;" IS EQU
AL TO";Y
140 GOTO 710
150 Y=TAN(X)
160 RETURN
170 Y=COS(X)
180 RETURN
190 Y=SIN(X)
```

```
200 RETURN
210 Y=1/COS(X)
220 RETURN
230 Y=1/SIN(X)
240 RETURN
250 Y=1/TAN(X)
260 RETURN
270 Y=ATN(X/SQR(-X*X+1))
280 RETURN
290 Y=-ATN(X/SQR(-X*X+1))+1.5708
300 RETURN
310 Y=ATN(X)
320 RETURN
330 Y=ATN(SQR(X*X-1))+(SGN(X)-1)*1.5
708
340 RETURN
350 Y=ATN(1/SQR(X*X-1))+(SGN(X)-1)*1
.5708
360 RETURN
370 Y=-ATN(X)+1.5708
380 RETURN
390 Y=(EXP(X)-EXP(-X))/2
400 RETURN
410 Y=(EXP(X)+EXP(-X))/2
420 RETURN
430 Y=-EXP(-X)/(EXP(X)+EXP(-X)*2+1
440 RETURN
450 Y=2/(EXP(X)+EXP(-X))
460 RETURN
470 Y=2/(EXP(X)-EXP(-X))
480 RETURN
490 Y=EXP(-X)/(EXP(X)-EXP(-X))*2+1
500 RETURN
510 Y=LOG(X+SQR(X*X+1))
520 RETURN
530 Y=LOG(X+SQR(X*X-1))
540 RETURN
550 Y=LOG((1+X)/(1-X))/2
560 RETURN
570 Y=LOG((SQR(-X*X+1)+1)/X)
580 RETURN
590 Y=LOG((SGN(X)*SQR(X*X+1)+1)/X)
600 RETURN
610 Y=LOG((X+1)/(X-1))/2
```

33

```
620 RETURN
630 DATA TANGENT,COSINE,SINE,SECANT,
COSECANT,COTANGENT
640 DATA INVERSE SINE,INVERSE COSINE
,INVERSE TANGENT
650 DATA INVERSE SECANT,INVERSE COSE
CANT,INVERSE COTANGENT
660 DATA HYPERBOLIC SINE,HYPERBOLIC
COSINE,HYPERBOLIC TANGENT
670 DATA HYPERBOLIC SECANT,HYPERBOLI
C COSECANT,HYPERBOLIC COTANGENT
680 DATA INVERSE HYPERBOLIC SINE,INV
ERSE HYPERBOLIC COSINE
690 DATA INVERSE HYPERBOLIC TANGENT,
INVERSE HYPERBOLIC SECANT
700 DATA INVERSE HYPERBOLIC COSECANT
,INVERSE HYPERBOLIC COTANGENT
710 PRINT "ALL VALUES OF X MUST BE I
N RADIANS FOR THIS PROGRAM"
720 PRINT "DO YOU NEED A CONVERSION:
"
730 PRINT "1) FROM DEGREES TO RADIAN
S"
740 PRINT "2) FROM RADIANS TO DEGREE
S"
750 PRINT "3) NEITHER-- CONTINUE PRO
GRAM"
760 PRINT "4) NEITHER-- TERMINATE PR
OGRAM"
770 INPUT "ENTER YOUR CHOICE (1, 2,
3, OR 4) ";R
780 ON R GOTO 810,830,790,800
790 CLS:GOTO 50
800 END
810 INPUT "DEGREES ";D:R=D*.017453:P
RINT "= ";R;" RADIANS"
820 GOTO 840
830 INPUT "RADIANS ";R:D=R*57.2958:P
RINT "= ";D;" DEGREES"
840 FOR K=1 TO 8:PRINT:NEXT K:GOTO 7
20
850 CLS:PRINT "NOTICE"
860 PRINT "I AM UNABLE TO PERFORM TH
E REQUESTED CALCULATION"
```

```
870 PRINT "PLEASE LOOK OVER YOUR VAL
UE OF X AND RE-ENTER"
880 INPUT "PRESS ENTER TO CONTINUE";
A$:CLS:RESUME 50
```

CALCULATING DAIRY CATTLE FEED RATIONS

Remarks

The use of computers in agricultural-related industries has increased tremendously as software has become available. A group of farmers in Oklahoma have been involved in an experimental program with a computer terminal in their homes linked via telephone modem to a large central computer. Here is a program that greatly simplifies the tedious chore of calculating nutritionally balanced feed rations for diary cattle on the basis of Crude Protein and Total Digestible Nutrients (TDN). The program uses the common Pearson Square approach to rationing and can also ration for heifers (large and small breeds) as well as pregnant animals.

Variables

Q3—Whether animal is heifer or not
I9—Whether animal is pregnant or not
P—Cumulative protein requirement
T—Cumulative TDN requirement
V3—Crude protein supplied by concentrate
W3—TDN supplied by concentrate
I—Crude protein supplied by roughages
L—TDN supplied by roughages
P5—Protein needed from concentrate
D1—Pounds concentrate required
D2—Percent crude protein needed in concentrate
R8—Percent of feed mixture that is protein supplement
R9—Percent of feed mixture that is grain mix

Suggested Variations

1) You may wish to expand the principles in this program and modify to ration for other types of livestock.

2) You may wish to update the protein and TDN requirements as new figures are released from your Cooperative Agriculture Extension Agent.

Sample Run

CALCULATING
DAIRY CATTLE
FEED RATIONS
PRESS ANY KEY TO CONTINUE
*** SECTION A ——— DAILY REQUIREMENTS FOR DAILY
ANIMAL ***
IF COW IS HEIFER ENTER 1, OTHERWISE ENTER 0? 0
IF COW IS PREGNANT ENTER 1, OTHERWISE ENTER 0? 0
HOW MUCH DOES COW WEIGH (LBS.)? 1430
1.71 ———— CRUDE PROTEIN   9.9 ———— TDN
HOW MANY LBS. MILK PER DAY? 60
TESTING AT WHAT PERCENT BUTTERFAT? 5.0
5.16 ———— CRUDE PROTEIN   22.8 ———— TDN
****

TOTAL DAILY REQUIREMENTS
CRUDE PROTEIN——— 6.87   TDN——— 32.7
PRESS ANY KEY TO CONTINUE
****

*** SECTION B ——— CONCENTRATE RATION ***
YOU MAY USE AS MANY DIFFERENT CONCENTRATES AS
YOU WISH AS LONG AS THEY ADD UP TO ONE HUNDRED
POUNDS TOTAL. ENTER 0 POUNDS WHEN YOU HAVE
ENTERED ALL OF YOUR CONCENTRATES.
HOW MANY POUNDS OF CONCENTRATE # 1? 100
WHAT IS THE PERCENT PROTEIN OF CONCENTRATE # 1?
.14
WHAT IS THE PERCENT TDN OF CONCENTRATE # 1? 12
HOW MANY POUNDS OF CONCENTRATE # 2? 0
****

TOTAL NUTRIENTS FROM CONCENTRATE
CRUDE PROTEIN——— .14   TDN——— 12
****
PRESS ANY KEY TO CONTINUE
*** SECTION C ——— ROUGHAGES ***
YOU MAY USE AS MANY ROUGHAGES AS YOU WISH.
ENTER 0 POUNDS WHEN YOU HAVE ENTERED ALL
ROUGHAGES.
HOW MANY POUNDS OF ROUGHAGE # 14? 40
WHAT IS THE PERCENT PROTEIN OF ROUGHAGE # 1? 1.24
WHAT IS THE PERCENT TDN OF ROUGHAGE # 1? 5 .
HOW MANY POUNDS OF ROUGHAGE # 2? 0
****

PRESS ANY KEY TO CONTINUE
TOTAL NUTRIENTS FROM ROUGHAGES
CRUDE PROTEIN——— .496   TDN——— 2
****
REMAINING TO BE SUPPLIED FROM CONCENTRATE
FEEDS
CRUDE PROTEIN——— 6.374   TDN——— 2
****
POUNDS CONCENTRATE REQUIRED——— 255.833
****
PERCENT CRUDE PROTEIN NEEDED IN CONCEN-
TRATE—— 2.49147
****
WHAT IS THE NAME OF THE PROTEIN SUPPLEMENT YOU
WILL USE
? S.B.O.M. 45%
WHAT IS THE PERCENT PROTEIN OF S.B.O.M. 45% ? 44.7
ENTER 1 FOR UNDOCUMENTED RESULTS OR 2 FOR
PEARSON SQUARE ? 1
PRESS ANY KEY TO CONTINUE
PROTEIN SUP. ———— 5.27708%
GRAIN MIX ———— 94.7229%
END OF PROGRAM
ENTER 1 FOR DRY MATTER IN FEED INSPECTION
ROUTINE OR 2 TO QUIT ? 2

Program for Calculating Diary Cattle Feed Rations

```
10  V3=0:Z9=0:I=0:L=0:W3=0:Z8=0:U=0
20  CLEAR 128
30  CLS:FOR N=1 TO 5:PRINT:NEXT N
40  PRINT "C A L C U L A T I N G "
50  PRINT "               D A I R Y
    C A T T L E"
60  PRINT "
          F E E D   R A T I O N S"
70  FOR N=1 TO 5:PRINT:NEXT N
80  GOSUB 90:GOTO 120
90  PRINT "PRESS ANY KEY TO CONTINUE"

100 A$=INKEY$:IF A$="" GOTO 100
110 CLS:RETURN
```

```
120 PRINT "*** SECTION A --- DAILY R
EQUIREMENTS FOR DAIRY ANIMAL ***"
130 INPUT "IF COW IS HEIFER ENTER 1,
 OTHERWISE ENTER 0 ";Q3
140 IF Q3=1 GOTO 1910
150 INPUT "IF COW IS PREGNANT ENTER
1, OTHERWISE ENTER 0 ";I9
160 PRINT
170 PRINT
180 INPUT "HOW MUCH DOES COW WEIGH (
LBS.) ";W
190 IF I9=1 GOTO 1700
200 GOSUB 1300
210 PRINT C1;" ---- CRUDE PROTEIN
    ";T1;" ---- TDN"
220 IF C1=0 GOTO 2660
230 INPUT "HOW MANY LBS. MILK PER DA
Y ";M1
240 INPUT "TESTING AT WHAT PERCENT B
UTTERFAT ";B1
250 GOSUB 1510
260 IF P2=0 GOTO 2710
270 PRINT P2;" ---- CRUDE PROTEIN
    ";T2;" ---- TDN"
280 P=C1+P2
290 T=T1+T2
300 GOSUB 3240
310 PRINT "TOTAL DAILY REQUIREMENTS"
320 PRINT "CRUDE PROTEIN---";P;"
    TDN---";T
330 GOSUB 90
340 GOSUB 3240
350 PRINT "*** SECTION B --- CONCENT
RATE RATION ***"
360 PRINT "YOU MAY USE AS MANY DIFFE
RENT CONCENTRATES AS YOU"
370 PRINT "WISH AS LONG AS THEY ADD
UP TO ONE HUNDRED POUNDS"
380 PRINT "TOTAL.   ENTER 0 POUNDS WH
EN YOU HAVE ENTERED ALL"
390 PRINT "OF YOUR CONCENTRATES."
400 Z8=Z8+1
410 PRINT "HOW MANY POUNDS OF CONCEN
TRATE #";Z8;"   ";::INPUT T3
```

```
420 IF T3=0 GOTO 520
430 U=U+T3
440 T3=T3/100
450 PRINT "WHAT IS THE PERCENT PROTE
IN OF CONCENTRATE #";Z8;"  ";:INPUT
T4
460 T5=T4*T3
470 V3=V3+T5
480 PRINT "WHAT IS THE PERCENT TDN O
F CONCENTRATE #";Z8;"  ";:INPUT S3
490 S4=S3*T3
500 W3=W3+S4
510 GOTO 400
520 IF U=100 GOTO 560
530 PRINT "YOUR TOTAL CONCETRATES AD
D UP TO ONLY ";U;" LBS."
540 PRINT "TOTAL MUST ADD UP TO 100
LBS. PLEASE ADJUST AND TRY AGAIN."
550 U=0:Z8=0:GOTO 350
560 GOSUB 3240
570 PRINT "TOTAL NUTRIENTS FROM CONC
ENTRATE"
580 PRINT "CRUDE PROTEIN---";V3;"
  TDN---";W3
590 GOSUB 3240
600 GOSUB 90
610 PRINT "*** SECTION C --- ROUGHAG
ES ***"
620 PRINT "YOU MAY USE AS MANY ROUGH
AGES AS YOU WISH."
630 PRINT "ENTER 0 POUNDS WHEN YOU H
AVE ENTERED ALL ROUGHAGES."
640 Z9=Z9+1
650 PRINT "HOW MANY POUNDS OF ROUGHA
GE #";Z9;"  ";:INPUT G
660 IF G<=0 GOTO 740
670 PRINT "WHAT IS THE PERCENT PROTE
IN OF ROUGHAGE #";Z9;"  ";:INPUT G1
680 G1=G1/100
690 I=I+(G1*G)
700 PRINT "WHAT IS THE PERCENT TDN O
F ROUGHAGE #";Z9;"  ";:INPUT H1
710 H1=H1/100
720 L=L+(H1*G)
```

39

```
730 GOTO 640
740 GOSUB 3240
750 GOSUB 90:PRINT "TOTAL NUTRIENTS
FROM ROUGHAGES"
760 PRINT "CRUDE PROTEIN--- ";I;"
  TDN--- ";L
770 GOSUB 3240
780 PRINT "REMAINING TO BE SUPPLIED
FROM CONCENTRATE FEEDS"
790 P5=P-I
800 T5=T-L
810 PRINT "CRUDE PROTEIN--- ";P5;"
   TDN--- ";L
820 IF P5<=0 GOTO 3250
830 GOSUB 3240
840 D1=T5/W3*100
850 IF D1<=0 GOTO 2760
860 PRINT "POUNDS CONCENTRATE REQUIR
ED--- ";D1
870 GOSUB 3240
880 D2=P5/D1*100
890 PRINT "PERCENT CRUDE PROTEIN NEE
DED IN CONCENTRATE-- ";D2
900 GOSUB 3240
910 PRINT "WHAT IS THE NAME OF THE P
ROTEIN SUPPLEMENT YOU WILL USE ":INP
UT C$
920 E$="GRAIN MIX   "
930 F$="PROTEIN SUP."
940 PRINT "WHAT IS THE PERCENT PROTE
IN OF ";C$;"   ";:INPUT V4
950 IF D2>V4 GOTO 980
960 R5=V4-D2
970 GOTO 990
980 R5=D2-V4
990 IF D2>V3 GOTO 1020
1000 R6=V3-D2
1010 GOTO 1030
1020 R6=D2-V3
1030 R7=R6+R5
1040 R8=(R6/R7)*100
1050 R9=(R5/R7)*100
1060 INPUT "ENTER 1 FOR UNDOCUMENTED
```

```
    RESULTS OR 2 FOR PEARSON SQUARE ";Z
5
1070 GOSUB 90
1080 IF Z5=2 GOTO 1170
1090 PRINT F$;" ---- ";R8;"%"
1100 PRINT E$;" ---- ";R9;"%"
1110 PRINT
1120 PRINT
1130 PRINT "        E N D    O F    P R O
   G R A M"
1140 INPUT "ENTER 1 FOR DRY MATTER I
N FEED INSPECTION ROUTINE OR 2 TO QU
IT ";T1
1150 IF T1=1 GOTO 2800
1160 GOTO 3260
1170 PRINT F$;" -- ";V4;"
   ";R6;" -- ";R8;"%"
1180 PRINT
1190 PRINT "
  ";D2
1200 PRINT
1210 PRINT E$;" -- ";V3;"
   ";R5;" -- ";R9;"%"
1220 PRINT "
                ------"
1230 PRINT "
             ";R7
1240 PRINT "BY WEIGHT:"
1250 PRINT (R8/100)*D1;" POUNDS ";C$
1260 PRINT (R9/100)*D1;" POUNDS GRAI
N MIX"
1270 U9=(R8/100)*D1
1280 U8=(R9/100)*D1
1290 GOTO 1130
1300 IF W<>770 GOTO 1320
1310 C1=1.03:T1=6.16
1320 IF W<>880 GOTO 1340
1330 C1=1.15:T1=6.82
1340 IF W<>990 GOTO 1360
1350 C1=1.29:T1=7.48
1360 IF W<>1100 GOTO 1380
1370 C1=1.41:T1=8.14
1380 IF W<>1210 GOTO 1400
1390 C1=1.52:T1=8.80
```

```
1400 IF W<>1320 GOTO 1420
1410 C1=1.62:T1=9.24
1420 IF W<>1430 GOTO 1440
1430 C1=1.71:T1=9.90
1440 IF W<>1540 GOTO 1460
1450 C1=1.83:T1=10.56
1460 IF W<>1650 GOTO 1480
1470 C1=1.92:T1=11.00
1480 IF W<>1760 GOTO 1500
1490 C1=2.02:T1=11.66
1500 RETURN
1510 IF B1<>2.5 GOTO 1530
1520 K=.006:J=.255
1530 IF B1<>3.0 GOTO 1550
1540 K=.070:J=.280
1550 IF B1<>3.5 GOTO 1570
1560 K=.074:J=.305
1570 IF B1<>4.0 GOTO 1590
1580 K=.078:J=.330
1590 IF B1<>4.5 GOTO 1610
1600 K=.082:J=.355
1610 IF B1<>5.0 GOTO 1630
1620 K=.086:J=.380
1630 IF B1<>5.5 GOTO 1650
1640 K=.090:J=.405
1650 IF B1<>6.0 GOTO 1670
1660 K=.094:J=.430
1670 P2=K*M1
1680 T2=J*M1
1690 RETURN
1700 IF W<>770 GOTO 1720
1710 C1=1.26:T1=7.92
1720 IF W<>880 GOTO 1740
1730 C1=1.43:T1=8.80
1740 IF W<>990 GOTO 1760
1750 C1=1.61:T1=9.68
1760 IF W<>1100 GOTO 1780
1770 C1=1.72:T1=10.56
1780 IF W<>1210 GOTO 1800
1790 C1=1.87:T1=11.44
1800 IF W<>1320 GOTO 1820
1810 C1=2.00:T1=12.32
1820 IF W<>1430 GOTO 1840
1830 C1=2.11:T1=13.20
```

```
1840 IF W<>1540 GOTO 1860
1850 C1=2.20:T1=13.86
1860 IF W<>1650 GOTO 1880
1870 C1=2.38:T1=14.74
1880 IF W<>1760 GOTO 1900
1890 C1=2.53:T1=15.62

1900 GOTO 210
1910 INPUT "ENTER 1 FOR SMALL BREED
OR 2 FOR LARGE BREED ";Q4
1920 IF Q4=1 GOTO 2320
1930 INPUT "HOW MUCH DOES HEIFER WEI
GH ";W
1940 IF W<>88 GOTO 1960
1950 P=.24:T=1.1
1960 IF W<>99 GOTO 1980
1970 P=.30:T=1.32
1980 IF W<>121 GOTO 2000
1990 P=.40:T=1.98
2000 IF W<>165 GOTO 2020
2010 P=.73:T=3.30
2020 IF W<>220 GOTO 2040
2030 P=.81:T=4.40
2040 IF W<>330 GOTO 2060
2050 P=.96:T=5.94
2060 IF W<>440 GOTO 2080
2070 P=1.10:T=7.48
2080 IF W<>550 GOTO 2100
2090 P=1.26:T=8.80

2100 IF W<>660 GOTO 2120
2110 P=1.41:T=9.90
2120 IF W<>770 GOTO 2140
2130 P=1.57:T=10.78
2140 IF W<>880 GOTO 2160
2150 P=1.76:T=11.44
2160 IF W<>990 GOTO 2180
2170 P=1.95:T=11.66
2180 IF W<>1100 GOTO 2200
2190 P=2.06:T=11.66

2200 IF W<>1210 GOTO 2220
2210 P=2.02:T=11.00
2220 IF W<>1320 GOTO 2240
2230 P=1.78:T=9.46
2240 IF P>0 GOTO 2310
```

```
2250 PRINT "YOUR WEIGHT OF ";W;" IS
ILLEGAL"
2260 PRINT "ONLY THE FOLLOWING WEIGH
TS CAN BE PROCESSED BY THIS PROGRAM:
"
2270 PRINT "88, 99, 121, 165, 220, 3
30, 440, 550, 660, 770, 880, 990,"
2280 PRINT "1100, 1210, AND 1320"
2290 PRINT "PLEASE ADJUST YOUR WEIGH
T AND REENTER."
2300 GOTO 1930
2310 GOTO 300
2320 INPUT "WHAT DOES HEIFER WEIGH "
;W
2330 IF W<>44 GOTO 2350
2340 P=.14:T=.7
2350 IF W<>55 GOTO 2370
2360 P=.20:T=.9
2370 IF W<>77 GOTO 2390
2380 P=.30:T=1.3
2390 IF W<>110 GOTO 2410
2400 P=.47:T=2.0
2410 IF W<>165 GOTO 2430
2420 P=.61:T=2.6
2430 IF W<>220 GOTO 2450
2440 P=.70:T=3.5
2450 IF W<>330 GOTO 2470
2460 P=.86:T=5.1
2470 IF W<>440 GOTO 2490
2480 P=1.02:T=6.4
2490 IF W<>550 GOTO 2510
2500 P=1.21:T=7.7
2510 IF W<>660 GOTO 2530
2520 P=1.30:T=8.4
2530 IF W<>770 GOTO 2550
2540 P=1.29:T=8.1
2550 IF W<>880 GOTO 2570
2560 P=1.22:T=7.9
2570 IF W<>990 GOTO 2590
2580 P=1.28:T=7.5
2590 IF P>0 GOTO 2650
2600 PRINT "YOUR WEIGHT OF ";W;" IS
ILLEGAL"
```

```
2610 PRINT "ONLY THE FOLLOWING WEIGH
TS CAN BE PROCESSED BY THIS PROGRAM:
"
2620 PRINT "44, 55, 77, 110, 165, 22
0, 330, 440, 550, 660, 770, 880, AND
 990"
2630 PRINT "PLEASE ADJUST YOUR WEIGH
T TO ONE OF THE ABOVE AND REENTER"
2640 GOTO 2320
2650 GOTO 300
2660 PRINT "YOUR WEIGHT OF ";W;" IS
ILLEGAL"
2670 PRINT "ONLY THE FOLLOWING WEIGH
TS CAN BE PROCESSED BY THIS PROGRAM"

2680 PRINT "770, 880, 990, 1100, 121
0, 1320, 1430, 1540, 1650, AND 1760"

2690 PRINT "PLEASE ADJUST YOUR WEIGH
T TO ONE OF THE ABOVE AND REENTER."
2700 GOTO 180
2710 PRINT "YOUR BUTTERFAT ENTRY OF
";B1;" IS ILLEGAL"
2720 PRINT "ONLY THE FOLLOWING PERCE
NTAGES CAN BE PROCESSED BY THIS PROG
RAM"
2730 PRINT " 2.5, 3.0, 3.5, 4.0, 4.5
, 5.0, 5.5, AND 6.0"
2740 PRINT "PLEASE ADJUST YOUR BUTTE
RFAT TO ONE OF THE ABOVE AND REENTER
"
2750 GOTO 230
2760 GOSUB 3240
2770 PRINT "YOU REQUIRE NO PROTEIN S
UPPLEMENT"
2780 GOSUB 3240
2790 GOTO 1130

2800 GOSUB 90:PRINT "***** DRY MATTE
R IN FEED INSPECTION ROUTINE *****"
2810 PRINT "THIS ROUTINE ASSUMES THA
T A NORMAL INTAKE OF DRY MATTER"
2820 PRINT "IS EQUAL TO 3.5 LBS. PER
 HUNDRED WEIGHT."
```

```
2830 PRINT "***** D.M.I.F.I.R SECTIO
N A: ROUGHAGES *****"
2840 Z=0
2850 PRINT "ENTER 0 POUNDS WHEN YOU
HAVE ENTERED ALL ROUGHAGES"
2860 R=1
2870 PRINT "HOW MANY POUNDS OF ROUGH
AGE #";R;"   ";:INPUT A1
2880 IF A1=0 GOTO 2940
2890 PRINT "WHAT IS PERCENT DRY MATT
ER FOR ROUGHAGE #";R;"   ";:INPUT A2
2900 A3=(A2/100)*A1
2910 Z=Z+A3
2920 R=R+1
2930 GOTO 2870
2940 GOSUB 90:PRINT "***** D.M.I.F.I
.R. SECTION B: GRAIN MIX *****"
2950 R=1
2960 GOTO 3180
2970 PRINT "ENTER 0 POUNDS WHEN ALL
GRAINS HAVE BEEN ENTERED"
2980 PRINT "HOW MANY POUNDS OF GRAIN
 #";R;"   ";:INPUT A1
2990 IF A1=0 GOTO 3050
3000 PRINT "WHAT IS PERCENT DRY MATT
ER FOR GRAIN #";R;"   ";:INPUT A2
3010 A3=(A2/100)*A1
3020 Z=Z+A3
3030 R=R+1
3040 GOTO 2980
3050 GOSUB 90:PRINT "***** D.M.I.F.I
.R. SECTION C: PROTEIN SUPPLEMENT **
***"
3060 PRINT "WHAT IS DRY MATTER PERCE
NT OF ";C$;"   ";:INPUT A1
3070 A3=(A1/100)*U9
3080 Z=Z+A3
3090 GOSUB 90:PRINT "***** D.M.I.F.I
.R. SECTION D: CONCLUSION *****"
3100 PRINT "TOTAL DRY MATTER IN RATI
ON--- ";Z;" POUNDS"
3110 X=(Z*100)/W
3120 PRINT "POUNDS DRY MATTER PER HU
NDRED WEIGHT--- ";X;" POUNDS"
```

```
3130 IF X>3.5 GOTO 3160
3140 PRINT "***** DOES NOT EXCEED DR
Y MATTER LIMITS *****"
3150 GOTO 3260
3160 PRINT "***** YOUR RATION EXCEED
S THE PRESCRIBED DRY MATTER LIMITS *
****"
3170 GOTO 3260
3180 PRINT "WHEN ENTERING EACH OF YO
UR GRAINS BY WEIGHT, REMEMBER THAT"
3190 PRINT "YOU HAVE A TOTAL OF ";U8
;" POUNDS OF GRAIN IN YOUR MIX."
3200 PRINT "THEREFORE, IF YOU ENTERE
D 50 POUNDS OF A CERTAIN GRAIN IN"
3210 PRINT "SECTION B OF THE DAIRY R
ATION PROGRAM, YOU WOULD ENTER"
3220 PRINT U8;" TIMES 50% OR ";U8*.5
;" POUNDS HERE."
3230 GOTO 2970
3240 PRINT STRING$(63,"*"):RETURN
3250 PRINT "YOU DO NOT REQIRE ANY AD
DITIONAL PROTEIN":END
3260 END
```

SCORECARD

Remarks

Here is a very useful program to aid those who might be called upon to score judging contests. In these contests, the head judge will score and place four subjects (such as animals in a livestock judging contest) and will assign different scores for other possible placings. The contestants will then score the same subjects, and write their placings on a score card along with their team number and contestant letter (A, B, C, or D). The contestants are then graded on the basis of how close their judging matches that of the head judge. There are four operations to be chosen from in this program:

☐ 1) *Clear memory* - This deletes all information stored in memory concerning previous contests, and readies the computer to score a new class.

☐ 2) *Score new class* - This is done after the head judge's placing scores have been entered via operation #4. This operation compares the contestant's placing with that of the judges, and scores the contestant appropriately.

□ 3) *Sort and list current class* - After the entire class has been scored through operation #2, this operation will print out all individual contestant's scores, as well as team cumulative scores.

□ 4) *Enter placing scores for new class* - This is where the head judge's score for each of the possible placings is entered into the computer.

Variables

CLASS (X, Y)—Contains score of contestant Y on team X

      S1—Score for current contestant being graded

      B(Z)—Score for placing #Z given by head judge

      TS—Team score of current team being sorted and listed.

Suggested Variations

1) You might wish to expand this program to accept the judging of more than four objects.

2) To increase the number of teams able to compete, change the value 50 in line #10 in the CLASS array to the number of teams you wish.

3) To make best use of this program, consider using a marked-card-reader peripheral. Otherwise, it is best to have two people involved in the grading. One person calls the placing off of each scorecard to the other person who types it into the computer.

Sample Run

TYPE IN NUMBER OF APPROPRIATE FUNCTION:
1) CLEAR MEMORY
2) SCORE NEW CLASS
3) SORT AND LIST CURRENT CLASS
4) ENTER PLACING SCORES FOR NEW CLASS
? 4
PLACING 1234
SCORE VALUE? 15
PLACING 1243
SCORE VALUE? 20
(the score values for all placings are entered)
TYPE IN NUMBER OF APPROPRIATE FUNCTION:
1) CLEAR MEMORY
2) SCORE NEW CLASS
3) SORT AND LIST CURRENT CLASS
4) ENTER PLACING SCORES FOR NEW CLASS
?2

TYPE OOOO TO TERMINATE CLASS
SCHOOL NUMBER ? 12
CONTESTANT LETTER ? A
CONTESTANT PLACING ? 1234
SCHOOL— — 12
CONTESTANT— — A
PLACING— — 1234
SCORE— — 15
PRESS ENTER TO CONTINUE?
TYPE OOOO TO TERMINATE CLASS
SCHOOL NUMBER? 0000
TYPE IN NUMBER OF APPROPRIATE FUNCTION:
1) CLEAR MEMORY
2) SCORE NEW CLASS
3) SORT AND LIST CURRENT CLASS
4) ENTER PLACING SCORES FOR NEW CLASS
? 3
ENTER SCHOOL (0000 OT QUIT)? 12
SCHOOL— — — 12
CONTESTANT

A	15
B	0
C	0
D	0

TEAM SCORE— — 15
ENTER SCHOOL (0000 TO QUIT)? 0000
TYPE IN NUMBER OF APPROPRIATE FUNCTION:

Program for Scorecard

```
10 CLS:DIM B(24),CLASS(50,4)
20 ON ERROR GOTO 630
30 DATA 1234,1243,1324,1342,1423,143
2,2134,2143,2314,2341,2413
40 DATA 2431,3124,3142,3214,3241,341
2,3421,4123,4132,4213,4231
50 DATA 4312,4321
60 CLS:REM ** MENU **
70 PRINT "TYPE IN NUMBER OF APPROPRI
ATE FUNCTION:"
80 PRINT:PRINT "1) CLEAR MEMORY"
90 PRINT "2) SCORE NEW CLASS"
```

```
100 PRINT "3) SORT AND LIST CURRENT
CLASS"
110 PRINT "4) ENTER PLACING SCORES F
OR NEW CLASS"
120 PRINT:PRINT:INPUT Z
130 CLS:ON Z GOTO 150,230,450,580
140 GOTO 60
150 FOR B=1 TO 24:B(B)=0:NEXT B
160 PRINT CHR$(23);"CLEARING.....";
170 FOR V=1 TO 50
180 FOR W=1 TO 4
190 CLASS(V,W)=0
200 NEXT W
210 NEXT V
220 GOTO 60
230 CLS:PRINT "TYPE 0000 TO TERMINAT
E CLASS"
240 PRINT:PRINT:INPUT "SCHOOL NUMBER
";SCHOOL
250 IF SCHOOL=0 GOTO 60
260 PRINT:INPUT "CONTESTANT LETTER "
;B$:IF B$="A" THEN C=1
270 IF B$="B" THEN C=2
280 IF B$="C" THEN C=3
290 IF B$="D" THEN C=4
300 PRINT:INPUT "CONTESTANT PLACING
";PLAC
310 P=0
320 P=P+1:READ A:IF PLAC=A GOTO 340
330 IF A=4321 GOTO 630ELSE GOTO 320
340 RESTORE:S1=B(P)
350 CLS:PRINT "SCHOOL-- ";SCHOOL
360 PRINT "CONTESTANT-- ";:IF C=1 TH
EN PRINT "A"
370 IF C=2 THEN PRINT "B"
380 IF C=3 THEN PRINT "C"
390 IF C=4 THEN PRINT "D"
400 PRINT "PLACING-- ";PLAC
410 PRINT:PRINT:PRINT:PRINT "SCORE--
";S1
420 PRINT:PRINT:PRINT:INPUT "PRESS E
NTER TO CONTINUE ";A$
430 IF A$="E" THEN PRINT "** CORRECT
ION **": GOTO 230
```

```
440 CLASS(SCHOOL,C)=S1:RESTORE:GOTO
230
450 INPUT "ENTER SCHOOL (0000 TO QUI
T)";S2
460 IF S2=0 GOTO 60
470 CLS:PRINT "SCHOOL--- ";S2
480 TS=0
490 PRINT "CONTESTANT","SCORE"
500 FOR Z1=1 TO 4
510 IF Z1=1 PRINT "A",
520 IF Z1=2 PRINT "B",
530 IF Z1=3 PRINT "C",
540 IF Z1=4 PRINT "D",
550 PRINT CLASS(S2,Z1)
560 TS=TS+CLASS(S2,Z1)
570 NEXT Z1:PRINT:PRINT "TEAM SCORE-
- ";TS:GOTO 450
580 FOR Z=1 TO 24
590 READ A:PRINT "PLACING ";A
600 INPUT "SCORE VALUE";B(Z)
610 CLS:NEXT Z
620 RESTORE:GOTO 60
630 PRINT "ERROR":FOR X5=1 TO 1000:N
EXT X5
640 RESTORE:GOTO 130
```

MATH TEACHER

Remarks

This program is designed for those users who wish to experiment with their computers as an educational tool. It will quiz a student on knowledge of simple mathematic fundamentals concerning addition, subtraction, multiplication and division. There are three levels of difficulty available to the student, corresponding to the range of the numbers used in the equations. The student is automatically scored at the end of the examination.

Variables

A —Number of questions to be asked
L —Difficulty level
C —Number of correct responses
I —Number of incorrect responses
B —Type of problems to be asked (addition, subtraction, multiplication, or division)

N   —Current question number
E, F—Numbers appearing in equation
G   —User's answer to problem
H   —Correct answer to problem
T   —User's percent correct responses

Suggested Variations

1) This program can expand to other areas of mathematics. Add other types of questions, such as fractions or square roots.

2) Instead of having all questions of one type, you may wish to mix them up in the quiz.

3) You might wish to add a pleasing graphics display to reward the user for correct responses, or perhaps a sound effects "razz" for incorrect answers. See the OUT routines in the Program Hints section of this book.

Sample Run

&&&&&&&&&&&&&&&&&&&&&&&&&&&&&&&&&&&&&
MATH   TEACHER
&&&&&&&&&&&&&&&&&&&&&&&&&&&&&&&&&&&&&

HOW MANY QUESTIONS? <u>2</u>
WHAT LEVEL OF DIFFICULTY:
1) BEGINNER
2) INTERMEDIATE
3) EXPERT
ENTER 1, 2, OR 3 ? <u>2</u>
ENTER 1 FOR ADDITION, 2 FOR SUBTRACTION, 3 FOR
DIVISION, OR 4 FOR MULTIPLICATION? <u>1</u>
SCRATCH PAPER NOT ALLOWED!
QUESTION # 1
$463 + 6 = ?$ <u>469</u>
ABSOLUTELY CORRECT!
QUESTION # 2
$299 + 411 = ?$ <u>710</u>
ABSOLUTELY CORRECT!
FINAL   TALLY
_____
CORRECT ANSWERS———— 2
INCORRECT ANSWERS—— 0
100% FOR THIS EXERCISE

Program for Math Teacher

```
10   CLS: PRINT "&&&&&&&&&&&&&&&&&&&&
&&&&&&&&&&&&&&&&&&&&&&&&&&&&&&&&"
20   PRINT
30   PRINT
40   PRINT
50   PRINT "    M A T H   T E A
  C H E R"
60   PRINT
70   PRINT
80   PRINT
90   PRINT        "&&&&&&&&&&&&&&&&&&&&&
&&&&&&&&&&&&&&&&&&&&&&&&&&&&&&&&"
100  FORZ=1TO1500:NEXTZ:CLS
110  INPUT "HOW MANY QUESTIONS";A
120  PRINT "WHAT LEVEL OF DIFFICULTY:
"
130  PRINT "1) BEGINNER"
140  PRINT "2) INTERMEDIATE"
150  PRINT "3) EXPERT"
160  INPUT "ENTER 1, 2, OR 3 ";L
170  C=0:I=0
180  PRINT "ENTER 1 FOR ADDITION, 2
FOR SUBTRACTION, 3 FOR"
190  INPUT"DIVISION, OR 4 FOR MULTIP
LICATION";B
200  PRINT "SCRATCH PAPER NOT ALLOWE
D!":FORZ=1TO1500:NEXTZ
210  IF B=1 GOTO 260
220  IF B=2 GOTO 400
230  IF B=3 GOTO 490
240  IF B=4 GOTO 590
250  PRINT "ILLEGAL PROBLEM CHOICE--
WE'LL START WITH ADDITION"
260  FOR N=1 TO A
270  PRINT "QUESTION #";N
280  E=RND(1000):F=RND(1000)
290 IF L=1 AND (E>100 OR F>100) THEN
  280
300 IF L=2 AND (E>500 OR F>500) THEN
  280
310  PRINT E;" + ";F;" = ";
320  INPUTG:H=E+F
```

```
330    IF G=H GOTO 360
340    PRINT "NOPE, THAT'S NOT CORRECT
"
350    I=I+1:GOTO380
360    PRINT "ABSOLUTELY CORRECT!"
370    C=C+1
380    NEXTN
390    GOTO 680
400    FOR N=1TOA
410    PRINT "QUESTION #";N
420    E=RND(1000):F=RND(1000)
430 IF L=1 AND (E>100 OR F>100) THEN
 420
440 IF L=2 AND (E>500 OR F>500) THEN
 420
450    PRINT E;" - ";F;" =";
460    INPUT G: H=E-F
470    IF G=H GOTO 360
480    GOTO 340
490    FOR N=1TOA
500    PRINT "QUESTION #";N
510 E=RND(10)
520 IF L=1 THEN F=RND(10)*E
530 IF L=2 THEN F=RND(500)*3
540 IF L=3 THEN F=RND(1000)*E
550    PRINT F;" / ";E;" = ";
560    INPUTG:H=F/E
570    IF G=H GOTO 360
580    GOTO 340
590    FORN=1TOA
600    PRINT "QUESTION #";N
610 IF L=1 THEN E=RND(10):F=RND(10)
620 IF L=2 THEN E=RND(15):F=RND(15)
630 IF L=3 THEN E=RND(20):F=RND(20)
640    PRINT E;" X ";F;" = ";
650    INPUT G:H=E*F
660    IF G=H GOTO 360
670    GOTO 340
680    FORZ=1TO1000:NEXTZ:CLS
690    PRINT "F I N A L    T A L L Y"
700    PRINT "----------------------"
710    PRINT "CORRECT ANSWERS----";C
720    PRINT "INCORRECT ANSWERS--";I
730    PRINT
```

```
740   T=C/A*100: PRINTT;"% FOR THIS E
XERCISE"
750   END
```

METRIC CONVERTER

Remarks

Having trouble switching over to the Metric System? Here's a handy little converter program that will have you thinking metric in no time. The program has been especially written with the user's modifications in mind.

Variables

U —Type of conversion (1= met. to eng. 2= eng. to met.)
A —Conversion choice (1 to 16)
A$—Abbreviated units of value to be converted
B$—Abbreviated units of converted value
C —Converted value of B
B —Value to be converted

Suggested Variations

1) The user can easily add as many conversion choices as memory allows.

2) This program might make a fine foundation for a Metric Teacher program for children.

Sample Run

METRIC CONVERTER
ENTER 1 FOR METRIC TO ENGLISH OR 2 FOR ENGLISH TO METRIC? 2
8) INCHES TO CENTIMETERS
9) YARDS TO METERS
10) CUBIC INCHES TO CUBIC CENTIMETERS
11) MILES TO KILOMETERS
12) GALLONS TO LITERS
13) OUNCES TO GRAMS
14) POUNDS TO KILOGRAMS
15) DEGREES F. TO DEGREES C.
16) DEGREES C. TO DEGREES F.
ENTER YOUR CHOICE NUMBER (1 TO 16)? 15
——————————————————————————————————————

HOW MANY DEG. F

55

? <u>32</u>
32 EG. F = 0 DEG. C

————————————————————————

TYPE 1 TO CONTINUE OR 2 TO QUIT? <u>2</u>

Program for Metric Converter

```
10   CLS:PRINT "M E T R I C    C O N V
 E R T E R"
20   INPUT "ENTER 1 FOR METRIC TO ENG
LISH OR 2 FOR ENGLISH TO METRIC";U
30   CLS:ONUGOTO40,120
40   PRINT "1) CENTIMETERS TO INCHES"

50   PRINT "2) METERS TO YARDS"
60   PRINT "3) CUBIC CENTIMETERS TO C
UBIC INCHES"
70   PRINT "4) KILOMETERS TO MILES"
80   PRINT "5) LITERS TO GALLONS"
90   PRINT "6) GRAMS TO OUNCES"
100   PRINT "7) KILOGRAMS TO POUNDS"
110   GOTO 210
120   PRINT "8) INCHES TO CENTIMETERS
"
130   PRINT "9) YARDS TO METERS"
140   PRINT "10) CUBIC INCHES TO CUBI
C CENTIMETERS"
150   PRINT "11) MILES TO KILOMETERS"

160   PRINT "12) GALLONS TO LITERS"
170   PRINT "13) OUNCES TO GRAMS"
180   PRINT "14) POUNDS TO KILOGRAMS"

190   PRINT "15) DEGREES F. TO DEGREE
S C."
200   PRINT "16) DEGREES C. TO DEGREE
S F."
210   INPUT "ENTER YOUR CHOICE NUMBER
 (1 TO 16)";A
220   IF (A>=1) * (A<=16) GOTO 240
230   PRINT "BAD CHOICE NUMBER":GOTO2
10
240   A=INT(A)
```

```
250     PRINT "--------------------------
----------------------------------------
-"
260     IF A=1  THEN A$="CM":B$="IN"
270     IF A=2  THEN A$="M":B$="YDS"
280     IF A=3  THEN A$="CC":B$="CI"
290     IF A=4  THEN A$="KM":B$="MI"
300     IF A=5  THEN A$="L":B$="GAL"
310     IF A=6  THEN A$="G":B$="OZ"
320     IF A=7  THEN A$="KG":B$="LBS"
330     IF A=8  THEN A$="IN":B$="CM"
340     IF A=9  THEN A$="YDS":B$="M"
350     IF A=10 THEN A$="CI":B$="CC"
360     IF A=11 THEN A$="MI":B$="KM"
370     IF A=12 THEN A$="GAL":B$="L"
380     IF A=13 THEN A$="OZ":B$="G"
390     IF A=14 THEN A$="LBS":B$="KG"
400 IF A=15 THEN A$="DEG. F":B$="DE
G. C"
410 IF A=16 THEN A$="DEG. C":B$="DE
G. F"
420     PRINT "HOW MANY ";A$:INPUTB
430     IF A=1  THEN C=B*.3937
440     IF A=2  THEN C=B*1.0936
450     IF A=3  THEN C=B*.061025
460     IF A=4  THEN C=B*.621377
470     IF A=5  THEN C=B*.26418
480     IF A=6  THEN C=B*.03527
490     IF A=7  THEN C=B*2.02046
500     IF A=8  THEN C=B*2.54
510     IF A=9  THEN C=B*.91441
520     IF A=10 THEN C=B*1.6386
530     IF A=11 THEN C=B*1.6093
540     IF A=12 THEN C=B*3.7852
550     IF A=13 THEN C=B*28.3527
560     IF A=14 THEN C=B*.49493
570     IF A=15 THEN C=(B-32)*(5/9)
580     IF A=16 THEN C=B*(9/5)+32
590     PRINT
600     PRINT B;" ";A$;" = ";C;" ";B$
610     PRINT "--------------------------
----------------------------------------
-"
```

```
620   INPUT "TYPE 1 TO CONTINUE OR 2
TO QUIT";V
630   IF V=1 GOTO 10
640   END
```

CODE/DECODE

Remarks

This program allows a message to be entered into the computer and scrambled into a very odd looking coded message. Like many other computerized coding programs, this program codes using the ASC(X) and CHR$(X) functions. The difference is that this program allows a "seed" number to be utilized. For each different seed number, an entirely different coding system is used. Be careful and understand what symbols your machine can process. A seed number over thirty-seven can result in graphic characters being entered into the coded message.

Variables

NP   —Operation choice (1=code 2=decode)
S   —Seed number
M$ —Message
T$ —Each letter in sequence to be coded
CD   —ASCII value of T$ plus the seed number
NU$ —The new coded message
OLD$ —The decoded message

Suggested Variations

1) There are many ways to mathematically manipulate strings. Experiment and you'll come up with some brand new code/decode schemes.

2) If these coded messages are to be sent to another computer via modems and automatically decoded, graphics and lower-case letters can be processed with little trouble and should add to the complexity of the codes.

Sample Run

DO YOU WISH TO:
1) CODE A MESSAGE OR 2) DECODE A MESSAGE
ENTER 1 OR 2? 1
A SEED GREATER THAN 37 MAY UTILIZE GRAPHIC CHARACTERS IN CODED MESSAGE.

ENTER SEED NUMBER? <u>4</u>
DO NOT USE COMMA (,) OR COLON (:).
ENTER MESSAGE:
? *HELLO BOB-I HAVE FOUND THE MAP TO THE LOST DUTCHMAN'S GOLD MINE. CONTACT ME FOR DE-TAILS-- ED.*
THE CODED MESSAGE IS:
LIPPS$FSF1$M$LEZI$JSYRHXLIQETXSXLI$PSWX$HYX
GLQER+W$KSPH$QMRI
2$$GSRXEGXQIJSV$HIXEMPW11$IH2

Program for Code/Decode

```
10 CLS:CLEAR 1000
20 PRINT "DO YOU WISH TO:"
30 PRINT "1) CODE A MESSAGE    OR    2
) DECODE A MESSAGE"
40 INPUT "ENTER 1 OR 2 ";NP
50 PRINT "A SEED GREATER THAN 37 MAY
 UTILIZE GRAPHIC CHARACTERS IN CODED
 MESSAGE."
60 INPUT "ENTER SEED NUMBER";S
70 IF NP=2 GOTO 280
80 CLS
90 PRINT "DO NOT USE COMMA (,) OR CO
LON (:)."
100 PRINT "ENTER MESSAGE:"
110 INPUT M$
120 FOR K=1 TO LEN(M$)
130 T$=MID$(M$,K,1)
140 CD=ASC(T$)+S:IF CD>255 THEN CD=C
D-255
150 NU$=NU$+CHR$(CD)
160 NEXT
170 PRINT "THE CODED MESSAGE IS:"
180 PRINT NU$
190 END
200 FOR K=1 TO LEN(NU$)
210 T$=MID$(NU$,K,1)
220 CD=ASC(T$)-S:IF CD<0 THEN CD=CD+
255
230 OLD$=OLD$+CHR$(CD)
240 NEXT
```

59

```
250  PRINT "THE DECODED MESSAGE IS:"
260  PRINT OLD$
270  END
280  PRINT "ENTER CODED MESSAGE"
290  INPUT NU$
300  GOTO 200
```

MATRIX ADDITION AND SUBTRACTION

Remarks

One of the most useful capabilities of the BASIC language is its ability to process huge matrices in the form of arrays with speed and reliability. Here is a program that demonstrates matrix manipulation for the operations of addition and subtraction. Both matrices must have the same dimensions.

Variables

A(RC, C)—Value in row R, column C in first matrix
B(R, C) —Value in row R, column C in second matrix
C(R, C) —Value in row R, column C in resulting matrix
T   —Type of operation (1=add 2=subtract)

Suggested Variations

1) You may wish to clean up your resulting matrix using an equal tabbing spaced format.

2) You may wish to expand this program to perform other useful matrix operations.

Sample Run

MATRIX ADDITION AND SUBTRACTION

WHAT ARE THE DIMENSIONS OF THE MATRICES (ROWS, COLUMNS)? 2,2
ENTER 1 FOR ADDITION OR 2 FOR SUBTRACTION? 1
*** ROW # 1 ***
VALUE OF COLUMN # 1 ? 3
VALUE OF COLUMN # 2 ? 8
*** ROW # 2 ***
VALUE OF COLUMN #1 ? 4
VALUE OF COLUMN # 2 ? 5
NOW ENTER THE VALUES OF THE SECOND MATRIX

*** ROW # 1 ***

60

ENTER THE VALUE OF COLUMN #1   ?<u>3</u>
ENTER THE VALUE OF COLUMN #2   ?<u>4</u>
*** ROW #2   ***
ENTER THE VALUE OF COLUMN #1   ?<u>-1</u>
ENTER THE VALUE OF COLUMN #2   ?<u>3</u>
RESULT:
6   12
3   8

Program for Matrix Addition and Subtraction

1

```
10 CLS:PRINT "MATRIX ADDITION AND SU
BTRACTION":PRINT:PRINT
20 INPUT "WHAT ARE THE DIMENSIONS OF
  THE MATRICES (ROWS,COLUMNS) ";R,C
30 DIM A(R,C),B(R,C),C(R,C)
40 INPUT "ENTER 1 FOR ADDITION OR 2
FOR SUBTRACTION ";T
50 FOR Z=1 TO R
60 PRINT "*** ROW #";Z;" ***"
70 FOR Y=1 TO C
80 PRINT "VALUE OF COLUMN #";Y;"   ";
:INPUT A(Z,Y)
90 NEXT Y:NEXT Z
100 CLS:PRINT "NOW ENTER THE VALUES
OF THE SECOND MATRIX":PRINT
110 FOR Z=1 TO R
120 PRINT "*** ROW #";Z;" ***"
130 FOR Y=1 TO C
140 PRINT "ENTER THE VALUE OF COLUMN
 #";Y;"   ";:INPUT K
150 IF T=2 THEN K=-K
160 A(Z,Y)=A(Z,Y)+K
170 NEXT Y:NEXT Z
180 CLS:PRINT "RESULT:"
190 FOR Z=1 TO R
200 FOR Y=1 TO C
210 PRINT A(Z,Y);"   ";
220 NEXT Y:PRINT " ":NEXT Z
230 END
```

MULTI-SORT

Remarks

This program accepts either numeric or alphanumeric data and sorts it either sequentially (or alphabetically) or in reverse order. The sorting method used is a common bubble sort. Please note that if you wish to sort mixed numeric/alphanumeric data with the numeric data on the far left side of the entered data string, trailing or preceding zeros will have to be maintained for a true sort.

Example:
If one of my data strings is:
         100   Anderson
I must enter subsequent data strings like this:
         087   Smith
All strings are compared character-to-character starting with the leftmost character. Consult the ASCII table for character precedence.

Variables

DIR — Sort choice-see menu in program text
S(X) — Value of data #X
S$(X) — Value of string (alphanumeric) data #X
NUMBER — Number of items to be sorted

Suggested Variations

1) If the bubble sort method used is too slow for your applications, you may wish to provide an additional sorting method for large groups of data.

Sample Run

NUMBER OF ITEMS? 6
TYPE OF SORT
NUMERIC, HIGHEST TO LOWEST————— 1
NUMERIC, LOWEST TO HIGHEST————— 2
ALPHANUMERIC, ALPHABETIZED——— 3
ALPHANUMERIC, REVERSED————— 4
ENTER SORT CHOICE (1,2,3, OR 4)? 3
ITEM #1   ? ANDERSON
ITEM #2   ? ZUCCHINI
ITEM #3   ? WATSON

62

ITEM #4 ? <u>TRS-80</u>
ITEM #5 ? <u>BALONEY</u>
ITEM #6 ? <u>AARDVARK</u>
SORT COMPLETE—PRESS ENTER FOR SORTED LIST?

AARDVARK
ANDERSON
BALONEY
TRS-80
WATSON
ZUCCHINI

END OF PROGRAM

Program for Multi-Sort

```
10 CLS
20 CLEAR 1000:INPUT "NUMBER OF ITEMS
  ";NUMBER
30 DIM S(NUMBER),S$(NUMBER)
40 PRINT "TYPE OF SORT":PRINT "NUMER
IC, HIGHEST TO LOWEST---- 1"
50 PRINT "NUMERIC, LOWEST TO HIGHEST
---- 2":PRINT "ALPHANUMERIC, ALPHABE
TIZED---- 3":PRINT "ALPHANUMERIC, RE
VERSED-------- 4"
60 INPUT "ENTER SORT CHOICE (1,2,3,
OR 4) ";DIR
70 IF DIR>2 GOTO 90
80 FOR INDEX=1 TO NUMBER:PRINT "ITEM
 #";INDEX;"  ";:INPUT S(INDEX):NEXT
INDEX:GOTO 100
90 FOR INDEX=1 TO NUMBER:PRINT "ITEM
 #";INDEX;"  ";:INPUT S$(INDEX):NEXT
  INDEX
100 OLD=1
110 OLD=2*OLD:IF OLD<NUMBER THEN 110

120 OLD=INT((OLD-1)/2)
130 IF OLD=0 THEN 290
140 LIMIT=NUMBER-OLD
150 FOR INDEX=1 TO LIMIT
160 HOLD=INDEX
```

```
170 KEEP=HOLD+OLD
180 IF DIR=1 GOTO 190ELSE IF DIR=2 G
OTO 210ELSE IF DIR=3 GOTO 230ELSE IF
 DIR=4 GOTO 250ELSE PRINT "ILLEGAL S
ORT CHOICE":GOTO 40
190 IF S(KEEP)<S(HOLD) THEN HANG=S(H
OLD):S(HOLD)=S(KEEP):S(KEEP)=HANG:HO
LD=HOLD-OLD:IF HOLD>0 THEN 170
200 GOTO 260
210 IF S(KEEP)>S(HOLD) THEN HANG=S(H
OLD):S(HOLD)=S(KEEP):S(KEEP)=HANG:HO
LD=HOLD-OLD:IF HOLD>0 THEN 170
220 GOTO 260
230 IF S$(KEEP)<S$(HOLD) THEN HANG$=
S$(HOLD):S$(HOLD)=S$(KEEP):S$(KEEP)=
HANG$:HOLD=HOLD-OLD:IF HOLD>0 THEN 1
70
240 GOTO 260
250 IF S$(KEEP)>S$(HOLD) THEN HANG$=
S$(HOLD):S$(HOLD)=S$(KEEP):S$(KEEP)=
HANG$:HOLD=HOLD-OLD:IF HOLD>0 THEN 1
70
260 NEXT INDEX
270 GOTO 120
280 INPUT "SORT COMPLETE-- PRESS ENT
ER FOR SORTED LIST ";A$
290 INPUT "SORT COMPLETE-- PRESS ENT
ER FOR SORTED LIST ";A$
300 CLS:FOR INDEX=1 TO NUMBER
310 IF DIR>2 GOTO 340
320 PRINT S(INDEX)
330 GOTO 350
340 PRINT S$(INDEX)
350 NEXT INDEX
360 PRINT:PRINT:PRINT "END OF PROGRA
M":END
```

BIORHYTHM CYCLES

Remarks

What!? You shelled out the big bucks for your very own
computer and you don't have even a single copy of a Biorhythm

program? Well, get to work typing in this program! After all, we computer genius types have a certain image to maintain.

Variables

A(X) —contains various constants. To name a few:
　　　IF X= 1 to 12 then A(X) is the number of elapsed days in the year to month X.
　　　If X= 101 to 112 then A(X) is the number of days in month X.

A,B,C—Month, day and year of current date

E,F,G,—Month, day and year of birthdate

0　　—Number of days to be plotted

V　　—Number of days passed since birthdate

L\$　—Type of graph cycles to be plotted

L　　—Current PRINT　or tabbing position

Suggested Variations

　　1) If you have a line printer, this is a great program with which to make a few bucks at your local carnival or flea market.

Sample Run

BIORHYTHM
+++++++
ENTER TODAY'S DATE
　　EXAMPLE: 6,2,1980? <u>8,5,1980</u>
ENTER BIRTHDATE
　　EXAMPLE: 9,9,1959? <u>9,9,1959</u>
HOW MANY DAYS ON GRAPH? <u>3</u>
ENTER YOUR GRAPH CHOICE:
P ————— PLOT PHYSICAL CYCLE ONLY
C ————— PLOT COGNITIVE CYCLE ONLY
S ————— PLOT SENSITIVITY CYCLE ONLY
A ————— PLOT ALL CYCLES
ENTER YOUR CHOICE (P,C,S, OR A)? <u>C</u>
THE POTENTIAL FOR ACCIDENTS TO OCCUR IS GREATEST WHEN
ONE OR MORE OF YOUR CYCLES CROSSES THE CENTER LINE.
GRAPH SYMBOLS:
X ——CENTER LINE
P ——PHYSICAL CYCLE　　(23-DAY)
S ——SENSITIVITY CYCLE　　(28-DAY)

C — COGNITIVE CYCLE   (33-DAY)
PRESS ENTER TO CONTINUE
YOUR BIRTHDAY IS SEPTEMBER 9 1959
YOU WERE BORN ON A WEDNESDAY, 7636 DAYS (20.92 YEARS) AGO!

HERE ARE YOUR BIORHYTHM CYCLES
STARTING AT AUGUST 5 1980
AND ENDING AT AUGUST 7 1980
PRESS ENTER TO CONTINUE?

DATE	(−)	(X)	(+)
TUE AUG 5 1980	X	C	
WED AUG 6 1980	X	C	
THU AUG 7 1980	X	C	

Program for Biorhythm Cycles

```
10 CLS:CLEAR 64:DIM A(150)
20 PRINT CHR$(23):PRINT TAB(12) "BIO
RYTHM":PRINT STRING$(32,"+"):PRINT
30   FOR I=1 TO 12:READ A(I):NEXT I
40   FOR I=101 TO 112:READ A(I):NEXT
I
50   DATA 0,31,59,90,120,151,181,212,
243,273,304,334
60   DATA 31,28,31,30,31,30,31,31,30,
31,30,31
70   A(55)=6.28318
80   GOTO 150
90   X=(V/X-INT(V/X))*A(55)
100  Y=SIN(X)
110   X=X*57.295755
120   Y=(Y*18)+44
130   Y=INT(Y)
140   RETURN
150 INPUT "ENTER TODAY'S DATE

    EXAMPLE: 6,2,1980 ";M,D,Y
160   A=M:B=D:C=Y
170   GOSUB 260
180   Z=T
190 INPUT "ENTER BIRTHDATE

    EXAMPLE: 9,9,1959 ";M,D,Y
```

66

```
200    E=M:F=D:G=Y
210    GOSUB 260
220    V=T-Z
230    V=ABS(V)
240  REM
250    GOTO 440
260    H=Y-1800
270    I=INT(H/4)
280    J=INT(I/25)
290    L=INT((H+200)/400)
300    K=0
310    IF I*4<>H GOTO 350
320    IF J*100<>H GOTO 350
330    IF L*400-200<>H GOTO 350
340    K=1
350    T=365*H+I-J+L-K
360    T=T+A(M)+D-1
370    IF M<3 GOTO 390
380    T=T+K
390    IF INT(H/4)<>H/4 GOTO 420
400    IF M>2 GOTO 420
410    T=T-1
420    N=T-7*INT(T/7)
430    RETURN
440    PRINT:PRINT
450    INPUT "HOW MANY DAYS ON GRAPH "
;O
460    CLS
470  GOTO 1460
480  PRINT "THE POTENTIAL FOR ACCIDEN
TS TO OCCUR IS GREATEST WHEN"
490  PRINT "ONE OR MORE OF YOUR CYCLE
S CROSSES THE CENTER LINE."
500    PRINT "GRAPH SYMBOLS:"
510  PRINT "X  --CENTER LINE"
520    PRINT "P  --PHYSICAL CYCLE
(23-DAY)"
530    PRINT "S  --SENSITIVITY CYCLE
(28-DAY)"
540    PRINT "C  --COGNITIVE CYCLE
(33-DAY)"
550    PRINT
560    INPUT "PRESS ENTER TO CONTINUE
";B$:CLS
```

```
570   PRINT "YOUR BIRTHDAY IS ";:P=E:
GOSUB1070:PRINT F;G
580 PRINT "YOU WERE BORN ON A ";:Q=N
+1:GOSUB1190
590   PRINT ", ";V;" DAYS (";INT((V/3
65)*100)/100;"YEARS) AGO!"
600   PRINT
610 PRINT "HERE ARE YOUR BIORYTHM CY
CLES"
620   PRINT "STARTING AT ";:P=A:GOSUB
 1070:PRINT B;C
630   PRINT "AND ENDING AT ";
640   S=A:R=B+O-1:T=C
650   IF S<12 GOTO 670
660   S=1:T=T+1:GOTO 700
670   IF S<>2 GOTO 700
680   IF INT(T/4)<>T/4 THEN 700
690   K=1
700   IF R<=A(S+100)+K GOTO 730
710   R=R-(A(S+100)+K):IF S<>1 THEN S
=S+1:K=0
720   GOTO 650
730   P=S:GOSUB 1070:PRINT R;T
740   INPUT "PRESS ENTER TO CONTINUE
";B$:CLS
750 PRINT TAB(7);"DATE";TAB(25)"(-)"
;TAB(43)"(X)";TAB(61)"(+)"
760   PRINT
770   U=V+N:U=U-7*INT(U/7):B=B-1:U=U-
1:V=V-1:K=0
780   FOR I=1 TO O:V=V+1:B=B+1:U=U+1:
IF A<>2 THEN 810
790   IF INT(C/4)<>C/4 THEN 810
800   K=1
810   IF B<=A(A+100)+K THEN 830
820   A=A+1:B=1
830   IF U<7 THEN 850
840   U=0
850   IF A<=12 THEN 870
860 A=1:C=C+1
870   IF (A<>E)+(B<>F) THEN 890
880   PRINTTAB(33);"** HAPPY ";ABS(C-
G);" BIRTHDAY **"
```

68

```
890   W=U+1:GOSUB 1380
900    PRINT "    ";:A(25)=A:GOSUB 1260
:PRINTB;C;
910 IF L$="P" OR L$="A" GOTO 920ELSE
  GOTO 930
920 X=23:GOSUB 90:A(30)=Y
930 IF L$="S" OR L$="A" GOTO 940ELSE
  GOTO 950
940 X=28:GOSUB 90:A(35)=Y
950 IF L$="C" OR L$="A" GOTO 960ELSE
  GOTO 970
960 X=33:GOSUB 90:A(40)=Y
970 M=0:FOR L=19 TO 66:PRINT TAB(L);

980   IF A(30)=L THEN PRINT "P";:GOTO
  1030
990    IF A(35)=L THEN PRINT "S";:GOTO
  1030
1000   IF A(40)=L THEN PRINT "C";:GOT
O 1030
1010   IF 44=L THEN PRINT "X";
1020   IF 66=L THEN PRINT
1030   M=M+1:IF M<>4 THEN 1040:L=100
1040   NEXT L
1050   NEXT I
1060   END
1070   IF P=1 THEN PRINT "JANUARY";:R
ETURN
1080   IF P=2 THEN PRINT "FEBRUARY";:
RETURN
1090   IF P=3 THEN PRINT "MARCH";:RET
URN
1100   IF P=4 THEN PRINT "APRIL";:RET
URN
1110   IF P=5 THEN PRINT "MAY";:RETUR
N
1120   IF P=6 THEN PRINT "JUNE";:RETU
RN
1130   IF P=7 THEN PRINT "JULY";:RETU
RN
1140   IF P=8 THEN PRINT "AUGUST";:RE
TURN
1150   IF P=9 THEN PRINT "SEPTEMBER";
:RETURN
```

```
1160   IF P=10 THEN PRINT "OCTOBER";:
RETURN
1170   IF P=11 THEN PRINT "NOVEMBER";
:RETURN
1180   PRINT "DECEMBER";:RETURN
1190   IF Q=1 THEN PRINT "WEDNESDAY";
:RETURN
1200   IF Q=2 THEN PRINT "THURSDAY";:
RETURN
1210   IF Q=3 THEN PRINT "FRIDAY";:RE
TURN
1220   IF Q=4 THEN PRINT "SATURDAY";:
RETURN
1230   IF Q=5 THEN PRINT "SUNDAY";:RE
TURN
1240   IF Q=6 THEN PRINT "MONDAY";:RE
TURN
1250   PRINT "TUESDAY";:RETURN
1260   IF A(25)=1 THEN PRINT "JAN";:R
ETURN
1270   IF A(25)=2 THEN PRINT "FEB";:R
ETURN
1280   IF A(25)=3 THEN PRINT "MAR";:R
ETURN
1290   IF A(25)=4 THEN PRINT "APR";:R
ETURN
1300   IF A(25)=5 THEN PRINT "MAY";:R
ETURN
1310   IF A(25)=6 THEN PRINT "JUN";:R
ETURN
1320   IF A(25)=7 THEN PRINT "JUL";:R
ETURN
1330   IF A(25)=8 THEN PRINT "AUG";:R
ETURN
1340   IF A(25)=9 THEN PRINT "SEP";:R
ETURN
1350   IF A(25)=10 THEN PRINT "OCT";:
RETURN
1360   IF A(25)=11 THEN PRINT "NOV";:
RETURN
1370   PRINT "DEC";:RETURN
1380   IF W=1 THEN PRINT "WED";:RETUR
N
```

```
1390  IF W=2 THEN PRINT "THU";:RETUR
N
1400  IF W=3 THEN PRINT "FRI";:RETUR
N
1410  IF W=4 THEN PRINT "SAT";:RETUR
N
1420  IF W=5 THEN PRINT "SUN";:RETUR
N
1430  IF W=6 THEN PRINT "MON";:RETUR
N
1440  PRINT "TUE";:RETURN
1450  END
1460 PRINT "ENTER YOUR GRAPH CHOICE:
"
1470 PRINT "P ----- PLOT PHYSICAL CY
CLE ONLY"
1480 PRINT "C ----- PLOT COGNITIVE C
YCLE ONLY"
1490 PRINT "S ----- PLOT SENSITIVITY
 CYCLE ONLY"
1500 PRINT "A ----- PLOT ALL CYCLES"
1510 PRINT
1520 INPUT "ENTER YOUR CHOICE (P, C,
 S, OR A) ";L$
1530 IF L$<>"P" AND L$<>"S" AND L$<>
"C" AND L$<>"A" GOTO 1520
1540 CLS:GOTO 480
```

LINEAR CORRELATION COEFFICIENT AND REGRESSION

Remarks

This program calculates the correlation between two sets of data and then interpolates points on the regression line. All variables used internally are listed during the program (and below) to allow the uses of these numbers in other statistical analysis programs. At the end of the program, you interpolate Y axis values by entering X axis values of your choice.

Variables

P   —Number of data pairs
X(P)   —X data # P
Y(P)   —Y data #P
XSUM   —Sum of all X values

71

YSUM—Sum of all Y values
XYSUM—Sum of the products of each X and Y pair
X2SUM—Sum of all squared X values
Y2SUM—Sum of all squared Y values
XBAR —Average of all X values
YBAR —Average of all Y values

Suggested Variations

1) Insert a routine to plot the regression line on the CRT screen or on a line printer.

2) Instead of interpolating a great number of points, why not just have the user specify the endpoints and an increment and plot all points within these parameters.

Sample Run

LINEAR CORRELATION COEFFICIENT AND REGRESSION

DEFINITION OF VARIABLES
XSUM= SUM OF ALL X VALUES
YSUM= SUM OF ALL Y VALUES
XYSUM= SUM OF PRODUCTS OF ALL X AND Y PAIRS
X2SUM= SUM OF ALL X VALUES SQUARED
Y2SUM= SUM OF ALL Y VALUES SQUARED
XBAR= AVERAGE OF THE X VALUES
YBAR= AVERAGE OF THE Y VALUES

HOW MANY PAIRS? 4
PAIR # 1
ENTER X ? 10
ENTER Y ? 4
PAIR # 2
ENTER X ? 15
ENTER Y ? 12
PAIR # 3
ENTER X ? 24
ENTER Y ? 32
PAIR # 4
ENTER X ? 13
ENTER Y ? 5
4 PAIRS

XSUM= 62

YSUM= 53
XYSUM= 1053
X2SUM= 1070
Y2SUM= 1209
XBAR= 15.5
YBAR= 13.25
CORRELATION= .98501 OR X'S AND Y'S ARE 98.501%
CORRELATED
REGRESSION LINE SLOPE= 2.12385
Y INTERCEPT=-19.6697
ENTER X ? 52
Y= 90.7706
ENTER 1 FOR MORE POINTS OR 2 TO QUIT ? 1
ENTER X ? 0
Y= -19.6697
ENTER 1 FOR MORE POINTS OR 2 TO QUIT ? 2

Program for Linear Correlation Coefficient and Regression

```
10 CLS:PRINT "LINEAR CORRELATION COE
FFICIENT AND REGRESSION"
20 PRINT:PRINT
30 XSUM=0:YSUM=0:XYSUM=0:X2SUM=0:Y2S
UM=0
40 GOSUB 520
50 PRINT:PRINT
60 INPUT "HOW MANY PAIRS";P
70 DIM X(P),Y(P)
80 CLS
90 FOR Z=1 TO P
100 PRINT "PAIR #";Z
110 INPUT "ENTER X ";X
120 INPUT "ENTER Y ";Y
130 X(Z)=X:Y(Z)=Y
140 CLS:NEXT Z
150 REM* FIND XSUM,YSUM,XYSUM,X2SUM,
Y2SUM
160 FOR Z=1 TO P
170 XSUM=XSUM+X(Z)
180 YSUM=YSUM+Y(Z)
190 U=X(Z)*Y(Z):XYSUM=XYSUM+U
200 U=X(Z)*X(Z):X2SUM=X2SUM+U
210 U=Y(Z)*Y(Z):Y2SUM=Y2SUM+U
```

```
220 NEXT Z
230 XBAR=XSUM/P:YBAR=YSUM/P
240 CLS
250 PRINT P;" PAIRS":PRINT
260 PRINT "XSUM= ";XSUM
270 PRINT "YSUM= ";YSUM
280 PRINT "XYSUM= ";XYSUM
290 PRINT "X2SUM= ";X2SUM
300 PRINT "Y2SUM= ";Y2SUM
310 PRINT "XBAR= ";XBAR
320 PRINT "YBAR= ";YBAR
330 REM *CALCULATE NUMERATOR
340 NUM=XYSUM-((XSUM*YSUM)/P)
350 REM *CALCULATE DENOMINATOR
360 DEN=(SQR(X2SUM-((XSUM↑2/P))))*(S
QR(Y2SUM-((YSUM↑2/P))))
370 REM *CALCULATE CORRELATION
380 R=NUM/DEN
390 PRINT "CORRELATION= ";R;" OR X'S
 AND Y'S ARE ";R*100;"% CORRELATED"
400 REM *CALCULATE SLOPE OF REGRESSI
ON LINE
410 B=(XYSUM-((XSUM*YSUM)/P))/(X2SUM
-(XSUM↑2/P))
420 PRINT "REGRESSION LINE SLOPE= ";
B
430 REM *CALCULATE Y INTERCEPT
440 A=YBAR-(B*XBAR)
450 PRINT "Y INTERCEPT= ";A
460 INPUT "ENTER X ";X
470 Y=B*X+A
480 PRINT "Y= ";Y
490 INPUT "ENTER 1 FOR MORE POINTS O
R 2 TO QUIT ";C
500 IF C=1 GOTO 460
510 END
520 PRINT "DEFINITION OF VARIABLES"
530 PRINT "XSUM= SUM OF ALL X VALUES
"
540 PRINT "YSUM= SUM OF ALL Y VALUES
"
550 PRINT "XYSUM= SUM OF PRODUCTS OF
 ALL X AND Y PAIRS"
```

```
560 PRINT "X2SUM= SUM OF ALL X VALUE
S SQUARED"
570 PRINT "Y2SUM= SUM OF ALL Y VALUE
S SQUARED"
580 PRINT "XBAR= AVERAGE OF THE X VA
LUES"
590 PRINT "YBAR= AVERAGE OF THE Y VA
LUES"
600 RETURN
```

DECIMAL TO BASE CONVERSION

Remarks

The perfect complement to your new *BASE TO DECIMAL CONVERSION* (what else). Like *BASE TO DECIMAL*, this program converts using bases two to sixteen and includes common symbolic nomenclature (like the letters A through F for Base 16). The converted number may be up to ten digits long.

Variables

BA   —Base to convert decimal number to
G,NU—Decimal number
A(Z) —Place holder in position BA to the Z power
B(Z) —Number of digits held in position Z of place holder.

Suggested Variations

1) As suggested before, you may wish to type this program in and merge it with *BASE TO DECIMAL CONVERSION* for a handy, all-in-one utility. Use a renumbering program to ensure no duplication of line numbers.

2) Provide a routine to recognize and report an overflow when the converted number exceeds ten places.

Sample Run

DECIMAL TO BASE CONVERSION

WHAT BASE (2-16) ?<u>16</u>
WHAT NUMBER (DECIMAL) ? <u>32767</u>
32767 (DECIMAL) = 0 0 0 0 0 0 0 7 F F F BASE 16

DECIMAL TO BASE CONVERSION

WHAT BASE (2-16) ? <u>2</u>

WHAT NUMBER (DECIMAL)? 9
9 (DECIMAL) = 00000001001 BASE 2

DECIMAL TO BASE CONVERSION

WHAT BASE (2-16)? 11
WHAT NUMBER (DECIMAL)? 50000
50000 (DECIMAL) = 00000034625 BASE 11

Program for Decimal to Base Conversion

```
10 DIM A(10),B(10)
20 CLS:PRINT "DECIMAL TO BASE CONVER
SION":PRINT:PRINT
30 INPUT "WHAT BASE (2-16) ";BA
40 IF BA<2 OR BA>16 THEN CLS:GOTO 20

50 INPUT "WHAT NUMBER (DECIMAL) ";G:
NU=G
60 GOSUB 240
70 FOR Z=10 TO 1 STEP -1
80 IF A(Z)>NU THEN B(Z)=0:NEXT Z:GOT
O 110
90 B(Z)=INT(NU/A(Z)):NU=NU-(B(Z)*A(Z
))
100 NEXT Z
110 B(0)=NU
120 PRINT G;" (DECIMAL)=   ";
130 FOR X=10 TO 0 STEP -1
140 IF B(X)=15 THEN PRINT "F ";
150 IF B(X)=14 THEN PRINT "E ";
160 IF B(X)=13 THEN PRINT "D ";
170 IF B(X)=12 THEN PRINT "C ";
180 IF B(X)=11 THEN PRINT "B ";
190 IF B(X)=10 THEN PRINT "A ";
200 IF B(X)<10 THEN PRINT B(X);
210 NEXT X
220 PRINT "   BASE";BA
230 END
240 K=1:FOR X=1 TO 10
250 A(X)=K*BA
260 K=A(X)
270 NEXT
280 RETURN
```

BASE TO DECIMAL CONVERSION

Remarks

Here's a snazzy program for you programmers who are really tired of digging into conversion tables to find the decimal equivalent of a base number. This program will convert numbers up to ten digits long in bases two through sixteen. It accepts the base numbers using the common symbolic nomenclature (such as the letters A through F for Base sixteen).

Variables

B —Base
A(X)—Contains value in compartment X of base chart
D —Number of digits in base number
E —Digit in base number
G —Decimal equivalent of E's

Suggested Variations

1) By adding to the number of symbols recognized, you can easily increase the number of bases that this program can convert.

2) You may wish to allow more than ten digit long base numbers.

3) By merging this program with the *Decimal To Base* program, you could have a very useful utility program that could even allow Base to Base conversion.

Sample Run

BASE TO DECIMAL CONVERSION
WHAT BASE (2 TO 16) ? <u>16</u>
THE BASE NUMBER MAY BE UP TO 10 DIGITS LONG.
HOW MANY DIGITS LONG IS BASE NUMBER ? <u>4</u>
ENTER DIGITS AS READ FROM LEFT TO RIGHT.
DIGIT # 1 — WHAT IS THE VALUE ? <u>7</u>
DIGIT # 2 — WHAT IS THE VALUE ? <u>F</u>
DIGIT # 3 — WHAT IS THE VALUE ? <u>F</u>
DIGIT # 4 — WHAT IS THE VALUE ? <u>F</u>
7FFF BASE 16 EQUALS 32767 BASE 10.

BASE TO DECIMAL CONVERSION

WHAT BASE (2 TO 16) ? <u>2</u>
THE BASE NUMBER MAY BE UP TO 10 DIGITS LONG.

HOW MANY DIGITS LONG IS BASE NUMBER? <u>4</u>
ENTER DIGITS AS READ FROM LEFT TO RIGHT.
DIGIT # 1 — WHAT IS THE VALUE? <u>1</u>
DIGIT # 2 — WHAT IS THE VALUE? <u>0</u>
DIGIT # 3 — WHAT IS THE VALUE? <u>0</u>
DIGIT # 4 — WHAT IS THE VALUE? <u>1</u>
1001 BASE 2 EQUALS 9 BASE 10.

Program for Base to Decimal Conversion

```
10  DIM A(150)
20   CLS:PRINT:PRINT:PRINT "BASE TO D
ECIMAL CONVERSION":PRINT
30  INPUT "WHAT BASE (2 TO 16) ";B
40  IF B<2 OR B>16 THEN PRINT "INVALI
D BASE":GOTO 30
50   C=1
60   A(1)=1
70   FOR V= 2 TO 10
80   C=C*B
90   A(V)=C
100  NEXTV
110   CLS:PRINT "THE BASE NUMBER MAY
BE UP TO 10 DIGITS LONG."
120  INPUT "HOW MANY DIGITS LONG IS
BASE NUMBER ";D
130 D1=D
140 IF D>10 OR D<1 THEN PRINT "NUMBE
R TOO LONG":FOR X=1 TO 2000:NEXT X:G
OTO 110
150   PRINT "ENTER DIGITS AS READ FRO
M LEFT TO RIGHT."
160   G=0
170   F=99
180   FOR H=1 TO D
190 PRINT "DIGIT #";H;"-- WHAT IS TH
E VALUE ";:INPUT E$
200 IF E$= "A" OR E$="B" OR E$="C" O
R E$="D" OR E$="E" OR E$="F" GOTO 41
0
210 IF E$>"F" GOTO 410
220 E=VAL(E$)
230 IF E>=B THEN PRINT "INVALID BASE
 DIGIT":GOTO 190
```

78

```
240  G=G+(E*A(D)):D=D-1
250  F=F+1
260  A(F)=E
270  NEXTH
280  L=(D1-1)+100
290  FOR I=100 TO L
300  IF A(I)>=10 GOTO 350
310 PRINT A(I);
320  NEXTI
330  PRINT " BASE ";B;" EQUALS ";G;"
  BASE 10."
340  END
350 IF A(I)=10 PRINT "A";:GOTO 320
360 IF A(I)=11 PRINT "B";:GOTO 320
370 IF A(I)=12 PRINT "C";:GOTO 320
380 IF A(I)=13 PRINT "D";:GOTO 320
390 IF A(I)=14 PRINT "E";:GOTO 320
400 PRINT "F";:GOTO 320
410 IF E$>"F" THEN E=B+1:GOTO 230
420 IF E$="A" THEN E=10:GOTO 230
430 IF E$="B" THEN E=11:GOTO 230
440 IF E$="C" THEN E=12:GOTO 230
450 IF E$="D" THEN E=13:GOTO 230
460 IF E$="E" THEN E=14:GOTO 230
470 IF E$="F" THEN E=15:GOTO 230
```

BINOMIAL DISTRIBUTION

Remarks

Another good program for you hard core statistics fans out
there (there *are* a few of you left, aren't there?). This program
calculates the probability of a number of successes occuring after a
number of trials, given the calculated probability of success. This
program uses double precision variables throughout for accuracy.
It is important to use the correct amount of significant digits. This
is left to the user's discretion.

Variables

    N#—Number of trials
    R#—Number of successes
    P#—Calculated probability for success
    Y#—Factorial of X#
    H#—Binomial distribution

Suggested Variations

1) You might wish to institute a coin flipping routine to clearly demonstrate the workings of this program.

2) You may wish to extract the factorial subroutine for use in other programs.

Sample Run

BINOMIAL DISTRIBUTION

NUMBER OF TRIALS ? 10
NUMBER OF SUCCESSES ? 4
PROBABILITY OF SUCCESS ? .50
PROBABILITY OF 4 SUCCESSES IN 10
TRIALS= .205078125 OR 20. 5078125%

BINOMIAL DISTRIBUTION

NUMBER OF TRIALS ? 5
NUMBER OF SUCCESSES ? 3
PROBABILITY OF SUCCESS ? .75
PROBABILITY OF 3 SUCCESSES IN 5
TRIALS= .263671986758709 or 26. 3671986758709%

Program for Binomial Distribution

```
10 CLS:PRINT "BINOMIAL DISTRIBUTION"

20 PRINT
30 INPUT "NUMBER OF TRIALS ";N#
40 INPUT "NUMBER OF SUCCESSES ";R#
50 INPUT "PROBABILITY OF SUCCESS ";P
#
60 X#=N#:GOSUB 150:NF#=Y#
70 X#=R#:GOSUB 150:RF#=Y#
80 X#=N#-R#:GOSUB 150:NRF#=Y#
90 K#=NF#/(RF#*NRF#)
100 J#=(P#ER#)*((1-P#)↑(N#-R#))
110 H#=J#*K#
120 PRINT "PROBABILITY OF ";R#;" SUC
CESSES IN ";N#
130 PRINT "TRIALS= ";H#;" OR";H#*100
;"%"
```

80

```
140 END
150 REM *FACTORIAL SUBROUTINE    IN X
 OUT Y
160 Y#=X#
170 FOR Z=1 TO X#-1:Y#=Y#*Z:NEXT Z
180 RETURN
```

DAYS BETWEEN TWO DATES

Remarks

Some of you sharpies might recognize this program as a subroutine of program *BIORHYTHM*. I don't apologize since this is a very useful program on its own, and is common throughout the computer grapevine. Did you know that July 4, 1776 fell on a Thursday?

Variables

A(X)　—If X= 1 to 12 then A(X) is number of elapsed days in the year up to month X.
　　　　　If X = 101 to 112 then A(X) is number of days in month X.
A,B,C—Month, date, and year of latest date
E,F,G—Month, date, and year of earliest date
V　　—Number of days between the two dates
P,Q　—Used in subroutines to print month and day

Suggested Variations

1) This program will not accept a date such as 2,4,80 and consider it the same as 2,4,1980. You may wish to insert a routine to recognize and question this in order to accept either input method.

Sample Run

DAYS BETWEEN TWO DATES
++++++++++++++++++++++++++

ENTER LATEST DATE
EXAMPLE: 6,2,1980 ? <u>8,5,1980</u>
ENTER EARLIEST DATE
EXAMPLE: 2,1,1977 ? <u>7,4,1776</u>
PRESS ENTER TO CONTINUE?
LATEST DATE// TUESDAY, AUGUST 5 1980

EARLIEST DATE-- THURSDAY, JULY 4 1776

A DIFFERENCE OF 74541 DAYS
(204.22 YEARS)

DAYS BETWEEN TWO DATES
++++++++++++++++++++++++++
ENTER LATEST DATE
EXAMPLE: 6,2,1980? 8,5,1980
ENTER EARLIEST DATE
EXAMPLE: 2,1,1977? 9,9,1959
PRESS ENTER TO CONTINUE?
LATEST DATE-- TUESDAY, AUGUST 5 1980

EARLIEST DATE-- WEDNESDAY, SEPTEMBER 9 1959

A DIFFERENCE OF 7636 DAYS
(20.92 YEARS)

Program for Days Between Two Dates

```
10 CLS:CLEAR 64:DIM A(150)
20 PRINT:PRINT TAB(12) "DAYS BETWEEN
 TWO DATES":PRINTTAB(7) STRING$(32,"
+"):PRINT
30  FOR I=1 TO 12:READ A(I):NEXT I
40  FOR I=101 TO 112:READ A(I):NEXT
 I
50  DATA 0,31,59,90,120,151,181,212,
243,273,304,334
60  DATA 31,28,31,30,31,30,31,31,30,
31,30,31
70 INPUT "ENTER LATEST DATE

  EXAMPLE: 6,2,1980 ";M,D,Y
80  A=M:B=D:C=Y
90  GOSUB 170
100  Z=T
110 INPUT "ENTER EARLIEST DATE

   EXAMPLE: 2,1,1977 ";M,D,Y
120  E=M:F=D:G=Y
130  GOSUB 170
```

```
140   V=T-Z
150   V=ABS(V)
160   GOTO 350
170   H=Y-1800
180   I=INT(H/4)
190   J=INT(I/25)
200   L=INT((H+200)/400)
210   K=0
220   IF I*4<>H GOTO 260
230   IF J*100<>H GOTO 260
240   IF L*400-200<>H GOTO 260
250   K=1
260   T=365*H+I-J+L-K
270   T=T+A(M)+D-1
280   IF M<3 GOTO 300
290   T=T+K
300   IF INT(H/4)<>H/4 GOTO 330
310   IF M>2 GOTO 330
320   T=T-1
330   N=T-7*INT(T/7)
340   RETURN
350 INPUT "PRESS ENTER TO CONTINUE "
;A$:CLS
360 PRINT "LATEST DATE-- ";:U=V+N:U=
U-7*INT(U/7)
370 Q=U+1:IF U=7 THEN U=0
380 GOSUB 570:P=A:PRINT ", ";:GOSUB
450:PRINT B;C
390 PRINT:PRINT "EARLIEST DATE-- ";:
Q=N+1:GOSUB 570:PRINT ", ";
400 P=E:GOSUB 450:PRINT F;G
410 PRINT:PRINT:
420 PRINT "A DIFFERENCE OF ";V;" DAY
S"
430 PRINT "(";INT((V/365)*100)/100;"
  YEARS)"
440 END
450   IF P=1 THEN PRINT "JANUARY";:RE
TURN
460   IF P=2 THEN PRINT "FEBRUARY";:R
ETURN
470   IF P=3 THEN PRINT "MARCH";:RETU
RN
```

```
480   IF  P=4  THEN  PRINT  "APRIL";:RETU
RN
490   IF  P=5  THEN  PRINT  "MAY";:RETURN

500   IF  P=6  THEN  PRINT  "JUNE";:RETUR
N
510   IF  P=7  THEN  PRINT  "JULY";:RETUR
N
520   IF  P=8  THEN  PRINT  "AUGUST";:RET
URN
530   IF  P=9  THEN  PRINT  "SEPTEMBER";:
RETURN
540   IF  P=10 THEN  PRINT  "OCTOBER";:R
ETURN
550   IF  P=11 THEN  PRINT  "NOVEMBER";:
RETURN
560   PRINT  "DECEMBER";:RETURN
570   IF  Q=1  THEN  PRINT  "WEDNESDAY";:
RETURN
580   IF  Q=2  THEN  PRINT  "THURSDAY";:R
ETURN
590   IF  Q=3  THEN  PRINT  "FRIDAY";:RET
URN
600   IF  Q=4  THEN  PRINT  "SATURDAY";:R
ETURN
610   IF  Q=5  THEN  PRINT  "SUNDAY";:RET
URN
620   IF  Q=6  THEN  PRINT  "MONDAY";:RET
URN
630   PRINT  "TUESDAY";:RETURN
```

GAMETES AND GAM-MEM

Remarks

In this program, the user enters a chromosome that has from one to nine gene pairs. This program then calculates the possible gametes (sperm or egg) that can be produced from this chromosome through meiosis. The user must note that as the number of genes increase, the number of possible gametes increases exponentially. For instance, if there are five genes on a chromosome, there can be a maximum of two to the fifth power of possible gametes. For this reason, I have included (at no extra charge!) the small utility program *GAM-MEM*. This program will tell you exactly how much memory to CLEAR in line #20 of *GAMETES*.

Notice that for nine genes, you must save over 13K of memory! Actually, in a program of this nature, we really don't need two separate sections for male and female chromosomes. I did include these exactly for the purpose of SUGGESTED VARIATION #1 below.

Variables

A$(X,Y)—the type of Allele #X, on gene #Y—male
B$(X,Y)—Female equivalent of A$(X,Y)
P(X)   —Used to count in binary
PA   —A pager increment for "clean" output with no scrolling
M$(X)   —Possible gamete #X—male
F$(X)   —Possible gamete #X—female

Suggested Variations

1) Chances are if you have use for this program, the next step in your work is the actual mating of the two chromosomes. Since the memory requirements for this program can be quite high, you may wish to output the possible gametes to a cassette file in order to be read later into a gamete crossing program.

2) Since most users will not have lower-case modifications and can only see upper case characters on their CRT I have arbitrarily in my work set recessive alleles symbolically equal to the upper case symbol (for the dominant allele would be typed in as A and the recessive allele would be typed in as A*. If you have lower-case capabilities, you might wish to make direct use of them (no modification to the program is necessary), since common nomenclature uses both upper and lower case.

3) Don't forget that *GAM-MEM* only gives you the number of bytes to CLEAR for only one chromosome. If you are going to use both male and female chromosomes, you will have to CLEAR twice as much as program *GAM-MEM* directs you.

Sample Run

HOW MANY GENE PAIRS? <u>4</u>
MALE CHROMOSOME
GENE PAIR # 1
FIRST ALLELE? <u>A</u>
SECOND ALLELE ? <u>A*</u>
GENE PAIR # 2
FIRST ALLELE ? <u>B</u>

SECOND ALLELE ? B*
GENE PAIR # 3
FIRST ALLELE ? C
SECOND ALLELE ? C*
GENE PAIR # 4
FIRST ALLELE ? D
SECOND ALLELE ? D*
THE POSSIBLE GAMETES ARE:
1—ABCD
2—ABCD*
3—ABC*D
4—ABC*D*
5—AB*CD
6—AB*CD*
7—AB*C*D
8—AB*C*D*
9—A*BCD
10—A*BCD*
11—A*BC*D
12—A*BC*D*
13—A*B*CD
PRESS ENTER TO CONTINUE
14—A*B*CD*
15—A*B*CD*
16—A*B*C*D*

Sample Run

GAM-MEM
FOR 1 PAIRS, (2 COMBINATIONS) CLEAR 6 BYTES.
FOR 2 PAIRS, (4 COMBINATIONS) CLEAR 24 BYTES.
FOR 3 PAIRS, (8 COMBINATIONS) CLEAR 72 BYTES.
FOR 4 PAIRS, (16 COMBINATIONS) CLEAR 192 BYTES.
FOR 5 PAIRS, (32 COMBINATIONS) CLEAR 480 BYTES.
FOR 6 PAIRS, (64 COMBINATIONS) CLEAR 1152 BYTES.
FOR 7 PAIRS, (128 COMBINATIONS) CLEAR 2688 BYTES.
FOR 8 PAIRS, (256 COMBINATIONS) CLEAR 6144 BYTES.
FOR 9 PAIRS, (512 COMBINATIONS) CLEAR 13824 BYTES.

Program for Games and Gam-Mem

```
10 CLS
20 CLEAR 5000:REM * RUN PROGRAM GAM-
MEM FOR MEMORY REQUIREMENTS
```

```
30 DIM A$(2,9),B$(2,9),M$(512),F$(51
2),P(9)
40 INPUT "HOW MANY GENE PAIRS";P
50 IF P>9 THEN PRINT "9 PAIRS IS MAX
IMUM--REENTER":GOTO 40
60 CLS
70 PRINT "MALE CHROMOSOME":PRINT
80 FOR X=1 TO P
90 PRINT "GENE PAIR #";X
100 INPUT "FIRST ALLELE ";A$(1,X)
110 INPUT "SECOND ALLELE ";A$(2,X)
120 CLS
130 NEXT X
140 PRINT "WORKING"
150 FOR X=1 TO P:P(X)=1:NEXT X
160 X=P:R=0:X1=0
170 R=R+1:FOR K=1 TO P:M$(R)=M$(R)+A
$(P(K),K)+" ":NEXT K
180 IF P(X)=1 THEN P(X)=2:X=P:GOTO 1
70
190 IF P(X)=2 THEN P(X)=1:GOTO 210
200 P(X-1)=2:X=P:GOTO 170
210 IF X=1 THEN 230
220 X=X-1:GOTO 180
230 H=R
240 PA=0:PRINT "THE POSSIBLE GAMETES
 ARE:"
250 FOR X=1 TO H
260 IF X=1 GOTO 280
270 FOR Z=1 TO X-1:IF M$(Z)=M$(X) TH
EN 300ELSE NEXT Z
280 PA=PA+1:IF PA=14 THEN GOSUB 570
290 X1=X1+1:PRINT X1;"--    ";M$(X)
300 NEXT X
310 PRINT:INPUT "PRESS ENTER TO CONT
INUE ";A$:CLS
320 PRINT "FEMALE CHROMOSOME"
330 FOR X=1 TO P
340 PRINT "GENE PAIR #";X
350 INPUT "FIRST ALLELE ";B$(1,X)
360 INPUT "SECOND ALLELE ";B$(2,X)
370 CLS
380 NEXT X
390 PRINT "WORKING"
```

```
400 FOR X=1 TO P:P(X)=1:NEXT X
410 X=P:R=0
420 R=R+1:FOR K=1 TO P:F$(R)=F$(R)+B
$(P(K),K)+" ":NEXT K
430 IF P(X)=1 THEN P(X)=2:X=P:GOTO 4
20
440 IF P(X)=2 THEN P(X)=1:GOTO 460
450 P(X-1)=2:X=P:GOTO 420
460 IF X=1 THEN 480
470 X=X-1:GOTO 430
480 H=R:PA=0:X1=0
490 PRINT "THE POSSIBLE GAMETES ARE:
"
500 FOR X=1 TO H
510 IF X=1 GOTO 530
520 FOR Z=1 TO X-1:IF F$(Z)=F$(X) TH
EN 550ELSE NEXT Z
530 PA=PA+1:IF PA=14 THEN GOSUB 570
540 X1=X1+1:PRINT X1;"--    ";F$(X)
550 NEXT X
560 END
570 PA=0:PRINT:INPUT "PRESS ENTER TO
CONTINUE";A$:CLS:RETURN
```

```
10 CLS:PRINT "GAM-MEM"
20 FOR X=1 TO 9
30 K=2↑X
40 Z=K*(3*X)
50 PRINT "FOR ";X;" PAIRS, (";K;" CO
MBINATIONS) CLEAR ";Z;" BYTES."
60 NEXT X
```

MEAN, VARIANCE, STANDARD DEVIATION, STANDARD ERROR

Remarks

This program calculates the mean, variance, standard deviation, and standard error of the mean from a set of ungrouped data. It is a useful statistical analysis program that has found its way into many different fields of use.

Variables

N   —Number of samples
A(X)—Value of sample #X
C   —Mean
D   —Variance
E   —Standard Deviation
F   —Standard error of the mean

Suggested Variations

1) In order to allow faster entry of samples, you may wish to modify this program to accept grouped data. In other words, if there are five samples with the value of nine, it would be entered as 5,9.

2) Depending on your use of this program, you may wish to allow for the data to be part of the population, or the entire population.

Sample Run

MEAN, VARIANCE, STANDARD DEVIATION, STANDARD ERROR OF THE MEAN

HOW MANY SAMPLES? 5
VALUE OF SAMPLE # 1 ? 20
VALUE OF SAMPLE # 2 ? 14
VALUE OF SAMPLE # 3 ? 16
VALUE OF SAMPLE # 4 ? 8
VALUE OF SAMPLE # 5 ? 35

NUMBER OF SAMPLES 5

MEAN 18.6
VARIANCE 102.8
STANDARD DEVIATION 10.139
STANDARD ERROR OF THE MEAN 4.53431

Program for Mean, Variance, Standard Deviation and Standard Error

```
10 CLS:PRINT "MEAN, VARIANCE, STANDA
RD DEVIATION, STANDARD ERROR"
20 PRINT "OF THE MEAN":PRINT:PRINT
```

```
30 INPUT "HOW MANY SAMPLES ";N
40 DIM A(N)
50 FOR X=1 TO N:PRINT "VALUE OF SAMP
LE #";X;:INPUT A(X)
60 NEXT X
70 A=0
80 FOR B=1 TO N:A=A+A(B):NEXT B:C=A/
N
90 CLS:PRINT "NUMBER OF SAMPLES ";N:
PRINT "MEAN ";C
100 FOR X=1 TO N:A(X)=((A(X)-C)↑2)
110 NEXT X
120 D=0:FOR X=1 TO N:D=D+A(X):NEXT X

130 D=D/(N-1)
140 PRINT "VARIANCE ";D
150 E=SQR(D):PRINT "STANDARD DEVIATI
ON ";E
160 F=E/SQR(N)
170 PRINT "STANDARD ERROR OF THE MEA
N ";F
180 END
```

FRACTION MATH

Remarks

No matter what the computer wizards try to tell us, the real world does *not* always function by decimal number alone. Sometimes, it is just plain desirable to use fractions! This program is written just for you people who would rather live with 2/3 than .66666666666666666666667. It adds, subtracts, multiplies and divides fractions in the blink of an eye, and even prints the answer in fraction form. This program uses the cross-multiplying method to obtain a common denominator, but a reducing subroutine is included to take a fraction down to its simplest form.

Variables

CH—Operation choice
A —Numerator of first fraction
B —Denominator of first fraction
C —Numerator of second fraction
D —Denominator of second fraction
CO—Common denominator
CA—Revised numerator of first fraction

CC—Revised numerator of second fraction
CE—Result of operation- numerator of answer
D —Incrementer for reduction routine

Suggested Variations

1) Using the common denominator and reduction routine in this program, you could easily add more arithmetic operations. The more, the merrier!

2) Hey! This is an excellent starting point for your educators to write a computerized fraction math program for youngsters.

Sample Run

FRACTION MATH
THIS PROGRAM WILL PERFORM THE FOLLOWING FUNCTIONS
ON TWO FRACTIONS:
1) ADDITION
2) SUBTRACTION
3) MULTIPLICATION
4) DIVISION
AND
5) REDUCTION OF A SINGLE FRACTION
ENTER THE NUMBER OF THE OPERATION OF YOUR CHOICE? 1
** ADDITION **

NUMERATOR OF FIRST FRACTION? 5
DENOMINATOR OF FIRST FRACTION? 8
NUMERATOR OF SECOND FRACTION 12
DENOMINATOR OF SECOND FRACTION? 13
⅝ + 12/13 = 161/104
WOULD YOU LIKE THIS REDUCED (YES OR NO)? YES
REDUCED FORM: 161-104

ENTER 1 FOR NEW DATA OR 2 TO QUIT? 2

Program for Fraction Math

```
10 CLS
20 PRINT "FRACTION MATH"
30 PRINT "THIS PROGRAM WILL PERFORM
THE FOLLOWING FUNCTIONS"
```

```
40 PRINT "ON TWO FRACTIONS:"
50 PRINT "1) ADDITION"
60 PRINT "2) SUBTRACTION"
70 PRINT "3) MULTIPLICATION"
80 PRINT "4) DIVISION"
90 PRINT "AND"
100 PRINT "5) REDUCTION OF A SINGLE
FRACTION"
110 PRINT:PRINT:INPUT "ENTER THE NUM
BER OF THE OPERATION OF YOUR CHOICE"
;CH
120 CLS:ON CH GOTO 130,140,150,160,4
80
130 PRINT "** ADDITION **":GOTO 170
140 PRINT "** SUBTRACTION **":GOTO 1
70
150 PRINT "** MULTIPLICATION **":GOT
O 170
160 PRINT "** DIVISION **":GOTO 170
170 PRINT:PRINT
180 INPUT "NUMERATOR OF FIRST FRACTI
ON ";A
190 INPUT "DENOMINATOR OF FIRST FRAC
TION ";B
200 INPUT "NUMERATOR OF SECOND FRACT
ION ";C
210 INPUT "DENOMINATOR OF SECOND FRA
CTION ";D
220 CLS
230 ON CH GOTO 240,240,340,370
240 CO=B*D
250 CA=A*D
260 CC=C*B
270 IF CH=2 GOTO 310
280 CE=CA+CC
290 PRINT A;"/";B;" +";C;"/";D;" =";
CE;"/";CO
300 GOTO 390
310 CE=CA-CC
320 PRINT A;"/";B;" -";C;"/";D;" =";
CE;"/";CO
330 GOTO 390
340 CE=A*C:CO=B*D
```

```
350 PRINT A;"/";B;"   X ";C;"/";D;" =
";CE;"/";CO
360 GOTO 390
370 CE=A*D:CO=B*C
380 PRINT A;"/";B;"   / ";C;"/";D;" =
";CE;"/";CO
390 INPUT "WOULD YOU LIKE THIS REDUC
ED (YES OR NO)";A$
400 IF A$<>"NO" GOTO 420
410 END
420 REM
430 IF CE>CO GOTO 550
440 D=CE
450 IF CE/D=INT(CE/D) AND CO/D=INT(C
O/D) GOTO 470
460 D=D-1:IF D<=1 GOTO 510ELSE GOTO
450
470 CE=CE/D:CO=CO/D:IF CE<=1 GOTO 51
0ELSE GOTO 440
480 INPUT "ENTER NUMERATOR ";CE
490 INPUT "ENTER DENOMINATOR ";CO
500 GOTO 420
510 PRINT "REDUCED FORM:    ";CE;"/";
CO
520 PRINT:PRINT
530 INPUT "ENTER 1 FOR NEW DATA OR 2
 TO QUIT ";P
540 IF P=1 GOTO 10ELSE GOTO 410
550 D=CO
560 IF CE/D=INT(CE/D) AND CO/D=INT(C
O/D) GOTO 580
570 D=D-1:IF D<=1 GOTO 510ELSE GOTO
560
580 CE=CE/D:CO=CO/D:IF CO<=1 GOTO 51
0ELSE GOTO 550
```

Chapter 5
Business and Personal
Management Programs

DEPRECIATION

Remarks

Here's a program that will clearly show you which is the most suitable way to depreciate an asset according to your needs. One of three commonly used depreciation methods can be used:

1) Straight Line
2) Sum of the Year's Digits
3) Double Declining Balance

Variables

Double Declining Balance
        C—Cost of the Asset
        S—Salvage value of the asset
        L—Life of the asset
        Y—Year of depreciation
        B—Beginning book balance
        T—Total depreciation
        E—Ending book value
        D—Year's depreciation
Sum of the Year's Digits
        A—Price of the asset
        B—Salvage value of asset
        D—Life of asset

G—Year
H—Depreciation
Straight Line
P—Purchase price of asset
L—Life of asset
D—Yearly depreciation

Suggested Variations

1) This is a good business program that can be merged with others as your needs direct.

2) If item is depreciated for more than one year, you might wish to show columnar totals at the end of the year.

Sample Run

DEPRECIATION

ENTER THE NUMBER OF THE DEPRECIATION YOU WISH TO USE:

1   DOUBLE DECLINING BALANCE
2   SUM OF THE YEAR'S DIGITS
3   STRAIGHT LINE
? <u>3</u>
STRAIGHT LINE DEPRECIATION

WHAT IS THE PURCHASE PRICE? <u>$1000.00</u>
WHAT IS THE ESTIMATED LIFETIME? <u>5</u>
DEPRECIATES $ 200 EACH YEAR
WHAT IS THE FIRST YEAR OF USE? <u>1980</u>

YEAR	VALUE
1980	$ 1000
1981	$ 800
1982	$600
1983	$ 400
1984	$ 200

Program for Depreciation

```
10 CLS:CLEAR 100
20 PRINT "DEPRECIATION ":PRINT:PRINT
```

```
30 PRINT "ENTER THE NUMBER OF THE DE
PRECIATION YOU WISH TO USE:"
40 PRINT "1        DOUBLE DECLINING BA
LANCE"
50 PRINT "2        SUM OF THE YEAR'S D
IGITS"
60 PRINT "3        STRAIGHT LINE"
70 PRINT:INPUT U
80 ON U GOTO 90,460,670
90 CLS:PRINT:PRINT:PRINT"DOUBLE DECL
INING DEPRECIATION":PRINT
100 INPUT "ENTER THE COST OF THE ASS
ET $";C
110 INPUT "ENTER THE SALVAGE VALUE O
F THE ASSET $";S
120 IF S>=C THEN PRINT "SALVAGE MUST
 BE LESS THAN COST":GOTO 100
130 INPUT "ENTER THE LIFE OF THE ASS
ET ";L
140 Y=1
150 T=0:E=0:B=C
160 R=((100/L)/100)*2
170 CLS
180 PRINT TAB(22)"BEGIN"TAB(33)"TOTA
L"TAB(44)"END"TAB(55)"YEAR"
190 PRINT "YEAR"TAB(11)"COST"TAB(22)
"BOOK VAL"TAB(33)"DEPREC";
200 PRINTTAB(44)"BOOK VAL"TAB(55)"DE
PREC"
210 PRINTSTRING$(63,"-")
220 D=B*R
230 E=B-D
240 T=T+D
250 IF E<=S GOTO 300
260 IF Y=L GOTO 370
270 GOSUB 430
280 B=E
290 GOTO 220
300 IF E=S GOTO 350
310 H=S-E
320 D=D-H
330 T=T-H
340 E=E+H
350 GOSUB 430
```

96

```
360 GOTO 420
370 H=E-S
380 D=D+H
390 T=T+H
400 E=E-H
410 GOSUB 430
420 END
430 PRINT Y;TAB(11);C;TAB(22);B;TAB(
33);T;TAB(44);E;TAB(55);D
440 Y=Y+1
450 RETURN
460 CLS:PRINT:PRINT:PRINT"SUM OF THE
 YEAR'S DIGITS DEPRECIATION":PRINT
470 INPUT "ENTER THE PRICE (ROUNDED
TO DOLLARS)";A
480 PRINT "ENTER THE SALVAGE (OR TRA
DE IN) VALUE YOU EXPECT WHEN"
490 INPUT "YOU DISPOSE OF THIS ITEM
(ROUNDED TO DOLLARS)";B
500 C=A-B
510 INPUT"ENTER THE NUMBER OF YEARS
YOU EXPECT TO OWN THIS ITEM";D
520 INPUT "WHAT IS THE FIRST YEAR OF
 USE--EX. 1980";G
530 E=0:F=D
540 E=E+D
550 D=D-1
560 IF D=0 GOTO 580
570 GOTO 540
580 CLS:PRINT"YEAR","DEPRECIATION","
VALUE AT END OF YEAR"
590 H=C*(F/E)
600 A=A-H
610 PRINTG,"$";H,"$";A
620 F=F-1
630 G=G+1
640 IF F=0 GOTO 660
650 GOTO 590
660 END
670 CLS:PRINT "STRAIGHT LINE DEPRECI
ATION"
680 PRINT:PRINT:PRINT
690 Q=0
```

```
700 INPUT "WHAT IS THE PURCHASE PRIC
E";P
710 IF P<=0 THEN PRINT "ERROR":GOTO
30
720 CLS:INPUT "WHAT IS THE ESTIMATED
 LIFETIME";L
730 IF L<=0 THEN PRINT "ERROR":GOTO
40
740 D=P/L
750 CLS:PRINT "DEPRECIATES $";D;" EA
CH YEAR"
760 PRINT:INPUT"WHAT IS THE FIRST YE
AR OF USE";Y
770 CLS:PRINT "YEAR";STRING$(23," ")
;"VALUE"
780 PRINT STRING$(32,"-")
790 IF P<=0 GOTO 850
800 PRINT Y;STRING$(22," ");"$";P
810 Q=Q+1:IF Q=10 GOTO 860
820 IF P<=0 GOTO 850
830 Y=Y+1:P=P-D
840 GOTO 790
850 END
860 INPUT "PRESS ENTER TO CONTINUE";
A$:CLS:Q=0:GOTO 820
```

LOAN

Remarks

This program calculates the various factors concerning secur-
ing a loan at a rate of interest. A balloon payment is automatically
calculated if neccessary. At the end of each year, the interest and
equity paid that year are automatically calculated and displayed.

Variables

AMT—Amount of loan
XIN —Interest rate (enter as a whole number: 15% as 15)
IRS —Number of years (no pun intended by this variable
    name!)
IIN —Yearly interest paid
IEQ —Yearly equity paid
I   —Payment number

R   —Gross payment
PIN   —Interest payment
PEQ —Equity payment
TIN   —Cumulative interest
TEQ —Cumulative equity
TPAY—Total paid in

Suggested Variations

1) I assumed when writing this program that the first payment is made January 31. Modify to allow first payment to be on the last day of any month.

2) From lines #640 on you will notice a payment display routine that is not used in this program. You may wish to modify the program to make use of this routine. It beats wearing out the ENTER key on a twenty year loan.

3) If you wish to have the data output on your CRT in columnar form, you will probably have to delete some columns to fit it all on the screen. I suggest deleting Cumulative Interest and Cumulative Equity if you do so.

Sample Run

AMOUNT? 1000.00
INTEREST? 11.5
YEARS? 1
PRESS ENTER TO CONTINUE?
PAYMENT NUMBER   1
OUTSTANDING BALANCE— 1000
GROSS PAYMENT— 88.62
INTEREST PAYMENT— 9.59
EQUITY PAYMENT— 79.03
CUMULATIVE INTEREST— 9.59
CUMULATIVE EQUITY— 79.03
TOTAL PAID IN— 88.62
PRESS ENTER TO CONTINUE?
       .
       .
       .
PAYMENT NUMBER— 12
OUTSTANDING BALANCE— 87.76
GROSS PAYMENT— 88.61
INTEREST PAYMENT— .85
EQUITY PAYMENT— 87.76

CUMULATIVE INTEREST— 63.43
CUMULATIVE EQUITY— 1000
TOTAL PAID IN— 1063.43
YEAR # 1
INTEREST PAID THIS YEAR— 63.44
EQUITY PAID THIS YEAR— 999.99

Program For Loan

```
10 CLS
20 IYR=12
30 IIN=0:IEQ=0:I=0:ISW=0:TEQ=0:TIN=0
:TPAY=0
40 INPUT "AMOUNT ";AMT
50 INPUT "INTEREST ";XIN
60 INPUT "YEARS ";IRS
70 IPR=IRS*12
80 XIN=XIN/1200
90 XF=(1-(1+XIN)↑(-IPR))/XIN
100 OAMT=AMT
110 R=AMT/XF
120 IVA=(R+.005)*100
130 R=IVA/100
140 I=I+1
150 PIN=AMT*XIN
160 IVA=(PIN+.005)*100
170 PIN=IVA/100
180 PEQ=R-PIN
190 IF I=IPR GOTO 330
200 REM
210 TIN=TIN+PIN
220 TEQ=TEQ+PEQ
230 TPAY=TPAY+R
240 IIN=IIN+PIN
250 IEQ=IEQ+PEQ
260 PRINT:INPUT "PRESS ENTER TO CONT
INUE ";A$
270 GOSUB 470
280 IF I=IYR GOTO 380
290 AMT=AMT-PEQ
300 IF ISW=1 THEN STOP
310 GOTO 140
320 GOTO 270
```

100

```
330 ISW=1
340 OOPS=OAMT-TEQ-PEQ
350 R=R+OOPS
360 PEQ=PEQ+OOPS
370 GOTO 210
380 IYR=IYR+12
390 IIN=IIN+.005:IIN=IIN*100:IIN=INT
(IIN):IIN=IIN/100
400 IEQ=IEQ+.005:IEQ=IEQ*100:IEQ=INT
(IEQ):IEQ=IEQ/100
410 PRINT "YEAR #";I/12:PRINT "INTER
EST PAID THIS YEAR-- ";IIN
420 PRINT "EQUITY PAID THIS YEAR-- "
;IEQ
430 PRINT
440 IIN=0:IEQ=0
450 IF ISW=1 THEN END
460 GOTO 290
470 CLS
480 PRINT "PAYMENT NUMBER-- ";I
490 AMT=AMT+.005:AMT=AMT*100:AMT=INT
(AMT):AMT=AMT/100
500 PRINT "OUTSTANDING BALANCE-- ";A
MT
510 R=R+.005:R=R*100:R=INT(R):R=R/10
0
520 PRINT "GROSS PAYMENT-- ";R
530 PIN=PIN+.005:PIN=PIN*100:PIN=INT
(PIN):PIN=PIN/100
540 PRINT "INTEREST PAYMENT-- ";PIN
550 PEQ=PEQ+.005:PEQ=PEQ*100:PEQ=INT
(PEQ):PEQ=PEQ/100
560 PRINT "EQUITY PAYMENT-- ";PEQ
570 TIN=TIN+.005:TIN=TIN*100:TIN=INT
(TIN):TIN=TIN/100
580 PRINT "CUMULATIVE INTEREST-- ";T
IN
590 TEQ=TEQ+.005:TEQ=TEQ*100:TEQ=INT
(TEQ):TEQ=TEQ/100
600 PRINT "CUMULATIVE EQUITY-- ";TEQ
610 TPAY=TPAY+.005:TPAY=TPAY*100:TPA
Y=INT(TPAY):TPAY=TPAY/100
620 PRINT "TOTAL PAID IN-- ";TPAY
```

```
630 RETURN
640 INPUT "HOW MANY PAYMENTS WOULD Y
OU LIKE DISPLAYED";N
650 DIM A(N)
660 PRINT "ENTER THE PAYMENT NUMBERS
 YOU WOULD LIKE DISPLAYED"
670 FOR X=1 TO N:INPUT A(X):NEXT X
680 RETURN
```

SINKING FUND AND FIXED INVESTMENT

Remarks

This program will perform two separate operations:

1) Calculate the amount of a sinking fund created by a fixed, end-of-the-year investment placed annually at compounded interest for a number of years;

2) The fixed investment placed annually at compounded interest for a number of years to create a sinking fund.

Variables

TY—Type of operation (see menu above)
N —Number of years
R —Rate of interest
FV—Fixed investment
S —Sinking fund

Suggested Variations

1) You may wish to use the example above and combine other related business programs into one utility package.

Sample Run

SINKING FUND OR FIXED INVESTMENT
THIS PROGRAM WILL CALCULATE:
1) THE AMOUNT OF A SINKING FUND CREATED BY A FIXED (END OF THE YEAR) INVESTMENT PLACED ANNUALLY AT COMPOUNDED INTEREST FOR A NUMBER OF YEARS;
OR
2) THE FIXED INVESTMENT PLACED ANNUALLY AT COMPOUNDED INTEREST FOR A NUMBER OF YEARS TO CREATE A SINKING FUND.

ENTER 1 OR 2?1

HOW MANY YEARS? 5
WHAT IS THE RATE OF INTEREST)ENTER AS A DECIMAL(
? .115
WHAT IS THE FIXED INVESTMENT? 10000
SINKING FUND = $62900.3

ENTER 1 FOR NEW DATA OR 2 TO QUIT? 2

Program For Sinking Fund And Fixed Investment

```
10 CLS
20 PRINT "SINKING FUND AND FIXED INV
ESTMENT"
30 PRINT "THIS PROGRAM WILL CALCULAT
E:"
40 PRINT "1) THE AMOUNT OF A SINKING
 FUND CREATED BY A FIXED"
50 PRINT "    (END OF THE YEAR) INVES
TMENT PLACED ANNUALLY AT"
60 PRINT "    COMPOUNDED INTEREST FOR
 A NUMBER OF YEARS."
70 PRINT "                        OR"
80 PRINT "2) THE FIXED INVESTMENT PL
ACED ANNUALLY AT COMPOUNDED"
90 PRINT "    INTEREST FOR A NUMBER O
F YEARS TO CREATE A SINKING"
100 PRINT "    FUND.
110 PRINT
120 INPUT "ENTER 1 OR 2 ";TY
130 CLS
140 INPUT "HOW MANY YEARS ";N
150 INPUT "WHAT IS THE RATE OF INTER
EST >ENTER AS A DECIMAL< ";R
160 IF TY=2 GOTO 280
170 INPUT "WHAT IS THE FIXED INVESTM
ENT ";FV
180 W=1+R
190 X=W↑N
200 Y=X-1
210 Z=Y/R
220 S=FV*Z
230 PRINT "SINKING FUND= $";S
240 PRINT
```

103

```
250 INPUT "ENTER 1 FOR NEW DATA OR 2
  TO QUIT ";R
260 IF R=1 GOTO 10
270 END
280 INPUT "WHAT IS THE SINKING FUND
";S
290 W=1+R
300 X=W↑N
310 Y=X-1

320 Z=R/Y
330 FV=S*Z
340 PRINT "FIXED INVESTMENT= $";FV
350 GOTO 240
```

ECONOMIC ORDER QUANTITY

Remarks

This program, used mainly for inventory management, calculates the most economical number of products to buy each time you place an order. Cost of other quantities are also shown for comparison.

Variables

C—Cost of product
D—Number of products sold per year
H—Storage cost per product
S—Cost to place an order
Q—Economic order quantity
T—Cost to order and stock Q items

Suggested Variations

1) You may wish to use this program as a subroutine for an inventory management program.

2) You may wish to delete the routine showing the cost of ordering and stocking various quantities of the product.

Sample Run

ECONOMIC ORDER QUANTITY

HOW MUCH DOES ONE UNIT COST $? 5.00
HOW MANY UNITS DO YOU SELL PER YEAR? 1000

HOW MUCH DOES IT COST TO STORE ONE UNIT FOR ONE
YEAR $? .10
HOW MUCH DOES IT COST TO PLACE AN ORDER $? 25.00
YOU SHOULD ORDER 707 UNITS PER ORDER.

PRESS ENTER TO CONTINUE?
FOR ORDER QUANTITIES OF 470 UNITS, THE ANNUAL
COST TO ORDER AND STOCK THIS ITEM IS $ 76.6915
PRESS ENTER TO CONTINUE?
FOR ORDER QUANTITIES OF 705 UNITS, THE ANNUAL
COST TO ORDER AND STOCK THIS ITEM IS $70.711
PRESS ENTER TO CONTINUE?
FOR ORDER QUANTITIES OF 940 UNITS, THE ANNUAL
COST TO ORDER AND STOCK THIS ITEM IS $ 73.5958
PRESS ENTER TO CONTINUE?
FOR ORDER QUANTITIES OF 1175 UNITS, THE ANNUAL
COST TO ORDER AND STOCK THIS ITEM IS $ 80.0266
PRESS ENTER TO CONTINUE?
FOR ORDER QUANTITIES OF 1410 UNITS, THE ANNUAL
COST TO ORDER AND STOCK THIS ITEM IS $ 88.2305
PRESS ENTER TO CONTINUE?
FOR ORDER QUANTITIES OF 1645 UNITS, THE ANNUAL
COST TO ORDER AND STOCK THIS ITEM IS $ 97.4476
PRESS ENTER TO CONTINUE?
FOR ORDER QUANTITIES OF 1880 UNITS, THE ANNUAL
COST TO ORDER AND STOCK THIS ITEM IS $ 107.298
TYPE 1 TO CONTINUE OR 2 TO QUIT? 2

Program For Economic Order Quantity

```
10   CLS:PRINT:PRINT:PRINT"ECONOMIC O
RDER QUANTITY":PRINT
20   INPUT "HOW MUCH DOES ONE UNIT CO
ST $";C
30   INPUT "HOW MANY UNITS DO YOU SEL
L PER YEAR ";D
40   INPUT "HOW MUCH DOES IT COST TO
STORE ONE UNIT FOR ONE YEAR $";H
50   INPUT "HOW MUCH DOES IT COST TO
PLACE AN ORDER $";S
60   X=(2*D*S)/H
70  Y=SQR(X)
```

```
80   Q=INT(Y)
90   PRINT "YOU SHOULD ORDER ";Q;" UN
ITS PER ORDER."

100  PRINT:PRINT:INPUT"PRESS ENTER T
O CONTINUE";A$:CLS
110  Q=Q/3
120  Q=INT(Q)
130  R=Q
140  N=0
150  N=N+1
160  Q=Q+R
170  T=D/Q*S+Q/2*H
180  IF N>7 GOTO 220
190  PRINT "FOR ORDER QUANTITIES OF
";Q;" UNITS, THE ANNUAL"
200  PRINT "COST TO ORDER AND STOCK
THIS ITEM IS $";T
210  PRINT:INPUT"PRESS ENTER TO CONT
INUE";A$:GOTO150

220  INPUT "TYPE 1 TO CONTINUE OR 2
TO QUIT";G
230  IF G=1 GOTO 10
240  END
```

PRESENT VALUE OF AN ANNUITY

Remarks

This program calculates the present value of an annuity to be paid out for a number of consecutive years at a rate of annually compounded interest.

Variables

AN—Annuity
R —Rate of interest
N —Number of years
PV —Present value of the annuity

Suggested Variations

1) Allow other types of interest to be used.
2) Allow program to accept and process parts of years, that is, months and years

Sample Run

PRESENT VALUE OF AN ANNUITY

THIS PROGRAM CALCULATES THE PRESENT VALUE OF AN ANNUITY
TO BE PAID OUT FOR A NUMBER OF CONSECUTIVE YEARS AT
A RATE OF ANNUALLY COMPOUNDED INTEREST.

PRESS ENTER TO CONTINUE?
WHAT IS THE ANNUITY? 5000.00
WHAT IS THE RATE OF INTEREST)ENTER AS A DECIMAL(
? .115
HOW MANY YEARS? 5

PRESENT VALUE- $ 18249.4

ENTER 1 FOR NEW DATA OR 2 TO QUIT? 2

Program For Present Value Of Annuity

```
10 CLS
20 PRINT "PRESENT VALUE OF AN ANNUIT
Y"
30 PRINT
40 PRINT
50 PRINT "THIS PROGRAM CALCULATES TH
E PRESENT VALUE OF AN ANNUITY"
60 PRINT "TO BE PAID OUT FOR A NUMBE
R OF CONSECUTIVE YEARS AT"
70 PRINT "A RATE OF ANNUALLY COMPOUN
DED INTEREST."
80 PRINT
90 INPUT "PRESS ENTER TO CONTINUE ";
A$
100 CLS
110 INPUT "WHAT IS THE ANNUITY ";AN
120 INPUT "WHAT IS THE RATE OF INTER
EST >ENTER AS A DECIMAL< ";R
130 INPUT "HOW MANY YEARS ";N
140 PRINT
150 W=1+R
160 X=W↑N
```

```
170 Y=X-1
180 Z=R*X
190 M=Y/Z
200 PV=AN*M
210 PRINT "PRESENT VALUE= $";PV
220 PRINT
230 INPUT "ENTER 1 FOR NEW DATA OR 2
 TO QUIT ";R
240 IF R=1 GOTO 10
250 END
```

ANNUITY

Remarks

This program calculates the annuity that a principle drawing annually compounded interest will give for a number of years. An annuity is fixed sum paid at regular intervals.

Variables

R—Rate of interest
N—Number of years
P —Principle
A—Annuity

Suggested Variations

1) Allow for different types of interest.
2) Allow program to accept parts of years, that is, months as well as years.

Sample Run

ANNUITY

THIS PROGRAM CALCULATES THE ANNUITY THAT A PRINCIPLE DRAWING ANNUALLY COMPOUNDED INTEREST WILL GIVE FOR A PERIOD OF YEARS.
AN ANNUITY IS A FIXED SUM PAID AT REGULAR INTERVALS.

PRESS ENTER TO CONTINUE?
WHAT IS THE RATE OF INTEREST(ENTER AS A DECIMAL ?.115
HOW MANY YEARS?5
WHAT IS THE PRINCIPLE? 1000.00
ANNUITY= $273.982

Program for Annuity

```
10 CLS
20 PRINT "ANNUITY"
30 PRINT
40 PRINT
50 PRINT "THIS PROGRAM CALCULATES TH
E ANNUITY THAT A PRINCIPLE"
60 PRINT "DRAWING ANNUALLY COMPOUNDE
D INTEREST WILL GIVE FOR"
70 PRINT "A PERIOD OF YEARS.
80 PRINT "AN ANNUITY IS A FIXED SUM
PAID AT REGULAR INTERVALS."
90 PRINT
100 INPUT "PRESS ENTER TO CONTINUE";
A$
110 CLS
120 INPUT "WHAT IS THE RATE OF INTER
EST >ENTER AS A DECIMAL< ";R
130 INPUT "HOW MANY YEARS ";N
140 INPUT "WHAT IS THE PRINCIPLE ";P

150 W=1+R
160 X=W↑N
170 Y=R*X
180 Z=X-1
190 M=Y/Z
200 A=P*M
210 PRINT "ANNUITY= $";A
220 PRINT
230 INPUT "ENTER 1 FOR NEW DATA OR 2
 TO QUIT ";R
240 IF R=1 GOTO 10
250 END
```

PRESENT VALUE
Remarks

This program calculates the present value of an amount of money due in a number of years at a specified rate of interest. The present value of an amount due in X years is the sum of money placed at interest for X years that will produce the given amount.

109

Both simple and compound interest can be processed by this program.

Variables

TY — Type of interest being used (1=simple 2=compound)
AN — Amount of money
N — Number of years
R — Rate of interest
Q — Number of compounding periods per year
P — Present value

Suggested Variations

1) You may wish to modify this program to process parts of years; for instance: three years and four months.

2) You may wish to combine this program with other related business software.

Sample Run

PRESENT VALUE

THIS PROGRAM CALCULATES THE PRESENT VALUE OF AN AMOUNT OF MONEY DUE IN A NUMBER OF YEARS AT A RATE OF INTEREST. THE PRESENT VALUE OF AN AMOUNT DUE IN X YEARS IS THE SUM OF MONEY WHICH PLACED AT INTEREST FOR X YEARS WILL PRODUCE THE GIVEN AMOUNT.

WHICH TYPE OF INTEREST WILL BE USED:
1) SIMPLE INTEREST
2) COMPOUNDED INTEREST
ENTER 1 OR 2 ? 2
*** COMPOUNDED INTEREST ***
WHAT IS THE AMOUNT ($) ? 1000.00
DUE IN HOW MANY YEARS ? 5
AT WHAT RATE OF INTEREST)ENTER AS A DECIMAL(?
.115
HOW MANY COMPOUNDING PERIODS PER YEAR ? 4
PRESENT VALUE = $ 567.288

ENTER! FOR NEW DATA OR 2 TO QUIT? 2

Program for Present Value

```
10 CLS
20 PRINT "PRESENT VALUE"
30 PRINT
40 PRINT
50 PRINT "THIS PROGRAM CALCULATES TH
E PRESENT VALUE OF AN"
60 PRINT "AMOUNT OF MONEY DUE IN A N
UMBER OF YEARS AT A"
70 PRINT "RATE OF INTEREST. THE PRES
ENT VALUE OF AN AMOUNT"
80 PRINT "DUE IN X YEARS IS THE SUM
OF MONEY WHICH PLACED"
90 PRINT "AT INTEREST FOR X YEARS WI
LL PRODUCE THE GIVEN"
100 PRINT "AMOUNT."
110 PRINT
120 PRINT "WHICH TYPE OF INTEREST WI
LL BE USED:"
130 PRINT "1) SIMPLE INTEREST"
140 PRINT "2) COMPOUNDED INTEREST"
150 INPUT "ENTER 1 OR 2 ";TY
160 CLS
170 IF TY=1 THEN PRINT "*** SIMPLE I
NTEREST ***" ELSE PRINT "*** COMPOUN
DED INTEREST ***"
180 INPUT "WHAT IS THE AMOUNT ($) ";
AN
190 INPUT "DUE IN HOW MANY YEARS ";N
200 INPUT "AT WHAT RATE OF INTEREST
>ENTER AS A DECIMAL< ";R
210 IF TY=1 GOTO 330
220 INPUT "HOW MANY COMPOUNDING PERI
ODS PER YEAR ";Q
230 W=R/Q
240 X=1+W
250 Y=N*Q
260 Z=X↑Y
270 P=AN/Z
280 PRINT "PRESENT VALUE = $";P
290 PRINT
```

111

```
300 INPUT "ENTER 1 FOR NEW DATA OR 2
    TO QUIT";R
310 IF R=1 GOTO 10
320 END
330 W=N*R
340 X=1+W
350 P=AN/X
360 GOTO 280
```

AMOUNT

Remarks

This program calculates the amount of a sum of money placed at a rate of interest for a number of years. This program can calculate for any number of compounding periods per year (1 for annually, 4 for quarterly, etc.).

Variables

TY —Type of interest (1=simple   2=compound)
P   —Principal
R   —Interest rate
N   —Number of years
Q   —Number of compounding periods per year
AM—Amount of money

Suggested Variations

1) You may wish to alter this program to accept parts of years, that is, months and years.

2) You may wish to combine this program with other related software, or use it even as a subroutine.

Sample Run

AMOUNT

THIS PROGRAM WILL CALCULATE THE AMOUNT OF A SUM OF MONEY PLACED AT A RATE OF INTEREST FOR A NUMBER OF YEARS.

WHICH OF THE FOLLOWING INTEREST TYPES WILL BE USED:
1) SIMPLE INTEREST
2) COMPOUND INTEREST
ENTER 1 OR 2?2

```
*** COMPOUNDED INTEREST ***
WHAT IS THE PRINCIPAL ? 2600.00
WHAT IS THE INTEREST RATE )ENTER AS A DECIMAL( ?
.115
HOW MANY YEARS ? 5
INTEREST IS COMPOUNDED HOW MANY TIMES A YEAR ? 4
AMOUNT IS $ 4583.21
ENTER 1 FOR NEW DATA OR 2 TO QUIT ? 2
```

Program for Amount

```
10 CLS
20 PRINT "AMOUNT"
30 PRINT
40 PRINT "THIS PROGRAM WILL CALCULAT
E THE AMOUNT OF A SUM OF"
50 PRINT "MONEY PLACED AT A RATE OF
INTEREST FOR A NUMBER OF"
60 PRINT "YEARS."
70 PRINT
80 PRINT
90 PRINT "WHICH OF THE FOLLOWING INT
EREST TYPES WILL BE USED:"
100 PRINT "1) SIMPLE INTEREST"
110 PRINT "2) COMPOUNDED INTEREST"
120 INPUT "ENTER 1 OR 2 ";TY
130 CLS
140 IF TY=1 THEN PRINT "*** SIMPLE I
NTEREST ***" ELSE PRINT "*** COMPOUN
DED INTEREST ***"
150 INPUT "WHAT IS THE PRINCIPAL ";P

160 INPUT "WHAT IS THE INTEREST RATE
 >ENTER AS A DECIMAL< ";R
170 INPUT "HOW MANY YEARS ";N
180 IF TY=1 GOTO 290
190 INPUT "INTEREST IS COMPOUNDED HO
W MANY TIMES A YEAR ";Q
200 U=N*Q
210 V=R/Q
220 W=(1+V)
230 X=W↑U
240 AM=P*X
250 PRINT "AMOUNT IS $";AM
```

```
260 INPUT "ENTER 1 FOR NEW DATA OR 2
  TO QUIT ";Z
270 IF Z=1 THEN GOTO 10
280 END
290 W=N*R
300 X=1+W
310 AM=P*X
320 GOTO 250
```

BUDGET DEFINED BY ACTIVITY CURVE

Remarks

Given a sketched graph of money expenditure over a number of months, this program will calculate a budget to match this activity curve. This budget can be output to a cassette file, labeled, saved, and recalled for future reference.

Variables

C — Job number, later redefined
A — Months between start and finish of job
B — Groups participating on job
A\$ — Name of current group
D — Money allotted current group
A(W) — Height of graph at month W
E — Total height of all months
F — Dollars allotted per unit on graph

Suggested Variations

1) You might wish to output to the cassette file data pertaining to the graph, so that it too can be reconstructed at a later date.

Sample Run

BUDGET DEFINED BY ACTIVITY CURVE

FOR EACH OF THE WORKFORCE GROUPS PARTICIPATING IN THIS JOB, A GRAPH OF PROPOSED SPENDING SHOULD BE OBTAINED.

WHAT IS THE JOB NUMBER OF THIS JOB ? 1234
HOW MANY MONTHS BETWEEN START AND FINISH DATES FOR THIS JOB ? 4

114

HOW MANY GROUPS WILL BE PARTICIPATING ON THIS JOB?1
INSERT A FRESH CASSETTE INTO THE RECORDER AND PLACE RECORDER IN THE 'RECORD' MODE.

PRESS ENTER WHEN THIS HAS BEEN DONE?
GROUP # 1
ENTER THE NAME OF THIS GROUP? <u>CIVIL ENGINEERING</u>
HOW MUCH MONEY IS ALLOTTED TO THIS GROUP FOR JOB # 1234? <u>20000.00</u>
MONTH 1
GRAPH IS HOW MANY UNITS HIGH? <u>4</u>
MONTH 2
GRAPH IS HOW MANY UNITS HIGH? <u>10</u>
MONTH 3
GRAPH IS HOW MANY UNITS HIGH? <u>8</u>
MONTH 4
GRAPH IS HOW MANY UNITS HIGH? <u>15</u>
PRESS ENTER FOR A MONTH BY MONTH BUDGET BREAKDOWN?

MONTH	BUDGET
1	2162.16
2	5405.41
3	4324.32
4	8108.11

PRESS ENTER TO CONTINUE
PLEASE WAIT..
DATA STORAGE COMPLETE FOR JOB # 1234
DENOTE ON CASSETTE LABEL—JOB # 1234, FILE A

PRESS ENTER TO CONTINUE?
FILE A—DATA PRINTOUT
IF YOU WISH TO PRINT OUT THE DATA CONTAINED IN FILE A, ENTER A 1. OTHERWISE ENTER A 2? <u>2</u>

Program for Budget Defined by Activity Curve

```
10   CLS:PRINT "BUDGET DEFINED BY ACT
IVITY CURVE":PRINT:PRINT
20 DIM A(500)
30   PRINT "FOR EACH OF THE WORKFORCE
 GROUPS PARTICIPATING IN"
```

```
40   PRINT "THIS JOB, A GRAPH OF PROP
OSED SPENDING SHOULD BE"
50   PRINT "OBTAINED. ":PRINT
60   INPUT "WHAT IS THE JOB NUMBER OF
 THIS JOB ";C
70   CLS
80   PRINT "HOW MANY MONTHS BETWEEN S
TART AND FINISH DATES FOR"
90   INPUT "THIS JOB ";A
100   CLS
110   PRINT "HOW MANY GROUPS WILL BE
PARTICIPATING ON THIS JOB";
120   INPUT B
130   CLS
140   PRINT "INSERT A FRESH CASSETTE
INTO THE RECORDER AND PLACE"
150   PRINT "RECORDER IN THE 'RECORD'
 MODE."
160   PRINT:INPUT "PRESS ENTER WHEN T
HIS HAS BEEN DONE";A$
170   CLS:PRINT"PLEASE WAIT.."
180   PRINT #-1,A;",";B;",";C
190   CLS
200   FOR Z=1 TO B
210   PRINT "GROUP #";Z
220   PRINT "ENTER THE NAME OF THIS G
ROUP ";
230   INPUTA$
240   PRINT "HOW MUCH MONEY IS ALLOTE
D TO THIS GROUP FOR JOB #";C;" ";
250   INPUT D
260   E=0
270   FOR W=1 TO A
280   CLS:PRINT"MONTH ";W
290   INPUT "GRAPH IS HOW MANY UNITS
HIGH ";A(W):E=E+A(W)
300   NEXTW
310   F=D/E:FORV=1 TO A:A(V)=A(V)*F:N
EXTV
320 GOSUB 710
330   FOR W=1 TO A:PRINT W,A(W)
340   NEXT W
350 INPUT "PRESS ENTER TO CONTINUE "
;A$
```

```
360    CLS:PRINT "PLEASE WAIT.."
370    PRINT#-1, Z;",";A$;",";D
380    FOR W=1 TO A:PRINT#-1, W;",";A(
W):NEXTW
390    CLS
400    NEXT Z
410    CLS
420    PRINT "DATA STORAGE COMPLETE FO
R JOB #";C
430    PRINT "DENOTE ON CASSETE LABEL-
- JOB #";C;", FILE A"
440    PRINT:INPUT "PRESS ENTER TO CON
TINUE ";A$:CLS
450    PRINT "FILE A-- DATA PRINTOUT"
460    PRINT "IF YOU WISH TO PRINT OUT
 THE DATA CONTAINED IN"
470    INPUT "FILE A, ENTER A 1.  OTHE
RWISE ENTER A 2 ";A
480    IF A=2 GOTO 700
490    PRINT "REWIND TAPE TO BEGINNING
 OF FILE A. PLACE RECORDER"
500    PRINT "IN 'PLAY' MODE."
510    PRINT:INPUT "PRESS ENTER WHEN Y
OU HAVE DONE SO ";A$:CLS
520    INPUT#-1,A,B,C
530    CLS
540    PRINT "      F  I  L  E      A"
550    PRINT:PRINT"JOB #";C
560    PRINT "NUMBER OF GROUPS ON JOB-
- ";B
570    PRINT "NUMBER OF MONTHS FROM ST
ART TO FINISH-- ";A
580    FOR X=1 TO B
590    INPUT "PRESS ENTER TO CONTINUE
";A$:CLS
600    INPUT#-1, Z,A$,D
610    PRINT "GROUP #";Z
620    PRINT "NAME-- ";A$
630    PRINT "ALLOTMENT FOR JOB #";C;"
-- $";D
640    PRINT:INPUT "PRESS ENTER FOR MO
NTH BY MONTH BUDGET PROPOSAL";A$:CLS

650    PRINT "MONTH #","BUDGET"
```

117

```
660   FOR W=1 TO A
670   INPUT#-1, W,A(W):PRINTW,"$";A(W
)
680   NEXTW
690   NEXTX
700   END
710 INPUT "PRESS ENTER FOR A MONTH B
Y MONTH BUDGET BREAKDOWN";A$
720 CLS
730 PRINT "MONTH","BUDGET"
740 RETURN
```

INTERNAL RATE OF RETURN

Remarks

This program accepts data of an investment and the returns over a number of years and calculates the internal rate of return for that investment. It also compares this rate with that given by a competitive investment (for instance, a bank savings account), and determines which is the best investment.

Variables

R(X) — Return for year X
CO — Total investment
I1 — Interest available from other medium
Y1 — Number of years
NPV — Net present value
IC — Incrementer for internal rate of return
GU — Internal rate of return
VA — Value variable to check status

Suggested Variations

1) You might wish to modify this program to accept the returns on two investments, compare the internal rate of return for each of the investments, and make an appropriate decision.

2) Look over the "high-low skip" routine used to calculate the variable GU through the variable IC. Can you think of other uses for this routine?

Sample Run

INTERNAL RATE OF RETURN

WHAT IS THE TOTAL INVESTMENT $? <u>10000.00</u>

118

WHAT IS THE BANK INTEREST RATE (SUCH AS 10.5)? 11.5
FOR HOW MANY YEARS? 5
RETURN FOR YEAR # 1 $? 2200.00
RETURN FOR YEAR # 2 $? 2200.00
RETURN FOR YEAR # 3 $? 2200.00
RETURN FOR YEAR # 4 $? 2200.00
RETURN FOR YEAR # 5 $? 2200.00

WORKING

INTERNAL RATE OF RETURN=   3.263%
YOU LOSE MONEY ON THIS INVESTMENT
YOU PAID   11.5%

Program for Internal Rate of Return

```
10 CLS
20 DIM R(50)
30 PRINT "INTERNAL RATE OF RETURN":P
RINT:PRINT
40 INPUT "WHAT IS THE TOTAL INVESTME
NT $";CO
50 INPUT "WHAT IS THE BANK INTEREST
RATE (SUCH AS 10.5) ";I1
60 INPUT "FOR HOW MANY YEARS ";Y1
70 FOR X=1 TO Y1
80 PRINT "RETURN FOR YEAR #";X;"   $"
;:INPUT R(X)
90 NEXT X
100 CLS
110 IC=10:IT=0:GU=0
120 GU=GU+IC:IT=GU/100
130 PRINT "WORKING"
140 SUM=0
150 FOR X=1 TO Y1
160 NPV=R(X)/((1+IT)↑X)
170 SUM=SUM+NPV
180 NEXT X
190 CLS
200 VA=SUM-CO
210 IF VA>0 GOTO 120
220 IF VA<0 THEN GU=GU-IC:IC=IC/10:I
F IC<.001 THEN 230ELSE GOTO 120
```

119

```
230 PRINT "INTERNAL RATE OF RETURN=
";GU;"%"
240 IF I1>GU THEN PRINT "YOU LOSE MO
NEY ON THIS INVESTMENT":PRINT "YOU P
AID ";I1;"%"
250 END
```

CASH REGISTER

Remarks

This program causes your computer to function as a cash register. It will keep separate track of cash, check and charge account sales, and will automatically compute sales tax charges. Sales data for each day can be output to cassette files for recall upon start-up the next business day.

Variables

YSA	—Yesterday's sales
SD	—Sales to date
AC	—Number of accounts on file
A(X)	—Account number
C(X)	—Total charges to account X
TAX	—Sales tax rate
PR	—Item price
Q	—Quantity
SUB	—Subtotal
AC(X), CC(X)	—Current account files and charges
DS	—Sales for day
P1	—Cash sales
P2	—Check sales
P3	—Charge sales

Suggested Variations

1) While this program may not be suitable for use as is, it is constructed with the end user in mind. Modification should be easy.

2) To make this a really functional system: if you have a line printer, insert a routine to print out a receipt for each sale.

Sample Run

CASH REGISTER

START DAY ROUTINE

120

WOULD YOU LIKE TO:
1) LOAD LAST FILE
2) START A NEW PERIOD
ENTER YOUR CHOICE (1 OR 2)? 2

ENTER SALES TAX RATE AS DECIMAL (I.E. .05)? .06
NEW CUSTOMER

ITEM PRICE (ENTER – 1 TO SUBTOTAL) $? 1.50
QUANTITY? 1
ITEM PRICE (ENTER – 1 TO SUBTOTAL) $? – 1
SUBTOTAL—$1.5
TAX—$.09

TOTAL—$1.59
PAYMENT TYPE (1=CASH   2=CHECK   3=CHARGE)? 2
PRESS SPACE BAR FOR NEXT CUSTOMER OR TYPE 'Q' TO
END DAY
Q
END DAY ROUTINE
TOTAL SALES TODAY—$1.59
YESTERDAY'S SALES—$0
TOTAL SALES TO DATE—$1.59
TOTAL CASH SALES TODAY—$0
TOTAL CHECK SALES TODAY—$1.59
TOTAL CHARGE SALES TODAY—$0
PRESS ENTER FOR TODAY'S ACCOUNT CHARGES?
NO ACCOUNTS RECORDED
WOULD YOU LIKE TO SEE ALL ACCOUNT CHARGES TO
DATE (YES/NO)? NO
POSITION CASSETTE TAPE FOR NEW FILE
PLACE RECORDER IN)RECORD(MODE.

Program for Cash Register

```
10  CLEAR 100
20  DIM A(50),C(50),AC(50),CC(50)
30  CLS:PRINT "CASH REGISTER":PRINT
40  PRINT "START DAY ROUTINE"
50  PRINT "-----------------"
60  PRINT "WOULD YOU LIKE TO:"
70  PRINT "1) LOAD LAST FILE"
80  PRINT "2) START A NEW PERIOD"
```

121

```
90 INPUT "ENTER YOUR CHOICE (1 OR 2)
";CH
100 IF CH=2 GOTO 210
110 PRINT "POSITION CASSETTE TAPE TO
 BEGINNING OF LAST FILE"
120 PRINT "PRESS >PLAY< KEY."
130 INPUT "PRESS ENTER WHEN READY";A
$:CLS
140 PRINT "LOADING DATA"
150 INPUT#-1,YSA,SD,AC
160 PRINT "LOADING ACCOUNT FILES"
170 FOR X=1 TO AC
180 INPUT#-1,A(X),C(X)
190 NEXT X
200 GOTO 220
210 SD=0:AC=0:YSA=0
220 CLS:INPUT "ENTER SALES TAX RATE
AS DECIMAL (I.E. .05) ";TAX
230 U=1
240 CLS:PRINT "NEW CUSTOMER":SUB=0
250 PRINT@320,"ITEM PRICE (ENTER -1
TO SUBTOTAL) $";:INPUT PR
260 IF PR=-1 GOTO 340
270 PRINT@384,"QUANTITY ";:INPUT Q
280 SUB=SUB+(PR*Q)
290 PRINT@320,STRING$(63," ");
300 PRINT@384,STRING$(63," ");
310 PRINT@704,STRING$(63," ");
320 PRINT@704,"CURRENT SUBTOTAL-- $"
;SUB;
330 GOTO 250
340 T=SUB*TAX
350 T=T+.005:T=T*100:T=INT(T):T=T/10
0
360 G=SUB+T
370 CLS:PRINT "SUBTOTAL-- $";SUB
380 PRINT "TAX-- $";T
390 PRINT:PRINT:PRINT
400 PRINT "TOTAL-- $";G
410 INPUT "PAYMENT TYPE (1=CASH  2=C
HECK  3=CHARGE) ";K
420 ON K GOTO 430,510,520
430 INPUT "MONEY RECEIVED $";M
```

```
440 C=M-G:C=C+.005:C=C*100:C=INT(C):
C=C/100
450 PRINT "CHANGE-- $";C
460 P1=P1+G
470 PRINT:PRINT
480 PRINT "PRESS SPACE BAR FOR NEXT
CUSTOMER OR TYPE 'Q' TO END DAY"
490 A$=INKEY$:IF A$=" " OR A$="Q" GO
TO 500ELSE GOTO 490
500 IF A$="Q" GOTO 560ELSE GOTO 240
510 P2=P2+G:GOTO 470
520 INPUT "ACCOUNT #";I
530 AC(U)=I:CC(U)=G:U=U+1
540 P3=P3+G
550 PRINT "ACCOUNT CHARGE RECORDED":
GOTO 470
560 PRINT "END DAY ROUTINE"
570 DS=P1+P2+P3
580 SD=DS+SD
590 PRINT "TOTAL SALES TODAY-- $";DS
600 PRINT "YESTERDAY'S SALES-- $";YS
A
610 PRINT "TOTAL SALES TO DATE-- $";
SD
620 PRINT "TOTAL CASH SALES TODAY--$
";P1
630 PRINT "TOTAL CHECK SALES TODAY--
 $";P2
640 PRINT "TOTAL CHARGE SALES TODAY-
- $";P3
650 PRINT:PRINT
660 INPUT "PRESS ENTER FOR TODAYS AC
COUNT CHARGES";A$:CLS
670 PRINT "ACCOUNT #","CHARGE"
680 FOR X=1 TO U-1
690 IF AC(1)=0 THEN PRINT "NO ACCOUN
TS RECORDED":GOTO 710
700 PRINT AC(X),CC(X)
710 NEXT X
720 INPUT "WOULD YOU LIKE TO SEE ALL
 ACCOUNT CHARGES TO DATE (YES/NO)";A
$
730 FOR X=1 TO U-1
```

```
740 FOR Z=1 TO AC
750 IF A(Z)=AC(X) GOTO 780
760 NEXT Z
770 AC=AC+1:A(AC)=AC(X):C(AC)=CC(X):
GOTO 790
780 C(Z)=C(Z)+CC(X)
790 NEXT X
800 IF A$="NO" GOTO 860
810 PRINT "ACCOUNT #","CHARGE"
820 FOR X=1 TO AC
830 IF A(1)=0 THEN PRINT "NO ACCOUNT
S RECORDED":GOTO 850
840 PRINT A(X),C(X)
850 NEXT X
860 PRINT "POSITION CASSETTE TAPE FO
R NEW FILE"
870 PRINT "PLACE RECORDER IN >RECORD
< MODE."
880 INPUT "PRESS ENTER WHEN READY";A
$:CLS
890 PRINT "SAVING DATA"
900 PRINT#-1,DS,SD,AC
910 IF A(1)=0 THEN 960
920 PRINT "SAVING ACCOUNT FILES"
930 FOR X=1 TO AC
940 PRINT#-1,A(X),C(X)
950 NEXT X
960 CLS:END
```

Chapter 6
Game and Simulation Programs

HANGMAN
Remarks

This is the computerized version of that classic word Game, Hangman. One player chooses a word that is kept secretly inside the computer. The other tries to guess the word one letter at a time. If he guesses an incorrect letter, a part of the hangman is drawn on the screen. The object of this game is to guess your opponent's word before the drawing of the hangman is completed. See Fig. 6-1.

Variables

A\$ —The secret word
L —How many letters in secret word
B\$ —Players letter guess
W —# of guesses player has made
A\$(X) —Contains #X letter in word

Suggested Variations

1) Add number of guesses allowed by adding parts of hangman to be drawn, for example: rope, neck

2) Show # of letters in word before player's first correct guess.

3) Add a vocabulary to the computer so this can be a one-player game.

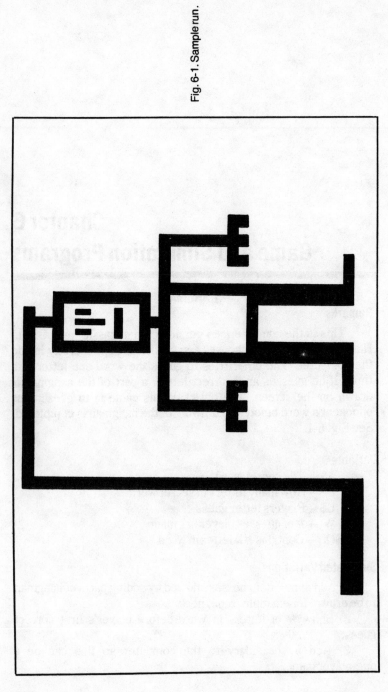

Fig. 6-1. Sample run.

Program for Hangman

```
10 DIM A(20),A$(20)
20 Q=64
30 CLS
40 INPUT "ENTER YOUR WORD";A$
50 L=LEN(A$)
60 IF L>20 THEN PRINT "WORD TOO LONG
":GOTO 40
70 FOR Z=1 TO L:A$(Z)=MID$(A$,Z,1):N
EXT Z
80 FOR Z=1 TO L:IF A$(Z)=" " THEN PR
INT "TWO WORDS":STOP
90 NEXT Z
100 CLS:GOSUB 340
110 PRINT @64,"USED LETTERS:";
120 PRINT@0,"WORD: ";
130 W=0
140 PRINT @768,"YOUR GUESS ";:INPUT
B$
150 PRINT @Q+14,B$;",";:Q=Q+2
160 J=0
170 FOR Z=1 TO L:IF B$=A$(Z) THEN A(
Z)=1:J=1
180 NEXT Z
190 IF J=1 GOTO 270
200 W=W+1
210 ON W GOSUB 390,460,520,570,620,6
50
220 IF W=6 GOTO 240
230 GOTO 140
240 PRINT @896,"THE WORD WAS: ";
250 FOR Z=1 TO L:PRINT A$(Z);:NEXT Z
260 END
270 FOR Z=1 TO L:IF A(Z)=0 THEN PRIN
T @Z+10,"-";
280 IF A(Z)=1 THEN PRINT@Z+10,A$(Z);
290 NEXT Z
300 R=0:FOR Z=1 TO L:R=R+A(Z):NEXT Z
310 IF R=L GOTO 330
320 GOTO 140
```

```
330 PRINT @704,"YOU GUESSED MY WORD!
":END
340 FOR X=0 TO 23:Y=34:SET(X,Y):SET(
X,Y+1):NEXT X
350 FOR Y=6 TO 33:X=22:SET(X,Y):SET(
X+1,Y):NEXT Y
360 FOR X=22 TO 57:Y=6:SET(X,Y):NEXT
 X
370 FOR Y=7 TO 8:X=54:SET(X,Y):SET(X
+1,Y):NEXT Y
380 RETURN
390 FOR X=49 TO 60:Y=9:SET(X,Y):NEXT
 X
400 FOR Y=9 TO 16:X=49:SET(X,Y):NEXT
 Y
410 FOR X=49 TO 60:Y=16:SET(X,Y):NEX
T X
420 FOR Y=9 TO 16:X=60:SET(X,Y):NEXT
 Y
430 SET(53,11):SET(57,11):SET(55,11)
:SET(55,12)
440 FOR X=53 TO 57:Y=14:SET(X,Y):NEX
T X
450 RETURN
460 FOR X=48 TO 61:Y=18:SET(X,Y):NEX
T X
470 FOR Y=18 TO 26:X=48:SET(X,Y):SET
(X+1,Y):NEXT Y
480 FOR Y=18 TO 26:X=60:SET(X,Y):SET
(X+1,Y):NEXT Y
490 FOR X=48 TO 61:Y=26:SET(X,Y):NEX
T X
500 SET(54,17):SET(55,17)
510 RETURN
520 FOR X=47 TO 38 STEP -1:Y=13:SET(
X,Y):NEXT X
530 FOR Y=18 TO 23:X=38:SET(X,Y):SET
(X+1,Y):NEXT Y
540 FOR X=36 TO 41:Y=24:SET(X,Y):NEX
T X
550 SET(36,25):SET(38,25):SET(39,25)
:SET(41,25)
560 RETURN
```

```
570 FOR X=62 TO 71:Y=18:SET(X,Y):NEX
T X
580 FOR Y=18 TO 24:X=70:SET(X,Y):SET
(X+1,Y):NEXT Y
590 FOR X=68 TO 73:Y=24:SET(X,Y):NEX
T X
600 SET(68,25):SET(70,25):SET(71,25)
:SET(73,25)
610 RETURN
620 FOR Y=27 TO 34:X=48:SET(X,Y):SET
(X+1,Y):SET(X+2,Y):SET(X+3,Y):NEXT Y

630 FOR X=42 TO 51:Y=34:SET(X,Y):NEX
T X
640 RETURN
650 FOR Y=27 TO 34:X=58:SET(X,Y):SET
(X+1,Y):SET(X+2,Y):SET(X+3,Y):NEXT Y

660 FOR X=58 TO 67:Y=34:SET(X,Y):NEX
T X
670 RETURN
```

MAZE

Remarks

In this game, the player must move his symbol (the asterisk) around and past the mines to the opening on the right side of the screen. The speed at which the asterisk moves can be one of 10 levels, and the number of mines in the maze can be from 20 to 200. The player can move his man in this real-time environment by pressing the following keys:

> Q — MOVE UP
> A — MOVE DOWN
> L — MOVE LEFT
> ; — MOVE RIGHT
> SPACEBAR— STOP

The symbol will continue to move in the last direction specified until a new direction key is pressed. Hitting a maze ends the game. Also there are 15 supermazes scattered in the maze. Hitting one of these will give you a brand new maze. See Fig. 6-2.

Variables

B(X)—Contents of position X in the maze.
If X = 4 the contents is a supermaze.

X = 3 the contents is exit of maze.

X = 2 the contents is a mine.

U —Speed

L —Number of mines in maze

Y —Argument of INKEY$

S —Moves player's symbol

A —Print @ position of player

Suggested Variations

1) To make the game more difficult, remove the space bar recognition from the game. The player will then not be able to stop his symbol once he has begun.

2) You might wish to add a time limit to this game.

3) If a player hits a mine you may wish to simulate an explosion with the "wavy screen" effect described in *Programming Tips*.

Sample Run

OBJECT—TRY TO MANEUVER THE * THROUGH THE OPENING IN THE RIGHT SIDE OF THE SCREEN WITHOUT HITTING ANY OF THE ¢'S BY USING THE FOLLOWING KEYS:

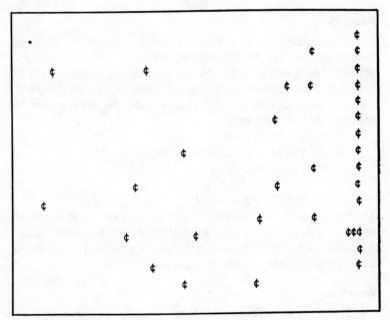

Fig. 6-2. Sample run.

Q—MOVE UP
A—MOVE DOWN
L—MOVE LEFT
;—MOVE RIGHT
SPACE BAR—STOP
ENTER SPEED 1 (FASTEST) TO 10 (SLOWEST)? 5
DEGREE OF MAZE DIFFICULTY (20 to 200)? 20
PLEASE WAIT...
HERE IS YOUR MAZE:

Program for Maze

```
10 CLS
20 DIM B(1024)
30 S=0
40 PRINT "OBJECT-- TRY TO MANEUVER T
HE * THROUGH THE OPENING"
50 PRINT "IN THE RIGHT SIDE OF THE S
CREEN WITHOUT HITTING ANY"
60 PRINT "OF THE <'S BY USING THE FO
LLOWING KEYS:"
70 PRINT "Q-- MOVE UP"
80 PRINT "A-- MOVE DOWN"
90 PRINT "L-- MOVE LEFT"
100 PRINT ";-- MOVE RIGHT"
110 PRINT "SPACE BAR-- STOP"
120 INPUT "ENTER SPEED 1 (FASTEST) T
O 10 (SLOWEST) ";U:U=INT(U)*10
130 INPUT "DEGREE OF MAZE DIFFICULTY
 (20 TO 200)";L
140 CLS:PRINT "PLEASE WAIT..."
150 IF L>200 OR L<20 GOTO 130
160 FOR X=0 TO 1023:B(X)=0:NEXT X
170 CLS:PRINT "HERE IS YOUR MAZE:"
180 S=0
190 P=0:FOR X=1 TO 16:B(P)=1:P=P+64:
NEXT X
200 P=63:Y=RND(15)
210 FOR X=1 TO 15:IF X=Y THEN B(P)=3
 ELSE B(P)=2
220 IF B(P)=3 THEN B(P-1)=1
230 P=P+64:NEXT X
240 FOR I=1 TO 15
```

131

```
250 O=RND(1023):IF B(O)>0 OR O=A GOT
O 250
260 B(O)=4:NEXT I
270 FOR X=1 TO L
280 B(1023)=4
290 H=RND(1023):IF B(H)>0 OR H=A GOT
O 290
300 B(H)=2
310 NEXT X
320 CLS
330 FOR X=1 TO 1023:IF B(X)=2 THEN P
RINT@X,"<";
340 NEXT X
350 S=0
360 Y$=INKEY$
370 FOR G=1 TO U:NEXT G
380 IF Y$=";" THEN S=1
390 IF Y$="L" THEN S=-1
400 IF Y$="Q" THEN S=-64
410 IF Y$="A" THEN S=64
420 IF Y$=" " THEN S=0
430 IF B(A)=1 AND Y$="L" THEN S=0
440 IF A+S>=0 AND A+S<=1023 THEN A=A
+S
450 PRINT @A,"*";
460 IF A-S=A GOTO 480
470 PRINT @A-S," ";
480 IF B(A)=2 GOTO 530
490 IF B(A)=3 GOTO 570
500 IF B(A)=4 GOTO 600
510 IF A<>1023 AND B(A+1)=2 THEN PRI
NT @A+1,"<";
520 GOTO 360
530 FOR X=1 TO 20:FOR Z=1 TO 10:NEXT
 Z:PRINT@A," ";
540 FOR Z=1 TO 10:NEXT Z:PRINT @A,"*
";:NEXT X
550 CLS:PRINT "YOU HAVE HIT A MINE,
YOU LOSE!"
560 END
570 FOR Z=1 TO 500:NEXT Z
580 CLS:PRINT CHR$(23);"HURRAY!!":PR
INT "YOU WIN!":PRINT:PRINT
590 END
```

```
600 CLS:PRINT CHR$(23);"SUPER MAZE!"

610 IF A=1023 THEN A=0
620 GOTO 160
630 FOR X=0 TO 1023:IF B(X)=3 THEN P
RINT X:NEXT X
640 NEXT X
```

CONCENTRATION

Remarks

In this popular game, two players take turns trying to match symbols on a grid made up of thirty-two squares. To look behind a square one must simply type the number of the square. Pressing the ENTER key is not necessary. However, if the square's number is less than ten, you must enter a leading zero (for instance 08 for square #8). If you make a mistake, press the space bar and re-enter your choice. If the symbols behind the two chosen squares match up, the player is awarded the match and the squares are removed from the screen. Otherwise, the squares once again cover the symbols and it is the next player's turn. At the end of the game, the player who has guessed the most matches wins. See Fig. 6-3.

Variables

A(X), B(X), C(X), J(X)—Contents and status of square #X

Y — Which digit of square choice is being entered

J —Number of square chosen

Fig. 6-3. Sample run.

CONCENTRATE							
FIRST PLAYER'S NAME? JIM							
OTHER PLAYER'S NAME? MIKE							
1	2	3	4	5	6	7	8
		JIM'S TURN					
9	10	11	12	13	14	15	16
17	18	19	20	21	22	23	24
25	26	27	28	29	30	31	32
**				FIRST			

PL$(X)—Name of player #X
PL(X) —Score of player #X

Suggested Variations

1) You might wish to make this a single player game against the computer.

2) You might wish to assign values to certain symbols. For example, matching the asterisks is worth a score of five matches.

Program for Concentration

```
10 CLS
20 CLEAR 200
30 DIM A(32),B(32),C(32),J(32)
40 DATA 33,33,35,35,36,36,37,37,38,3
8,42,42,43,43,47,47,60,60,61,61,62,6
2,63,63,64,64,91,91,92,92,88,88
50 M=0
60 GOTO 450
70 X$=" "+STRING$(6,191)
80 FOR Z=1 TO 7:X$=X$+"  "+STRING$(6
,191):NEXT Z
90 T=0
100 FOR X=1 TO 4:FOR Z=1 TO 3
110 PRINT@T,X$:T=T+64:NEXT Z:T=T+64:
NEXT X
120 T1=1:T=66:FOR K=1 TO 4:FOR X=1 T
O 8:PRINT@T,T1;:A(T1)=T:T=T+8:T1=T1+
1:NEXT X:T=T+192:NEXT K
130 REM * PICK THE PLACES
140 FOR X=1 TO 32:C(X)=0:NEXT X
150 FOR X=1 TO 32:READ K
160 T=RND(32):IF C(T)<>0 GOTO 160
170 C(T)=K:NEXT X
180 GOTO 550
190 FOR Y=1 TO 2
200 PRINT@209,STRING$(30,32);:PRINT@
209,PL$(H);"'S TURN";
210 PRINT@960,"    ** ";
220 IF Y=1 THEN PRINT@990,"FIRST   "
; ELSE PRINT@990,"SECOND  ";
230 PRINT@960,"    ** ";
240 A$=INKEY$:IF A$= "" GOTO 240
```

134

```
250 PRINT @960,A$;
260 IF A$=" " THEN B$=" ":GOTO 280
270 B$=INKEY$:IF B$="" GOTO 270
280 IF B$=" " THEN PRINT@960," ";:G
OTO 230
290 PRINT@961,B$;
300 C$=A$+B$:J=VAL(C$):B(Y)=J
310 IF J>32 OR J<=0 GOTO230
320 IF J(J)=1 GOTO 230
330 P=A(J)-66:B(Y+2)=P:FOR K=1 TO 3:
PRINT@P,STRING$(7,C(J));:P=P+64:NEXT
340 IF B(1)=B(2) THEN PRINT@990,"ILL
EGAL";:FOR X=1 TO 500:NEXT:PRINT@990
,"       ";:GOTO 370
350 NEXT Y
360 IF C(B(1))=C(B(2)) GOTO 400
370 PRINT @990,"NO MATCH";:FOR X=1 T
O 1000:NEXT
380 FOR K=1 TO 2:B=B(K+2):FOR R1=1 T
O 3:PRINT@B," "+STRING$(6,191);:B=B+
64:NEXT R1:PRINT@A(B(K)),B(K);:NEXT
K
390 GOTO 560
400 PRINT@990,"A MATCH!";:FOR X=1 TO
 1000:NEXT X:PL(H)=PL(H)+1:M=M+1
410 IF M=16 GOTO 500
420 FOR K=1 TO 2:B=B(K+2):FOR R1=1 T
O 3:PRINT@B,STRING$(7,128);:B=B+64:N
EXT R1:NEXT K
430 J(B(1))=1:J(B(2))=1
440 GOTO 560
450 CLS:PRINT "C O N C E N T R A T E
":PRINT "----------------------":PRIN
T:PRINT
460 INPUT "FIRST PLAYER'S NAME ";PL$
(1)
470 INPUT "OTHER PLAYER'S NAME ";PL$
(2)
480 CLS
490 GOTO 70
500 CLS:PRINT "FINAL SCORE"
510 PRINT
520 PRINT PL$(1);"----   ";PL(1)
```

```
530 PRINT PL$(2);"----   ";PL(2)
540 PRINT:PRINT:END
550 FOR H=1 TO 2:GOTO 190
560 FOR Z=1 TO 4:B(Z)=0:NEXT Z:NEXT
H:GOTO 550
```

KALEIDO

Remarks

Everyone has to have at least one kaleidoscope program to show off his computer! This program produces two and four quadrant symmetrical patterns using your choice of display characters. These are ever-changing patterns and can be very eye-pleasing. See Fig. 6-4.

Variables

A —Horizontal width of pattern
B —Vertical length of pattern

```
KALEIDOSCOPE TYPES
1)  SIMPLE GRAPHICS BLOCKS
2)  DEFINE GRAPHIC CHARACTER
3)  RANDOM GRAPHIC CHARACTERS
4)  DEFINE ALPHANUMERIC CHARACTER
5)  RANDOM ALPHANUMERIC CHARACTERS

ENTER THE NUMBER OF YOUR CHOICE ? 4
ENTER THE ASCII CODE NUMBER OF YOUR DESIRED CHARACTER ? 88
HORIZONTAL WIDTH (1-63) ? 15
VERTICAL LENGTH (1-23) ? 5

 X X      X X
XXX X X XXX
XXX X X XXX
 X X    X X


   X X    X  X
X X XX    XX X X
X X XX    XX X X
   X X    X X


X X          X X
X X XX    XX X X
X X XX    XX X X
X X          X X
```

Fig. 6-4. Sample run.

TY—The type of display character being used
X,Y,U,R—position for character to be plotted
CHAR—ASCII code if display character to be plotted

Suggested Variations

1) You may wish to define your horizontal and vertical limits more closely than I have to avoid illegal Function Call errors from occurring. This is not a big problem, but it may bother some folks.

2) In all but the simple graphics block display mode, you may notice that the pattern has only right/left symmetry. Can you see why? If so, you may wish to convert these to four quadrant.

Program for Kaleido

```
10 CLS
20 PRINT "KALEIDOSCOPE TYPES"
30 PRINT "1) SIMPLE GRAPHICS BLOCKS"
40 PRINT "2) DEFINE GRAPHIC CHARACTE
R"
50 PRINT "3) RANDOM GRAPHIC CHARACTE
RS"
60 PRINT "4) DEFINE ALPHANUMERIC CHA
RACTER"
70 PRINT "5) RANDOM ALPHANUMERIC CHA
RACTERS"
80 PRINT:PRINT
90 INPUT "ENTER THE NUMBER OF YOUR C
HOICE ";TY
100 ON TY GOTO 110,360,110,360,110
110 INPUT "HORIZONTAL WIDTH (1-63) "
;A
120 INPUT "VERTICAL LENGTH (1-23) ";
B
130 CLS
140 IF TY=1 GOTO 380
150 X=RND(A):Y=RND(B)
160 Y=RND(B)
170 U=X:R=Y:GOSUB 310
180 GOSUB 320:T=1
190 U=2*A-X+1:R=Y:GOSUB 310
200 GOSUB 320
210 U=X:R=2*B-Y+1:GOSUB 310
```

```
220 GOSUB 320
230 U=2*A-X+1:R=2*B-Y+1:GOSUB 310
240 GOSUB 320:T=0
250 X=RND(A):Y=RND(B)
260 U=X:R=Y:GOSUB 310:PRINT@P," ";
270 U=2*A-X+1:R=Y:GOSUB 310:PRINT@P,
" ";
280 U=X:R=2*B-Y+1:GOSUB 310:PRINT@P,
" ";
290 U=2*A-X+1:R=2*B-Y+1:GOSUB 310:PR
INT@P," ";
300 GOTO 150
310 C=INT(U/2):R=INT(R/3):P=(R*64)+C
:RETURN
320 ON TY GOTO 0000,330,340,330,350
330 PRINT@P,CHR$(CHAR);:RETURN
340 IF T=1 THEN GOTO 330ELSE CHAR=RN
D(62)+128:GOTO 330
350 IF T=1 THEN GOTO 330ELSE CHAR=RN
D(61)+32:GOTO 330
360 INPUT "ENTER THE ASCII CODE NUMB
ER OF YOUR DESIRED CHARACTER ";CHAR
370 GOTO 110
380 X=RND(A):Y=RND(B)
390 SET(X,Y):SET(2*A-X+1,Y):SET(X,2*
B-Y+1):SET(2*A-X+1,2*B-Y+1)
400 RESET(X+1,Y+1):RESET(2*A-X,Y+1)
410 RESET(X+1,2*B-Y):RESET(2*A-X,2*B
-Y)
420 GOTO 380
```

BLOCKERS

Remarks

Another popular video game that every computer user should have! In this program, two players control the direction of their moving blocks. The blocks leave a trail behind them, creating a sort of wall. The object is to force your opponent into hitting either your wall or his own. This is a very fine game with ten speed levels! This version uses the PEEK function to read the keyboard, so it is much more efficient than those versions using single key strobes such as the INKEY$ function. See Fig. 6-5.

Variables

GO—Number of points needed to win game.

SK—Skill (speed) level

```
HOW MANY POINTS TO WIN GAME ? 1
WHAT IS THE SKILL LEVEL ( 0=HARDEST   10=EASIEST) ? 10
PLAYER 1 ----
CONTROL KEY    DIRECTION
       Q           LEFT
       W           RIGHT
       R           UP
       S           DOWN
PLAYER 2 ----
       ,           LEFT
       .           RIGHT
       ;           UP
       /           DOWN

PRESS ENTER TO BEGIN?
```

Fig. 6-5. Sample run.

A1—PRINT @ position of player 1 + 15360
A2—PRINT @ position of player 2 + 15360
D1—Direction of player 1
D2—Direction of player 2
A —PEEK locations for keyboard scan
S1—Score of player 1
S2—Score of player 2

Suggested Variations

1) After a player has made a trail so many blocks long, you may wish to start deleting blocks from the end of the trail as the player moves.

Program for Blockers

```
10 CLS
20 INPUT "HOW MANY POINTS TO WIN GAM
E ";GO
```

```
30 INPUT "WHAT IS SKILL LEVEL (0=HAR
DEST  10=EASIEST)";SK
40 PRINT "PLAYER 1--- ";
50 PRINT CHR$(183);CHR$(187)
60 PRINT "CONTROL KEY            DIRECTI
ON"
70 PRINT "    Q                    LEFT"
80 PRINT "    W                    RIGHT
"
90 PRINT "    R                    UP"
100 PRINT "   S                    DOWN
"
110 PRINT "PLAYER 2--- ";
120 PRINT CHR$(191);CHR$(191)
130 PRINT "    ,                    LEFT
"
140 PRINT "    .                    RIGH
T"
150 PRINT "    ;                    UP"
160 PRINT "    /                    DOWN
"
170 PRINT
180 INPUT "PRESS ENTER TO BEGIN ";A$
:CLS
190 FOR X=0TO127:SET(X,0):SET(X,47):
NEXT X
200 FOR X=0 TO 47:SET(0,X):SET(127,X
):NEXT
210 A1=15810:D1=1
220 A2=15868:D2=2
230 POKE A1,183:POKE A1+1,187:POKE A
2,191:POKE A2+1,191
240 PRINT@275,"PRESS ANY KEY TO BEGI
N";
250 A$=INKEY$:IF A$="" GOTO 250
260 PRINT@275,"
";
270 A=PEEK(14340)
280 FOR X=1 TO (25*SK):NEXT X
290 IF A=2 THEN D1=2:GOTO 330
300 IF A=4 THEN D1=3:GOTO 330
310 IF A=8 THEN D1=4:GOTO 330
320 IF A=128 THEN D1=1
```

140

```
330 IF D1=1 THEN G=2:GOTO 370
340 IF D1=2 THEN G=-2:GOTO 370
350 IF D1=3 THEN G=-64:GOTO 370
360 IF D1=4 THEN G=64
370 IF PEEK(A1+G)<>32 OR PEEK(A1+1+G)<>32 GOTO 510
380 A1=A1+G:POKE A1,183:POKE A1+1,187
390 A=PEEK(14368)
400 IF A=16 THEN D2=2:GOTO 440
410 IF A=64 THEN D2=1:GOTO 440
420 IF A=8 THEN D2=3:GOTO 440
430 IF A=128 THEN D2=4
440 IF D2=1 THEN P=2:GOTO 480
450 IF D2=2 THEN P=-2:GOTO 480
460 IF D2=3 THEN P=-64:GOTO 480
470 IF D2=4 THEN P=64
480 IF PEEK(A2+P)<>32 OR PEEK(A2+1+P)<>32 GOTO 610
490 A2=A2+P:POKE A2,191:POKE A2+1,191
500 GOTO 270
510 PRINT@0, "PLAYER 1 LOSES THIS ROUND  *PRESS SPACE BAR*";
520 A$=INKEY$:IF A$<>" " GOTO 520
530 CLS
540 S2=S2+1:IF S2=GO GOTO 650
550 PRINT "CURRENT SCORE:"
560 PRINT "PLAYER 1-- ";S1
570 PRINT "PLAYER 2-- ";S2
580 PRINT:PRINT:PRINT "*PRESS ANY KEY*"
590 A$=INKEY$:IF A$="" GOTO 590
600 CLS:GOTO 190
610 PRINT@0,"PLAYER 2 LOSES THIS ROUND *PRESS SPACE BAR*;
620 A$=INKEY$:IF A$<>" " GOTO 620
630 S1=S1+1:IF S1=GO GOTO 650
640 CLS:GOTO 550
650 CLS:PRINT "FINAL SCORE"
660 PRINT "PLAYER 1--   ";S1
670 PRINT "PLAYER 2--   ";S2
680 PRINT:END
```

ROULETTE

Remarks

This is a regulation game of casino Roulette played on an American-style roulette wheel (includes the numbers 0 and 00). The numbers have been placed around the wheel randomly and fifty separate bets (including 38 single number bets) are on the menu. The number finally chosen is done so completely randomly, but you may wish to insert a RANDOM command at the beginning of the program just to get a new pseudo-random seed number each time you run the program. Good luck, at your personal casino!

Variables

A$(X) —Number in slot X of the wheel
AC   —Money in player's account
B   —Bet choice number
A   —Amount of player's bet
X,X1,Y —Used to plot roulette wheel
U   —Number of slots wheel will turn before stopping
G   —Current number of slots passed while wheel is turning
WIN$, WIN—Winning number

Suggested Variations

1) If you would rather play on a European-style roulette wheel, simply delete the double zero (00) from the wheel.

2) You may wish to set an amount of money won that will "break the bank" and declare the player champion of the gambling universe.

Sample Run

ROULETTE
YOUR ACCOUNT BEGINS AT $500
PLEASE WAIT...

1	2	3	COLUMN
1+	2*	3+	+ = RED
4*	5+	6*	* = BLACK
7+	8*	9+	# = GREEN
10*	11*	12+	
13*	14+	15*	PRESS
16+	17*	18+	ANY

19+	20*	21+	KEY
22*	23+	24*	TO
25+	26*	27+	CONTINUE
28*	29*	30+	
31*	32+	33*	
34+	35*	36+	

0#   00#

YOUR ACCOUNT STANDS AT $ 500
PRESS ANY KEY TO CONTINUE

1-36)SINGLE NUMBER BET	35:1	
37) NUMBER 0	35:1	
38) NUMBER 00	35:1	HERE
39) NUMBERS 1-12	2:1	ARE
40) NUMBERS 13-24	2:1	THE
41) NUMBERS 25-36	2:1	BETS
42) FIRST COLUMN	2:1	AND
43) SECOND COLUMN	2:1	THEIR
44) THIRD COLUMN	2:1	PAYOFF
45) NUMBERS 1-18	1:1	ODDS
46) NUMBERS 19-36	1:1	
47) EVEN NUMBER	1:1	
48) ODD NUMBER	1:1	
49) RED	1:1	
(50) BLACK	1:1	

ENTER YOUR BET CHOICE NUMBER (1-50) ? 49
ENTER THE AMOUNT OF YOUR BET ? 500
PRESS ANY KEY TO GET THE BALL ROLLING!

II
II
17
13   07
00   20
18   27

WHERE SHE STOPS, NOBODY KNOWS!
NUMBER 17 IS THE WINNER!
SORRY BUB, NO BUCKS—NO GAMBLING.

Program for Roulette

```
10 CLEAR 500
20 CLS:DIM A$(152),C(38),CO(38):AC=5
00
30 RESTORE
40 K=0
50 PRINT "ROULETTE"
```

143

```
60 PRINT "YOUR ACCOUNT BEGINS AT $";
AC
70 PRINT "PLEASE WAIT..."
80 DATA 28,8,35,10,25,6,11,31,29,16,
34,7,32,23,33,19,18,38,13
90 DATA 17,37,20,27,12,14,21,22,24,1
,30,15,5,26,4,2,36,3,9
100 DATA 1,2,1,2,1,2,1,2,1,2,2,1,2,1
,2,1,2,1,1,2,1,2,1,2,1,2,1,2,2,1,2,1
,2,1,2,1
110 DATA 0,18,18,12,36,9,56,6,76,9,9
4,12,112,18
120 T=0:FOR Z=1 TO 4:FOR X=1 TO 38:R
EAD A:IF A=37 THEN A$=" 0" ELSE IF A
=38 THEN A$=" 00" ELSE A$=STR$(A):IF
 A>0 AND A<10 THEN A$=A$+" "
130 A$(T+X)=A$:NEXT X
140 T=T+38:RESTORE:NEXT Z
150 FOR X=1 TO 38:READ Z:NEXT X
160 GOSUB 1090
170 RESTORE:FOR X=1 TO 74:READ Z:NEX
T X
180 GOSUB 910
190 CLS:PRINT "YOUR ACCOUNT STANDS A
T $";AC
200 PRINT:PRINT
210 PRINT "PRESS ANY KEY TO CONTINUE
 "
220 K=0
230 A$=INKEY$:IF A$="" GOTO 230
240 PRINT "1-36) SINGLE NUMBER BET
          35:1"
250 PRINT "37) NUMBER 0
          35:1"
260 PRINT "38) NUMBER 00
          35:1    HERE"
270 PRINT "39) NUMBERS 1-12
          2:1     ARE"
280 PRINT "40) NUMBERS 13-24
          2:1     THE"
290 PRINT "41) NUMBERS 25-36
          2:1     BETS"
300 PRINT "42) FIRST COLUMN
          2:1     AND"
```

```
310 PRINT "43) SECOND COLUMN
            2:1     THEIR"
320 PRINT "44) THIRD COLUMN
            2:1     PAYOFF"
330 PRINT "45) NUMBERS 1-18
            1:1     ODDS"
340 PRINT "46) NUMBERS 19-36
            1:1"
350 PRINT "47) EVEN NUMBER
            1:1"
360 PRINT "48) ODD NUMBER
            1:1"
370 PRINT "49) RED
            1:1"
380 PRINT "50) BLACK
            1:1"
390 INPUT "ENTER YOUR BET CHOICE NUM
BER (1-50) ";B
400 B=INT(B):IF B>50 OR B<1 THEN CLS
:GOTO 240
410 INPUT "ENTER THE AMOUNT OF YOUR
BET ";A
420 IF A<=AC GOTO 450
430 CLS:PRINT "YOU BET $";A;" AND YO
U ONLY HAVE $";AC
440 PRINT "NICE TRY, SLICK...":FOR X
=1 TO 1000:NEXT X:CLS:GOTO 240
450 RESTORE:FOR X=1 TO 74:READ Z:NEX
T X:CLS:FOR Z=1 TO 7:READ X:READ Y:G
OSUB 470:NEXT Z
460 GOTO 520
470 FOR X1=0 TO 7:SET(X,X1+Y):SET(X+
1,Y+X1)
480 SET(X+14,X1+Y):SET(X+15,X1+Y):SE
T(X1*2+X,Y):SET(X1*2+1+X,Y)
490 SET(X1*2+X,7+Y):SET(I*2+1+X,7+Y)

500 NEXT X1
510 RETURN
520 PRINT@95,CHR$(92);CHR$(92);:PRIN
T@31,CHR$(92);CHR$(92);
530 PRINT@896,"PRESS ANY KEY TO GET
THE BALL ROLLING!";
540 A$=INKEY$:IF A$="" GOTO 540
```

```
550 PRINT@896,"                          ";
560 PRINT@719,"ROUND AND ROUND SHE G
OES!";
570 T=0:U=100+RND(38):FOR G=1 TO U
580 T=T+1
590 PRINT@450,A$(T);:PRINT@331,A$(T+
1);:PRINT@276,A$(T+2);
600 PRINT@222,A$(T+3);:PRINT@296,A$(
T+4);:PRINT@369,A$(T+5);
610 PRINT@506,A$(T+6);
620 IF G>=U-10 THEN PRINT@719,"WHERE
 SHE STOPS, NOBODY KNOWS!";:K=K+15:F
OR N=1 TO K:NEXT N
630 NEXT G
640 WIN$=A$(T+3)
650 FOR Z=1 TO 5:FOR X=1 TO 250:NEXT
 X
660 PRINT@896,"NUMBER ";WIN$;" IS TH
E WINNER!"
670 FOR X=1 TO 250:NEXT X:PRINT@896,
"                          ";:NE
XT Z
680 IF WIN$=" 0" THEN WIN=37 ELSE IF
 WIN$=" 00" THEN WIN=38 ELSE WIN=VAL
(WIN$)
690 IF B=WIN THEN AC=AC+(35*A):GOTO
870
700 IF B=37 AND WIN$=" 0" THEN 870
710 IF B=38 AND WIN$=" 00" THEN 870
720 IF B=39 AND WIN>=1 AND WIN<=12 T
HEN 850
730 IF B=40 AND WIN>=13 AND WIN<=24
THEN 850
740 IF B=41 AND WIN>=25 AND WIN<=36
THEN 850
750 IF B=42 AND C(WIN)=1 THEN 850
760 IF B=43 AND C(WIN)=2 THEN 850
770 IF B=44 AND C(WIN)=3 THEN 850
780 IF B=45 AND WIN>=1 AND WIN<=18 T
HEN 860
790 IF B=46 AND WIN>=19 AND WIN<=36
THEN 860
```

146

```
800 IF B=47 AND WIN/2=INT(WIN/2) THE
N 860
810 IF B=48 AND WIN/2<>INT(WIN/2) TH
EN 860
820 IF B=49 AND CO(WIN)=1 THEN 860
830 IF B=50 AND CO(WIN)=2 THEN 860
840 AC=AC-A:GOTO 880
850 AC=AC+(2*A):GOTO 880
860 AC=AC+A:GOTO 880
870 AC=AC+(35*A)
880 IF AC<=0 GOTO 900
890 GOSUB 910:GOTO 190
900 PRINT "SORRY BUB, NO BUCKS--NO G
AMBLING.":END
910 REM
920 PRINT" 1              2
   3       COLUMN"
930 PRINT"--------------------------
------"
940 PRINT "1+          2*
   3+     + = RED"
950 PRINT "4*          5+
   6*      * = BLACK"
960 PRINT "7+          8*
   9+      # = GREEN"
970 PRINT "10*         11*
   12+"
980 PRINT "13*         14+
   15*   PRESS"
990 PRINT "16+         17*
   18+    ANY"
1000 PRINT "19+         20*
   21+    KEY"
1010 PRINT "22*         23+
   24*    TO"
1020 PRINT "25+         26*
   27+    CONTINUE"
1030 PRINT "28*         29*
   30+"
1040 PRINT "31*         32+
   33*"
1050 PRINT "34+         35*
   36+"
1060 PRINT "    0#              00#"
```

```
1070 A$=INKEY$:IF A$="" GOTO 1070
1080 RETURN
1090 T=0
1100 FOR X=1 TO 3:T=T+1:C(T)=X:IF T=
38 GOTO 1120
1110 NEXT X:GOTO 1100
1120 RESTORE:FOR X=1 TO 38:READ Z:NE
XT X:C(0)=4:FOR X=1 TO 36:READ CO(X)
:NEXT X
1130 RETURN
1140 A$=INKEY$:IF A$="" GOTO 1140
1150 CLS:RETURN
```

SLED

Remarks

One of my personal favorites, and an excellent way to make a game out of teaching projectile science. The instructions are self explanatory and the graphics are really snazzy. You are allowed three tries to jump your sled accurately, and wait until you see what happens if you miss on the third attempt! Take heart when typing in this relatively lengthy program: it is *well* worth the time!

Variables

S5 —Horizontal width of sleds to be jumped
S —Speed at which sled left ramp (mph)
V —Speed at which sled left ramp (ft/sec)
A5 —Angle of ramp to the horizontal
D —Total time of flight
C —Time to highest altitude
E —Maximum altitude reached in flight
G7 —Total horizontal range covered by flight
DF—Distance to closest edge of receiving ramp
J —Jump number
W —Attempt number
SL—Number of rocket sleds to jump over
BE—Greatest number of sleds jumped over successfully

Suggested Variations

1) If you add an air resistance factor to the calculations, you can change the scenario to a motorcycle daredevil jumping over school buses (a big hit with kids).

148

2) If your rocket overshoots the ramp on the first or second attempt, the pilot seems to fall quite slowly (execution time for graphics). You might want to give him a parachute for realism. (But teacher, I thought he was in a vacuum!)

Sample Run

WELCOME TO THE PLANET R-45!
YOU (THE GALAXY'S GREATEST DAREDEVIL) HAVE BEEN HIRED TO PERFORM THE MOST SPECTACULAR STUNT BEFORE A SELL/OUT CROWD IN THE SUPER-VACUUM-ARENA (THAT'S RIGHT, NO AIR INSIDE!), WHICH IS JUMPING YOUR TURBO ROCKET SLED OVER A NUMBER OF ROCKET SLEDS USING RAMPS. EACH ROCKET SLED IS 7.5 FEET WIDE. YOU CAN CHOOSE THE NUMBER OF SLEDS TO JUMP OVER AS WELL AS THE ANGLE OF YOUR RAMPS AND THE SPEED YOU WILL LEAVE THE TAKE-OFF RAMP AT THE LENGTH OF YOUR LANDING RAMP IS 40 FEET THE ARTIFICIAL GRAVITY IN THE ARENA IS THE SAME AS EARTH'S.

HOW MANY JUMPS WOULD YOU LIKE TO TRY? 1
JUMP # 1
ATTEMPT # 1
WHAT IS THE ANGLE OF YOUR TAKE/OFF RAMP? 45
HOW MANY SLEDS DO YOU WISH TO JUMP OVER? 5
HERE WE GO ...

4.2 MPH

PRESS ANY KEY WHEN YOU HAVE REACHED THE DESIRED SPEED.
SLED LEFT RAMP AT 4.2 MPH OR 6.16 FT/SEC
RAMP WAS SET AT 45 DEGREES TO THE HORIZONTAL
NEEDED TO LAND BETWEEN 37.5 AND 77.5 FEET.

TOTAL TIME OF FLIGHT ------------------------.325826 SECONDS
TIME TO HIGHEST ALTITUDE ----------------.162913 SECONDS
MAXIMUM ALTITUDE -----------------------------.426959 FEET
TOTAL HORIZONTAL RANGE ------------------1.05437 FEET
PRESS ENTER TO CONTINUE?

Program For Sled

```
10 DIM A(12)
20 S5=(RND(150)+50)/10
30 CLS:GOTO 270
40   X=A
50   GOSUB 240
60   C= (V*Y)/32.174
70   D=((2*V)*Y)/32.174
80   E=((V*V)*(Y*Y))/64.348
90   X=2*A
100   GOSUB 240
110   G=((V*V)*Y)/32.174
120 G7=G
130 DI=G
140 A5=A
150 RETURN
160 PRINT "SLED LEFT RAMP AT ";S;" M
PH OR ";V;" FT/SEC"
170 PRINT "RAMP WAS SET AT ";A5;" DE
GREES TO THE HORIZONTAL"
180 PRINT "NEEDED TO LAND BETWEEN ";
DF;" AND ";DF+40;" FEET."
190   PRINT "-------------------------
-------------------------------"
200   PRINT "TOTAL TIME OF FLIGHT----
----------------";D;" SECONDS"
210   PRINT "TIME TO HIGHEST ALTITUDE
----------------";C;" SECONDS"
220   PRINT "MAXIMUM ALTITUDE--------
----------------";E;" FEET"
230   PRINT "TOTAL HORIZONTAL RANGE--
----------------";G7;" FEET"
240 Y=SIN(X)
250 RETURN
260 PRINT@512,S;
270 PRINT "WELCOME TO THE PLANET R-4
5!"
280 PRINT "YOU (THE GALAXY'S GREATES
T DAREDEVIL) HAVE BEEN"
290 PRINT "HIRED TO PERFORM THE MOST
  SPECTACULAR STUNT BEFORE"
300 PRINT "A SELL-OUT CROWD IN THE S
UPER-VACUUM-ARENA (THAT'S"
```

```
310 PRINT "RIGHT, NO AIR INSIDE!), W
HICH IS JUMPING YOUR"
320 PRINT "TURBO ROCKET SLED OVER A
NUMBER OF ROCKET SLEDS"
330 PRINT "USING RAMPS.  EACH ROCKET
 SLED IS ";S5;" FEET WIDE."
340 PRINT "YOU CAN CHOOSE THE NUMBER
 OF SLEDS TO JUMP OVER"
350 PRINT "AS WELL AS THE ANGLE OF Y
OUR RAMPS AND THE SPEED"
360 PRINT "YOU WILL LEAVE THE TAKE-O
FF RAMP AT."
370 PRINT "THE LENGTH OF YOUR LANDIN
G RAMP IS 40 FEET"
380 PRINT "THE ARTIFICIAL GRAVITY IN
 THE ARENA IS THE SAME AS EARTH'S."
390 PRINT:INPUT "HOW MANY JUMPS WOUL
D YOU LIKE TO TRY ";N5:CLS
400 J=0
410 J=J+1:W=0
420 IF J>N5 GOTO 1910
430 W=W+1
440 PRINT "JUMP #";J
450 PRINT "ATTEMPT #";W
460 S=0
470 INPUT "WHAT IS THE ANGLE OF YOUR
 TAKE-OFF RAMP ";AN
480 IF AN>=90 THEN PRINT "NO GOOD, C
HUMP!":GOTO 470
490 IF W<>1 GOTO 530
500 INPUT "HOW MANY SLEDS DO YOU WIS
H TO JUMP OVER ";SL
510 IF SL>15 THEN PRINT "THE PLANET
DOESN'T HAVE THAT MANY!":GOTO 500
520 DF=SL*S5
530 CLS:PRINT "HERE WE GO...":FOR X=
1 TO 500:NEXT X
540 PRINT@832,"PRESS ANY KEY WHEN YO
U HAVE REACHED THE DESIRED SPEED";
550 A$=INKEY$:IF A$<>"" GOTO 580
560 PRINT@512,"                    ";:PRINT
@512,S;" MPH";
570 S=S+.2:S=S+.005:S=S*10:S=INT(S):
S=S/10:GOTO 550
```

```
580 S=S-.2:PRINT@512,S;" MPH";:FOR Z
=1 TO 500:NEXT Z
590 IF S<=0 GOTO 530
600 F=S/3600:V=F*5280:A=AN
610 GOSUB 40
620 CLS:G=14:H=40
630 FOR X=1 TO 8
640 FOR K=G TO 15
650 SET(K,H):NEXT K
660 H=H+1:G=G-2:NEXT X
670 G=18
680 FOR K=1 TO SL:H=45:FOR T=1 TO 3:
FOR H1=G TO G+3:SET(H1,H):NEXT H1:H=
H+1:NEXT T:G=G+6:NEXT K
690 Y=40:G1=G+1:FOR X=1 TO 8
700 FOR K=G TO G1
710 SET(K,Y):NEXT K
720 Y=Y+1:G1=G1+2:NEXT X
730 P=G1+2:FOR Y=17 TO 43:SET(P,Y):N
EXT Y
740 ST=15:EN=G:DT=EN-ST
750 HF=INT(DT/2)

760 IF G7>DF+40 THEN HF=HF+25
770 IF G7<DF THEN HF=HF-3:IF SL/2=IN
T(SL/2) THEN HF=HF-1
780 X=4:Y=44
790 SET(X,Y):SET(X+1,Y)
800 SET(X-2,Y+1):SET(X-1,Y+1)
810 SET(X-4,Y+2):SET(X-3,Y+2)
820 IF X>=HF+15 GOTO 840
830 RESET(X-4,Y+2):RESET(X-3,Y+2):X=
X+2:Y=Y-1:GOTO 790
840 RESET(X-2,Y+1):RESET(X-1,Y+1)
850 RESET(X-4,Y+2):RESET(X-3,Y+2)
860 SET(X,Y):SET(X+1,Y)
870 SET(X-1,Y-1):SET(X-2,Y-1)
880 SET(X-3,Y-2):SET(X-4,Y-2)
890 IF POINT(X+1,Y+1)=-1 GOTO 910ELS
E IF POINT(X+2,Y)=-1 GOTO 910ELSE IF
 Y=45 GOTO 1330
900 RESET(X-3,Y-2):RESET(X-4,Y-2):X=
X+2:Y=Y+1:GOTO 860
910 IF DI<DF GOTO 1400
```

152

```
920 GOSUB 1520:SET(X-1,Y):SET(X-2,Y)
:SET(X-3,Y-1)
930 RESET(X-1,Y):RESET(X-2,Y):RESET(
X-3,Y-1)
940 SET(X-4,Y-1):SET(X-4,Y):SET(X-4,
Y+1)
950 RESET(X-4,Y-1):RESET(X-4,Y):RESE
T(X-4,Y+1)
960 SET(X-5,Y-2):SET(X-6,Y-1):SET(X-
7,Y)
970 IF W=3 GOTO 1710
980 FOR Z=1 TO 500:NEXT Z
990 X=X-2
1000 GOSUB 1010:GOSUB 1030:GOSUB 105
0:GOSUB 1070:GOSUB 1090:GOSUB 1110:G
OTO 1130
1010 SET(X,Y):SET(X-5,Y)
1020 RETURN
1030 SET(X,Y+1):SET(X-2,Y+1):SET(X-3
,Y+1):SET(X-5,Y+1)
1040 RETURN
1050 FOR Z=X TO X-5 STEP-1:SET(Z,Y+2
):NEXT Z
1060 RETURN
1070 FOR Z=X-1 TO X-4 STEP -1:SET(Z,
Y+3):NEXT Z
1080 RETURN
1090 SET(X-1.Y+4):SET(X-4.Y+4)
1100 RETURN
1110 SET(X,Y+5):SET(X-1,Y+5):SET(X-4
,Y+5):SET(X-5,Y+5)
1120 RETURN
1130 FOR Z=1 TO 500:NEXT Z
1140 I=16:IF SL/2=INT(SL/2) THEN I=1
7
1150 FOR K=1 TO I
1160 Y=Y+1:GOSUB 1010:GOSUB 1030:GOS
UB 1050:GOSUB 1070:GOSUB 1090:GOSUB
1110
1170 RESET(X,Y-1):RESET(X-1,Y+1):RES
ET(X-2,Y):RESET(X-3,Y)
1180 RESET(X-4,Y+1):RESET(X-5,Y-1):R
ESET(X,Y+4):RESET(X-5,Y+4)
1190 NEXT K
```

```
1200 FOR Z=1 TO 250:NEXT Z
1210 FOR K=1 TO 30
1220 PRINT@672,"HE'S O.K. !!";
1230 RESET(X,Y):RESET(X,Y+1):RESET(X
-5,Y):RESET(X-5,Y+1)
1240 SET(X+1,Y+2):SET(X+2,Y+2):SET(X
-7,Y+2):SET(X-6,Y+2)
1250 RESET(X-7,Y+2):RESET(X+2,Y+2)
1260 SET(X+1,Y+3):SET(X-6,Y+3)
1270 RESET(X+1,Y+3):RESET(X-6,Y+3)
1280 SET(X-7,Y+2):SET(X+2,Y+2)
1290 RESET(X+1,Y+2):RESET(X+2,Y+2):R
ESET(X-6,Y+2):RESET(X-7,Y+2)
1300 SET(X,Y+1):SET(X,Y):SET(X-5,Y+1
):SET(X-5,Y)
1310 NEXT K
1320 GOTO 1660
1330 IF D1>DF GOTO 1400
1340 PRINT@0,"A SPLENDID JUMP OF ";G
7;" FEET!"
1350 PRINT@64,"THE CROWD IS REALLY L
OVING YOU!"
1360 IF SL>BE THEN BE=SL
1370 PRINT@192,"PRESS ANY KEY TO CON
TINUE"
1380 A$=INKEY$:IF A$="" GOTO 1380
1390 CLS:GOTO 410
1400 GOSUB 1520
1410 SET(X,Y-1):SET(X-1,Y-2):SET(X-2
,Y-2)
1420 RESET(X,Y-1):RESET(X-1,Y-2):RES
ET(X-2,Y-2)
1430 SET(X-2,Y-6):SET(X-3,Y-5):SET(X
-4,Y-4):SET(X-5,Y-3)
1440 RESET(X-2,Y-6):RESET(X-3,Y-5):R
ESET(X-4,Y-4):RESET(X-5,Y-3)
1450 SET(X-5,Y-3):SET(X-6,Y-4):SET(X
-7,Y-5):SET(X-8,Y-6)
1460 FOR Z=1 TO 250:NEXT Z
1470 IF W=3 GOTO 1820
1480 X=X+3:Y=Y-7:GOSUB 1110:GOSUB 10
90:GOSUB 1070:GOSUB 1050:GOSUB 1030:
GOSUB 1010
1490 FOR Z=1 TO 250:NEXT Z
```

154

```
1500 GOTO 1210
1510 GOTO 1660
1520 A=RND(10):ON A GOTO 1530,1540,1
550,1560,1570,1580,1590,1600,1610,16
20
1530 A$="KA-POW":GOTO 1630
1540 A$="WHOOPS!":GOTO 1630
1550 A$="CRASH!":GOTO 1630
1560 A$="YOWEEE!!":GOTO 1630
1570 A$="KA-BLOOEY!":GOTO 1630
1580 A$="SPLAT!":GOTO 1630
1590 A$="GROAN!":GOTO 1630
1600 A$="AIEEEE!!":GOTO 1630
1610 A$="PA-TOOEY!":GOTO 1630
1620 A$="BOO! HISS!"
1630 PA=((INT(Y/3)*64)+INT(X/2))
1640 FOR Z=1 TO 5:PRINT@PA-138,A$;:F
OR L=1 TO 100:NEXT L
1650 PRINT@PA-138,"               ";:
FOR L=1 TO 100:NEXT L:NEXT Z:RETURN
1660 PRINT@128,"PRESS ANY KEY FOR LA
ST JUMP'S DATA";
1670 A$=INKEY$:IF A$="" GOTO 1670
1680 CLS:GOSUB 160
1690 INPUT "PRESS ENTER TO CONTINUE"
;A$:CLS
1700 IF W=3 GOTO 410ELSE GOTO 430
1710 A(1)=X-5:A(2)=Y-1:A(3)=X-3:A(4)
=Y:A(5)=X-1:A(6)=Y
1720 A(7)=X-5:A(8)=Y+1:A(9)=X-3:A(10
)=Y+2:A(11)=X-1:A(12)=Y+2
1730 FOR K=1 TO 11 STEP 2:SET(A(K),A
(K+1)):NEXT K
1740 FOR Z=1 TO 21
1750 FOR K=1 TO 11 STEP2:RESET(A(K),
A(K+1)):NEXT K
1760 FOR K=2 TO 12 STEP 2:A(K)=A(K)+
1:NEXT K
1770 FOR K=1 TO 11 STEP 2:SET(A(K),A
(K+1)):NEXT K
1780 FOR K=1 TO 11 STEP 2:RESET(A(K)
,A(K+1)-1):NEXT K
1790 NEXT Z
```

```
1800 FOR K=1 TO 11 STEP 2:RESET(A(K)
,A(K+1)):NEXT K
1810 PRINT@336,"I GUESS HE DIDN'T SU
RVIVE.";:GOTO 1660
1820 X=X-1:Y=Y-2
1830 PA=((INT(Y/3)*64)+INT(X/2)):PRI
NT@PA-205,"SMOKE-->";
1840 FOR Z=1 TO 5:FOR C=1 TO 2:SET(X
,Y):SET(X+1,Y-1)
1850 Y=Y-2:SET(X,Y):SET(X-1,Y-1)
1860 FOR K=1 TO 100:NEXT K
1870 NEXT C
1880 NEXT Z
1890 PRINT@320,"LOOKS LIKE HE BURNED
 UP IN THIS ONE.";
1900 GOTO 1660
1910 CLS:PRINT "THAT'S ALL FOR THIS
PERFORMANCE!!"
1920 PRINT "YOUR BEST JUMP OF THE NI
GHT WAS ";BE;" SLEDS."
```

AIR RAID

Remarks

In this real-time game, the player uses three missile launchers
to shoot down from one to four targets. At the end of the game, the
player's hits, misses, and accuracy rating is displayed. The player
can participate in as many rounds as he wishes. See Fig. 6-6.

Variables

W —Number of rounds
A —PEEK location for keyboard read
R(X)—Right side PRINT @ limit for target #X
L(X)—Left side PRINT @ limit for target #X
D(X)—Direction of travel for target #X (1= right – 1= left)
T(X)—PRINT @ position of target #X
M2 —PRINT @ position of missile
HI —Number of hits
MI —Number of misses
V —How many targets per round

Suggested Variations

1) Allow the targets to keep moving while missile is being
fired. See program SAUCERS for this routine.

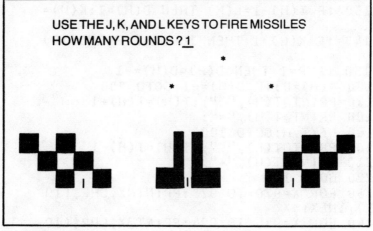

Fig. 6-6. Sample run.

2) Assign a time limit to each round.

3) Assign a limit to the number of missiles that can be shot from each launcher each round.

Program For Air Raid

```
10 CLS
20 PRINT "USE THE J, K, AND L KEYS T
O FIRE MISSLES"
30 INPUT "HOW MANY ROUNDS ";W
40 V=RND(4)
50 FOR Q=1 TO W:CLS
60 FOR C=1 TO 4:T(C)=-1:NEXT C
70 R(1)=64:L(1)=-1:R(2)=128:L(2)=63:
R(3)=192:L(3)=127:R(4)=256:L(4)=191
80 T(1)=RND(64)-1:IF V=1 GOTO 90ELSE
 T(2)=RND(64)+63:IF V=2 GOTO 90ELSE
T(3)=RND(64)+127:IF V=3 GOTO 90ELSE
T(4)=RND(64)+191
90 GOTO 230
100 A=PEEK(14338):IF A<4 OR A>16 GOT
O 120
110 ON A/4 GOTO 350,390,120,430
120 FOR H=1 TO V:IF T(H)=-1 THEN 190
ELSE IF T(H)+1=R(H) THEN D(H)=-1:K(H
)=1
```

157

```
130 IF T(H)-1=L(H) THEN D(H)=1:K(H)=
1
140 IF K(H)=1 THEN 160ELSE P=RND(10)

150 IF P=1 THEN D(H)=D(H)*-1
160 K(H)=0:IF D(H)=-1 GOTO 200
170 PRINT@T(H)," ";:T(H)=T(H)+1
180 PRINT@T(H),"*";
190 NEXT H:GOTO 100
200 PRINT@T(H)," ";:T(H)=T(H)-1
210 PRINT@T(H),"*";
220 GOTO 190
230 FOR X=970 TO 978:PRINT@X,CHR$(19
1);:NEXT X
240 FOR X=986 TO 994:PRINT@X,CHR$(19
1);:NEXT X
250 FOR X=1003 TO 1011:PRINT@X,CHR$(
191);:NEXT X
260 Z=974:FOR X=1 TO 4:PRINT@Z,CHR$(
191);:Z=Z-65:NEXT X
270 Z=976:FOR X=1 TO 4:PRINT@Z,CHR$(
191);:Z=Z-65:NEXT X
280 Z=1005:FOR X=1 TO 4:PRINT@Z,CHR$
(191);:Z=Z-63:NEXT X
290 Z=1007:FOR X=1 TO 4:PRINT@Z,CHR$
(191);:Z=Z-63:NEXT X
300 Z=925:FOR X=1 TO 3:PRINT@Z,CHR$(
191);:Z=Z-64:NEXT X
310 Z=927:FOR X=1 TO 3:PRINT@Z,CHR$(
191);:Z=Z-64:NEXT X
320 GOTO 330
330 PRINT@M1," ";:PRINT@M2," ";:PRIN
T@M3," ";:M1=975:PRINT@M1,"↑";:M2=99
0:PRINT@M2,"↑";:M3=1006:PRINT@M3,"↑"
;
340 GOTO 100
350 IF M1-65<0 THEN M1=M1+1:GOTO 330

360 PRINT@M1," ";:M1=M1-65:PRINT@M1,
"↑";
370 IF M1=T(1) OR M1=T(2) OR M1=T(3)
 OR M1=T(4) GOTO 470
380 GOTO 350
```

```
390 IF M2-64<=0 THEN MI=MI+1:GOTO 33
0
400 PRINT@M2," ";:M2=M2-64:PRINT@M2,
"↑";
410 IF M2=T(1) OR M2=T(2) OR M2=T(3)
 OR M2=T(4) GOTO 470
420 GOTO 390
430 IF M3-63<=0 THEN MI=MI+1:GOTO 33
0
440 PRINT@M3," ";:M3=M3-63:PRINT@M3,
"↑";
450 IF M3=T(1) OR M3=T(2) OR M3=T(3)
 OR M3=T(4) GOTO 470
460 GOTO 430
470 IF T(1)=M1 OR T(1)=M2 OR T(1)=M3
 THEN L=1
480 IF T(2)=M1 OR T(2)=M2 OR T(2)=M3
 THEN L=2
490 IF T(3)=M1 OR T(3)=M2 OR T(3)=M3
 THEN L=3
500 IF T(4)=M1 OR T(4)=M2 OR T(4)=M3
 THEN L=4
510 FOR X=1 TO 50:PRINT@T(L),"*";:PR
INT@T(L)," ";:NEXT X
520 T(L)=-1
530 TT=0:FOR K=1 TO V:TT=TT+T(K):NEX
T K
540 IF TT=V*-1 THEN 580
550 HI=HI+1:GOTO 330
560 CLS:PRINT"YOU MADE ";HI;" HITS A
ND ";MI;" MISSES FOR AN ACCURACY"
570 PRINT "RATING OF ";(HI/(HI+MI))*
100;"%":END
580 V=RND(4):HI=HI+1:NEXT Q
590 GOTO 560
```

SPACE POTATOES

Remarks

Neat name, huh? The player is being chased by the deadly space potato monsters. The player is also surrounded by a number of black holes (a must for every serious space game) as well as an unknown object and space warps. Hitting a black hole destroys the player and ends the game (See Fig. 6-7). Hitting a space warp places the player randomly elsewhere in space. The unknown object moves at random, destroying anything in its path. The player wins by luring the rather stupid space potatoes into black holes before they catch up and destroy the player. This is a real time game, and the player can move by pressing the following keys:

Q— MOVE UP
A— MOVE DOWN
L— MOVE LEFT

; — MOVE RIGHT (Note: the program directions state that the R key is used to move right. This is a tricky problem for the uninitiated to solve.)
Space Bar — STOP

Fig. 6-7. Sample run.

Variables

A(X)—Print @ positions if the various objects.

　　If X = 1 it is position of player

　　　　X = 2 - 5 it is position of space potatoes

　　　　X = 6 it is position of unknown object

　　　　X = 10 - 30 it is position of black holes

　　　　X = 31 - 40 it is position of space warps

I$ 　—Argument of INKEY$

S 　—Number of PRINT positions to move player

T 　—Which potato is moving

H2, V2, H1,

V1 —Converted Row, Column #s of potatoes and player

H 　—Number of PRINT positions to move @ unknown object.

Suggested Variations

1) Change the number of space potatoes, black holes, space warps and unknowns.

2) Hide some black holes in the maze, that is, do not show their position on the screen.

Program For Space Potatoes

```
10 CLS:DIM A(40)
20 PRINT "-------- SPACE POTATOES --
------"
30 PRINT "+    --   YOU"
40 PRINT "X    --   SPACE POTATOES"
50 PRINT "?    --   WHO KNOWS?"
60 PRINT "*    --   CONVENIENT BLACK H
OLES"
70 PRINT "@    --   SPACE WARP"
80 PRINT "INSTRUCTIONS-- TRY TO AVOI
D THE DEADLY SPACE POTATOES"
90 PRINT "AND RUN THEM INTO THE BLAC
K HOLES.  IF YOU RUN INTO"
100 PRINT "A SPACE WARP, YOU MAY EIT
HER BE DESTROYED OR PLACED"
110 PRINT "RANDOMLY ELSEWHERE."
120 PRINT "USE THESE KEYS TO MOVE YO
UR SHIP:"
130 PRINT "Q-- UP"
140 PRINT "A-- DOWN"
150 PRINT "L-- LEFT"
```

161

```
160 PRINT "R-- RIGHT"
170 PRINT "SPACE BAR-- STOP          PR
ESS ENTER TO BEGIN";
180 INPUT A$:CLS
190 FOR X=64 TO 127:PRINT @X,"O";:NE
XT X
200 FOR X=127 TO 959 STEP 64:PRINT@X
,"O";:NEXT X
210 FOR X=959 TO 896 STEP -1:PRINT@X
,"O";:NEXT X
220 FOR X=896 TO 64 STEP -64:PRINT@X
,"O";:NEXT X
230 FOR Q=1 TO 6
240 GOSUB 1060
250 A(Q)=W:NEXT Q
260 FOR Q=10 TO 30
270 GOSUB 1060
280 A(Q)=W
290 NEXT Q
300 FOR Q=31 TO 40
310 GOSUB 1060
320 A(Q)=W
330 NEXT Q
340 PRINT @A(1),"+";:FOR Z=2 TO 5:PR
INT@ A(Z),"X";:NEXT Z
350 PRINT@A(6),"?";:FOR Z=10 TO 30:P
RINT@A(Z),"*";:NEXT Z
360 FOR Z=31 TO 40:PRINT@A(Z),"@";:N
EXT
370 FOR X=1 TO 1000:NEXT X
380 I$=INKEY$
390 PRINT @0,I$;
400 IF I$="Q" THEN S=-64
410 IF I$="A" THEN S=64
420 IF I$=";" THEN S=1
430 IF I$="L" THEN S=-1
440 IF I$=" "THEN S=0
450 IF S=0 GOTO 600
460 IF A(1)+S<129 THEN S=0
470 IF A(1)+S>894 THEN S=0
480 FOR Z=63 TO 1023 STEP 64:IF A(1)
+S=Z THEN S=0
490 NEXT Z
```

```
500 FOR Z=0 TO 960 STEP 64:IF A(1)+S
=Z THEN S=0
510 NEXT Z
520 IF S=0 GOTO 540
530 A(1)=A(1)+S:PRINT @A(1),"+";:PRI
NT @A(1)-S," ";
540 FOR Z=2 TO 6:IF A(1)=A(Z) GOTO 1
160
550 NEXT Z
560 FOR Z=10 TO 30:IF A(1)=A(Z) GOTO
 1160
570 NEXT Z
580 FOR Z=31 TO 40:IF A(1)=A(Z) THEN
 GOSUB 1200:GOTO 600
590 NEXT Z
600 FOR T=2 TO 5
610 PRINT @50,T;
620 IF A(T)<0 GOTO 960
630 A=A(1):GOSUB 980
640 H1=H:V1=V:A=A(T):GOSUB 980
650 H2=H:V2=V
660 E=RND(2):ON E GOTO 670,700
670 IF H2<H1 THEN G=64:IF A(T)+64>89
4 THEN G=-64:GOTO 740
680 IF H2>H1 THEN G=-64:IF A(T)-64 <
128 THEN G=64:GOTO 740
690 GOTO 740
700 IF V2=V1 AND H2=H1 GOTO 1160
710 IF V2=V1 GOTO 670
720 IF V2<V1 THEN G=1
730 IF V2>V1 THEN G=-1
740 A(T)=A(T)+G:PRINT@A(T),"X";::PRIN
T@A(T)-G," ";
750 IF A(T)=A(1) GOTO 1160
760 FOR L=10 TO 30:IF A(T)=A(L) THEN
 A(T)=-1:PRINT@A(L),"#";
770 NEXT L
780 NEXT T
790 U=RND(4)
800 IF U=1 THEN H=2
810 IF U=2 THEN H=-2
820 IF U=3 THEN H=128
830 IF U=4 THEN H=-128
840 IF A(6)+H<129 GOTO 790
```

163

```
850 IF A(6)+H>894 GOTO 790
860 FOR Z=0 TO 960 STEP 64:IF A(6)+H
=Z GOTO 790
870 NEXT Z
880 FOR Z=63 TO 1023 STEP 64:IF A(6)
+H=Z GOTO 790
890 A(6)=A(6)+H:PRINT@A(6),"?";:PRIN
T@ A(6)-H," ";
900 IF A(6)=A(1) GOTO 1160
910 FOR Z=2 TO 5:IF A(6)=A(Z) GOTO 9
30
920 NEXT Z:GOTO 950
930 A(Z)=-1:PRINT@960,"ATTACKER DEST
ROYED BY UNKNOWN";
940 FOR X=1 TO 1000:NEXT X:PRINT @ 9
60,"                                ";
950 GOTO 580
960 IF A(2)<0 AND A(3)<0 AND A(4)<0
AND A(5)<0 GOTO 1180
970 GOTO 780
980 I=1:I1=127
990 IF A<=I1 THEN H=I:GOTO 1010
1000 I=I+1:I1=I1+64:GOTO 990
1010 H=H-1
1020 A=A-64:IF A<=63 GOTO 1040
1030 GOTO 1020
1040 V=A
1050 RETURN
1060 W=RND(394)
1070 IF W<=127 GOTO 1060
1080 FOR Z=63 TO 1023 STEP 64:IF W=Z
 GOTO 1060
1090 NEXT Z
1100 FOR Z=0 TO 960 STEP 64:IF W=Z G
OTO 1060
1110 NEXT Z
1120 FOR Z=40 TO 1 STEP -1:IF W=Z GO
TO 1140
1130 IF A(Z)=W GOTO 1060
1140 NEXT Z
1150 RETURN
1160 FOR X=1 TO 99:PRINT@A(1)," ";:P
RINT @A(1),"+";:NEXT X
```

```
1170 PRINT "YOU HAVE BEEN DESTROYED"
:END
1180 CLS:PRINT "YOU HAVE DESTROYED A
LL OF THE ATTACKERS!"
1190 END
1200 IF RND(10)>5 THEN CLS:GOTO 1170

1210 PRINT@A(1),"@";:GOSUB 1060:A(1)
=W:PRINT@A(1),"+";:RETURN
```

TRI-FIGHT

Remarks

Here's a fast-paced real-time game that will keep you on your toes to the very end! In this game you are fighting two alien spaceships. All ships are equally armed and equipped. However, both alien ships are on opposing sides, making this a three way galactic free-for-all! If you choose not to fire your weapons or move, you can rest and produce ten units of reserve energy while preparing your missile tubes for reloading. When you have at least fifty units of energy in reserve, you can transfer your reserve energy to the main energy banks and reload your ten missile tubes. If you choose, you can make use of the sound prompt routine in line # 1340 by doing the following:

1) Remove any cassette from your recorder.

2) Find the small metal lever in the rear left corner of the tape compartment of your recorder.

3) While pressing the lever towards the back of the recorder, simultaneously press the *PLAY* and *RECORD* buttons on the recorder.

4) Disconnect the earphone and motor control cables from the recorder. Leave the auxiliary cable connected.

5) Plug in an eight ohm speaker or earphone to the earphone jack.

6) Keep all cassettes away from the speaker. The magnet can erase them!

Variables

A —Distance from ship 1 (yours) to ship 2

B —Distance from ship 1 to ship 3

C —Distance from ship 2 to ship 3

D —Available energy in ship 1

E —Available energy in ship 2
F —Available energy in ship 3
D1—Reserve energy in ship 1
E1—Reserve energy in ship 2
F1—Reserve energy in ship 3
D2—Missiles loaded in ship 1
E2—Missiles loaded in ship 2
F2—Missiles loaded in ship 3
A1—PEEK location for keyboard scan
C0—Command number for key pressed (A1)
H —Units of energy removed by hit
X —Number of enemy ship acting (1 = ship 2   2 = ship 3)

Suggested Variations

1) You may wish to add additional weapons, effective at only certain ranges.

2) You may wish to increase the maximum amount of space that can be covered by an approach or retreat, or at least cut down the amount of energy utilized in executing these commands (50 units).

3) Remember that in order to have a command read by the computer, you must continue to hold down the command key until the command read has been verified. If this is bothersome, you might wish to substitute an INKEY$ function instead of the PEEK routine.

Sample Run

LIST OF COMMANDS

H—FIRE MISSILE AT SHIP 2
I—FIRE MISSILE AT SHIP 3
J—APPROACH SHIP 2
K—APPROACH SHIP 3
L—RETREAT FROM SHIP 2
M—RETREAT FROM SHIP 3
N—MANUFACTURE 10 UNITS OF ENERGY AND PREPARE
    NEW MISSILES FOR LOADING
0—TRANSFER RESERVED ENERGY AND LOAD MISSILE
TUBES

PRESS ANY KEY TO BEGIN
STATUS REPORT

DISTANCE 1-2: 5162 KM.
          1-3: 8760 KM.
          2-3: 7817 KM.
ENERGY AVAILABLE: 500
MISSILES LOADED: 10
RESERVE ENERGY: 0
COMMAND H READ
MISSILE MISSED TARGET
SHIP 2 HAS FIRED A MISSILE!
SHIP 3 HAS FIRED A MISSILE!

Program For Tri-Fight

```
10 GOSUB 1210
20 A=RND(10000):B=RND(10000):C=RND(1
0000)
30 D=500:E=500:F=500:D1=0:E1=0:F1=0:
D2=10:E2=10:F2=10
40 IF D<=0 THEN GOTO 1170
50 CLS:PRINT "STATUS REPORT"
60 PRINT "DISTANCE  1-2: ";A;" KM."
70 PRINT "          1-3: ";B;" KM."
80 PRINT "          2-3: ";C;" KM."
90 PRINT "ENERGY AVAILABLE: ";D
100 PRINT "MISSLES LOADED: ";D2
110 PRINT "RESERVE ENERGY: ";D1
120 A1=PEEK(14338)
130 CO=0
140 IF A1=1 THEN CO=1:GOTO 220
150 IF A1=2 THEN CO=2:GOTO 220
160 IF A1=4 THEN CO=3:GOTO 220
170 IF A1=8 THEN CO=4:GOTO 220
180 IF A1=16 THEN CO=5:GOTO 220
190 IF A1=32 THEN CO=6:GOTO 220
200 IF A1=64 THEN CO=7:GOTO 220
210 IF A1=128 THEN CO=8
220 IF CO=0 PRINT "NO COMMAND READ":
GOTO 570
230 ON CO GOTO 240,290,340,300,440,4
50,530,550
240 PRINT "COMMAND H READ"
250 IF D2=0 THEN PRINT "MISSLE TUBES
  EMPTY":GOTO 570
260 K=RND(2):IF K=1 THEN PRINT "MISS
LE MISSED TARGET":D2=D2-1:GOTO 570
```

```
270 K=A:GOSUB 1350
280 PRINT H;" UNIT HIT ON SHIP 2":E=
E-H:D2=D2-1:GOTO 570
290 PRINT "COMMAND I READ"
300 IF D2=0 GOTO 250
310 K=RND(2):IF K=1 THEN PRINT "MISS
LE MISSED TARGET":D2=D2-1:GOTO 570
320 K=B:GOSUB 1350
330 PRINT H;" UNIT HIT ON SHIP 3":F=
F-H:D2=D2-1:GOTO 570
340 PRINT "COMMAND J READ"
350 GOTO 370

360 PRINT "COMMAND K READ"
370 IF CO=3 AND A<1000 THEN 380ELSE
IF CO=4 AND B<1000 THEN 380ELSE 390
380 PRINT "I CAN'T ALLOW THAT!":GOTO
 570
390 K=RND(500)+500
400 IF CO=3 THEN A=A-K:GOTO 420
410 IF CO=4 THEN B=B-K
420 PRINT K;" KM APPROACH MADE":D=D-
50
430 GOTO 570
440 PRINT "COMMAND L READ":GOTO 460
450 PRINT "COMMAND M READ"
460 IF CO=5 AND A>9000 THEN 470ELSE
IF CO=6 AND B>9000 THEN 470ELSE 480
470 PRINT "I CAN'T ALLOW THAT!":GOTO
 570
480 K=RND(500)+500
490 IF CO=5 THEN A=A+K:GOTO 510
500 IF CO=6 THEN B=B+K
510 PRINT K;" KM RETREAT MADE"
520 D=D-50:GOTO 570
530 PRINT "COMMAND N READ"
540 D1=D1+10:GOTO 570
550 PRINT "COMMAND O READ":IF D1<50
THEN PRINT "NOT ENOUGH IN RESERVE FO
R TRANSFER":GOTO 570
560 D=D+D1:D1=0:D2=10
570 T=0:FOR X=1 TO 2:IF X=1 AND E<=0
 THEN GOTO 1140ELSE IF X=2 AND F<=0
GOTO 1140
```

```
580 IF X=1 AND E<80 THEN 1080ELSE IF
  X=2 AND F<80 THEN 1080
590 IF X=1 AND A>9000 THEN OB=1:GOTO
  860
600 IF C>9000 THEN OB=2:GOTO 860
610 IF X=2 AND B>9000 THEN OB=3:GOTO
  860
620 IF X=1 AND A<1000 THEN OB=1:GOTO
  970
630 IF C<1000 AND C<>0 THEN OB=2:GOT
O 970
640 IF X=2 AND B<1000 THEN OB=3:GOTO
  970
650 K=RND(20):IF K=5 THEN T=1:GOTO 8
60
660 IF K=7 THEN T=1:GOTO 970
670 K=RND(10):IF K=5 GOTO 1080
680 IF X=1 AND E2=0 THEN 1080
690 IF X=2 AND F2=0 THEN 1080
700 IF X=1 THEN K=RND(2):IF K=1 THEN
  OB=1 ELSE OB=3
710 IF X=2 THEN K=RND(2):IF K=1 THEN
  OB=1 ELSE OB=2
720 IF OB=3 AND F=0 THEN OB=1
730 IF OB=2 AND E=0 THEN OB=1
740 IF X=1 THEN PRINT "SHIP 2"; ELSE
  PRINT "SHIP 3";
750 PRINT " HAS FIRED A MISSLE!"
760 K=RND(2):IF K=1 AND X=1 THEN E2=
E2-1:GOTO 1140
770 IF K=1 AND X=2 THEN F2=F2-1:GOTO
  1140
780 IF X=1 AND OB=1 THEN K=A ELSE IF
  X=1 AND OB=3 THEN K=C
790 IF X=2 AND OB=1 THEN K=B ELSE IF
  X=2 AND OB=2 THEN K=C
800 GOSUB 1350
810 IF OB=1 THEN PRINT H;" UNIT HIT
SUSTAINED":D=D-H
820 IF OB=2 THEN PRINT "SENSORS RECE
IVE HIT ON SHIP 2":E=E-H
830 IF OB=3 THEN PRINT "SENSORS RECE
IVE HIT ON SHIP 3":F=F-H
840 IF X=1 THEN E2=E2-1 ELSE F2=F2-1
```

```
850 GOTO 1140
860 IF T<>1 GOTO 920
870 P=RND(2)
880 IF X=1 AND P=1 THEN OB=1:IF A<10
00 THEN OB=2
890 IF X=1 AND P=2 THEN OB=2:IF C<10
00 AND A<1000 THEN 970ELSE IF C<1000
 THEN OB=1
900 IF X=2 AND P=1 THEN OB=3:IF B<10
00 THEN OB=2
910 IF X=2 AND P=2 THEN OB=2:IF C<10
00 AND B<1000 THEN 970ELSE IF C<1000
 THEN OB=3
920 K=RND(500)+500
930 IF OB=1 THEN A=A-K:E=E-50:PRINT
"SHIP 2 APPROACHES"
940 IF OB=2 THEN C=C-K:IF X=1 THEN E
=E-50 ELSE F=F-50:IF X=1 THEN PRINT
"SHIP 2 APPROACHES SHIP 3" ELSE PRIN
T "SHIP 3 APPROACHES SHIP 2"
950 IF OB=3 THEN B=B-K:F=F-50:PRINT
"SHIP 3 APPROACHES"
960 GOTO 1140
970 IF T<>1 GOTO 1030
980 P=RND(2)
990 IF X=1 AND P=1 THEN OB=1:IF A>90
00 THEN OB=2
1000 IF X=1 AND P=2 THEN OB=2:IF C>9
000 AND A>9000 THEN 860ELSE IF C>900
0 THEN OB=1
1010 IF X=2 AND P=1 THEN OB=3:IF B>9
000 THEN OB=2
1020 IF X=2 AND P=2 THEN OB=2:IF C>9
000 AND B>9000 THEN 970ELSE IF C>900
0 THEN OB=3
1030 K=RND(500)+500
1040 IF OB=1 THEN A=A+K:E=E-50:PRINT
 "SHIP 2 RETREATS"
1050 IF OB=2 THEN C=C+K:IF X=1 THEN
E=E-50 ELSE F=F-50:IF X=1 THEN PRINT
 "SHIP 2 RETREATS FROM SHIP 3" ELSE
PRINT "SHIP 3 RETREATS FROM SHIP 2"
1060 IF OB=3 THEN B=B+K:F=F-50:PRINT
 "SHIP 3 RETREATS"
```

```
1070 GOTO 1140
1080 IF X=1 AND E1<50 GOTO 1120
1090 IF X=2 AND F1<50 GOTO 1120
1100 IF X=1 THEN E=E+E1:E1=0:E2=10:P
RINT "SENSORS RECEIVE MASSIVE ENERGY
 TRANSFER ON SHIP 2":GOTO 1140
1110 IF X=2 THEN F=F+F1:F1=0:F2=10:P
RINT "SENSORS RECIEVE MASSIVE ENERGY
 TRANSFER ON SHIP 3":GOTO 1140
1120 IF X=1 THEN E1=E1+10
1130 IF X=2 THEN F1=F1+10
1140 IF E<=0 AND F<=0 GOTO 1190ELSE
IF E<=0 PRINT "SHIP 2 DEAD":A=0:C=0:
GOTO 1160
1150 IF F<=0 THEN PRINT "SHIP 3 DEAD
":B=0:C=0
1160 NEXT X:GOSUB 1340:GOTO 40
1170 PRINT "YOU HAVE RUN OUT OF ENER
GY AND HAVE DESTROYED YOUR"
1180 PRINT "SPACESHIP.  EARTH IS DEA
D THANKS TO YOU!":END
1190 PRINT "YOU DID IT CAPTAIN!  EAR
TH HAS BEEN SAVED FROM THE"
1200 PRINT "ALIENS!  HOORAY!":END
1210 CLS:PRINT "LIST OF COMMANDS"
1220 PRINT "-----------------"
1230 PRINT "H-- FIRE MISSLE AT SHIP
2"
1240 PRINT "I-- FIRE MISSLE AT SHIP
3"
1250 PRINT "J-- APPROACH SHIP 2"
1260 PRINT "K-- APPROACH SHIP 3"
1270 PRINT "L-- RETREAT FROM SHIP 2"

1280 PRINT "M-- RETREAT FROM SHIP 3"

1290 PRINT "N-- MANUFACTURE 10 UNITS
 OF ENERGY AND PREPARE"
1300 PRINT "    NEW MISSLES FOR LOAD
ING"
1310 PRINT "O-- TRANSFER RESERVED EN
ERGY AND LOAD MISSLE TUBES"
1320 PRINT:PRINT "PRESS ANY KEY TO B
EGIN"
```

```
1330 A$=INKEY$:IF A$="" GOTO 1330ELS
E RETURN
1340 FOR X=1 TO 400:OUT 255,1:OUT 25
5,2:NEXT X:RETURN
1350 L=K/1000:H=(10-L)*10:H=H+(RND(0
)*10)
1360 RETURN
```

DICE

Remarks

This program simulates the casino game of Chug-A-Lug. The player bets on a number from one to six. Three dice are rolled, and the player is paid 1:1 odds for each die that his bet matches. This program uses a nifty graphics dice routine that you may wish to extract and use for other programs. See Fig. 6-8.

Variables

AC   — Money remaining in player's account
BET   — Amount of player's bet
NUM   — Number player bets on
OD   — Payoff odds to player (if 0 then player loses bet)
K   — Value of die#D in loop

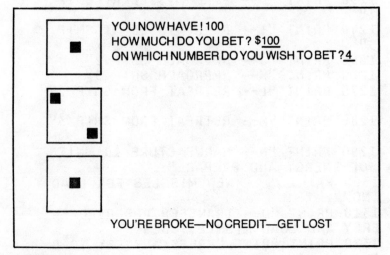

Fig. 6-8. Sample run.

D—Which die is being rolled
X,Y,G—Used to plot graphic dice

Suggested Variations

1) You may wish to allow more than one player to participate.
2) You may wish to set an upper limit on how much a player can win before he "breaks the bank".

Program for Dice

```
10 CLS
20 AC=100
30 PRINT@151,"YOU NOW HAVE $";AC
40 PRINT@215,"HOW MUCH DO YOU BET ";
:INPUT BET
50 IF BET>AC THEN PRINT@279,"THAT'S
MORE THAN YOU HAVE!";:GOTO 40
60 PRINT@279,"ON WHICH NUMBER DO YOU
 WISH TO BET ";:INPUT NUM
70 OD=0
80 FOR D=1 TO 3:K=RND(6)
90 IF K=NUM THEN OD=OD+1
100 GOSUB 320
110 NEXT D
120 IF OD=0 GOTO 160
130 PRINT@0, "YOU WIN AT ";OD;" TO 1
  PAYOFFS!"
140 AC=AC+(OD*BET)
150 PRINT@64,"PRESS ENTER TO CONTINU
E ";:INPUT G$:CLS:GOTO 30
160 PRINT@0,"YOU LOSE YOUR BET!"
170 AC=AC-BET:IF AC<=0 GOTO 180ELSE
GOTO 150
180 PRINT@913, "YOU'RE BROKE--NO CRE
DIT--GET LOST":END
190 FOR X=G TO G+17:SET(X,Y):NEXT X
200 IF P=1 THEN RETURN ELSE Y=Y+1:GO
SUB 270:RETURN
210 SET(G,Y):SET(G+1,Y):SET(G+4,Y):S
ET(G+5,Y):SET(G+12,Y):SET(G+13,Y):SE
T(G+16,Y):SET(G+17,Y)
220 Y=Y+1:GOSUB 270:RETURN
230 SET(G,Y):SET(G+1,Y):SET(G+4,Y):S
ET(G+5,Y):SET(G+16,Y):SET(G+17,Y)
```

```
240 Y=Y+1:GOSUB 270:RETURN
250 SET(G,Y):SET(G+1,Y):SET(G+16,Y):
SET(G+17,Y)
260 Y=Y+1:GOSUB 270:RETURN
270 SET(G,Y):SET(G+1,Y):SET(G+16,Y):
SET(G+17,Y):RETURN
280 SET(G,Y):SET(G+1,Y):SET(G+8,Y):S
ET(G+9,Y):SET(G+16,Y):SET(G+17,Y)
290 Y=Y+1:GOSUB 270:RETURN
300 SET(G,Y):SET(G+1,Y):SET(G+12,Y):
SET(G+13,Y):SET(G+16,Y):SET(G+17,Y)
310 Y=Y+1:GOSUB 270:RETURN
320 IF D=1 THEN G=4:Y=9:GOTO 350
330 IF D=2 THEN G=4:Y=20:GOTO 350
340 IF D=3 THEN G=4:Y=31:GOTO 350
350 P=0:GOSUB 190
360 Y=Y+1:ON K GOSUB 250,230,230,210
,210,210
370 Y=Y+1:ON K GOSUB 280,250,280,250
,280,210
380 Y=Y+1:ON K GOSUB 250,300,300,210
```

MICRO-INVADERS

Remarks

In this real-time shooting gallery game, you will try to shoot
down as many of the moving targets as possible in the allotted time.
This program uses a revolving string routine for moving the targets
which should be interesting for you to dissect and examine. The
player uses the right and left arrow keys to move his gun. Pressing
the space bar will fire a missile and pressing any other key will stop
the movement of the gun. Hitting the force field surrounding each
target will subtract points from your score. Also, the targets will
fire missiles back at you! There are five skill levels available.

Variables

TI	—Time remaining
Z$	—Argument of INKEY$ (returns last key pressed)
D	—Number of spaces to move gun
X	—PRINT @ position of gun
M	—PRINT @ position of missile
T$	—Large string containing targets
CO	—Counter used for string T$ to position targets
V$,U$	—Used to revolve T$

SC   —Current score
H2   —Skill level
Z4   —PRINT @ position of target's missile

Suggested Variations

1) You might wish to move the targets gradually closer to the bottom of the screen as the game progresses.

2) You may wish to add more time or allot bonus time for attaining a certain score.

3) You may wish to insert an end game routine if the player destroys all of the targets before time runs out.

Sample Run

MICRO-INVADERS
****
DO YOU WANT INSTRUCTIONS (YES OR NO)? <u>YES</u>
YOU CAN MOVE YOURSELF LEFT AND RIGHT BY USING THE APPROPRIATE ARROW KEYS.
PRESS THE SPACE BAR TO FIRE A MISSILE AND ANY OTHER KEY BESIDES THOSE ABOVE TO STOP YOURSELF.
PRESS ENTER TO CONTINUE?
HERE ARE THE ALIEN'S SCORE VALUES:
!-------5 POINTS
"-------10 POINTS
#-------15 POINTS
$ -------20 POINTS
%-------25 POINTS
&-------30 POINTS
HITTING THE (OR) PARTS OF THE TARGET SUBTRACTS 1 POINT FROM YOUR SCORE.
ALSO WATCH OUT FOR THE ALIEN'S MISSILES!
PRESS ENTER TO CONTINUE?
ENTER YOUR SKILL LEVEL (1-5)
1=HARDEST   5=EASIEST ? <u>5</u>
PLEASE WAIT . . .

(%)	(#)	(#)	(")	(#)	(%)
(%)	(&)	(%)	(#)	(#)	(#)
(")	(%)	(!)	(&)	(")	($)
(#)	(!)	(")	(#)	(&)	(")

@

TIME—500

175

Program for Micro-Invaders

```
10 CLS
20 CLEAR 3000
30 TI=501:X=RND(60)+897:GOSUB 690:PR
INT CHR$(23),"PLEASE WAIT...":GOTO 2
00
40 REM
50 TI=TI-1:PRINT@1000,"TIME-- ";TI;:
IF TI=0 GOTO 680ELSE IF S1=1 GOTO 14
0
60 Z$=INKEY$:IF Z$="" THEN GOTO 100
70 IF Z$=" " GOTO 130
80 A=ASC(Z$)
90 IF A=9 THEN D=4 ELSE IF A=8 THEN
D=-4 ELSE D=0
100 IF X+D>958 OR X+D<898 THEN D=0
110 PRINT@X-1,"    ";:X=X+D:PRINT@X-1
,"(@)";
120 GOTO 350
130 M=X-64:PRINT@M,"↑";:S1=1
140 K=-64:IF M+K<0 THEN S1=0:PRINT@M
," ";:GOTO 120
150 PRINT@M," ";:M=M+K:PRINT@M,"↑";
160 IF Z4=M OR Z4+1=M OR Z4+2=M GOTO
 460
170 IF M>255 GOTO 190
180 L$=MID$(T$,M+1,1):IF L$<>" " GOT
O 520
190 GOTO 350
200 REM START SETUP- ALIENS
210 T$="             "
220 CO=0:TA=0
230 CO=CO+1:IF CO=11 THEN CO=1
240 IF CO=1 THEN S$="<"
250 IF CO=2 THEN S$=CHR$(RND(6)+32)
260 IF CO=3 THEN S$=">":TA=TA+1
270 IF CO>3 THEN S$=" "
280 T$=T$+S$
290 IF TA=6 GOTO 310
300 GOTO 230
310 IF LEN(T$)=255 GOTO 320ELSE T$=T
$+"              ":GOTO 220
320 CLS:PRINT@0,T$;
```

176

```
330 PRINT@896,"PRESS ANY KEY TO BEGI
N";:J$=INKEY$:IF J$="" GOTO 330
340 PRINT@896,STRING$(23," ");
350 REM * MOVE ALIENS
360 U$=RIGHT$(T$,1):V$=LEFT$(T$,254)
370 T$=U$+V$
380 PRINT@0,T$;
390 IF S2=1 GOTO 480
400 H3=RND(H2):IF H3<>1 GOTO 40ELSE
S2=1:GOTO 420
410 GOTO 40
420 Z4=RND(61)+512:PRINT@Z4,STRING$(
3,191)
430 GOTO 440
440 FOR Z9=1 TO 6:Z4=Z4+64:PRINT@Z4,
STRING$(3,191);
450 IF Z4=M OR Z4+1=M OR Z4+2=M GOTO
 460ELSE GOTO 470
460 PRINT@Z4,"   ";:PRINT@Z4-64,"
";:Z4=990:M=0:S1=0:S2=0:GOTO 40
470 IF Z9<>6 GOTO 40
480 PRINT@Z4-64,"    ";:NEXT Z9:PRINT
@Z4,"   ";
490 IF Z4=X OR Z4+1=X OR Z4+2=X OR Z
4+3=X OR Z4-1=X GOTO 510
500 S2=0:GOTO 40
510 PRINT@576,"HA HA! YOU GOT BLOWN
TO BITS!   YOUR FINAL SCORE WAS ";SC;
" POINTS.":END
520 IF L$="<" OR L$=">" THEN VA=-1:G
OTO 670
530 L=ASC(L$)
540 IF L=33 THEN VA=5:GOTO 600
550 IF L=34 THEN VA=10:GOTO 600
560 IF L=35 THEN VA=15:GOTO 600
570 IF L=36 THEN VA=20:GOTO 600
580 IF L=37 THEN VA=25:GOTO 600
590 IF L=38 THEN VA=30:
600 SC=SC+VA
610 PRINT@960,"SCORE-- ";SC;
620 REM *REMOVE HIT TARGET FROM STRI
NG
630 F$=LEFT$(T$,M-1):U1=(LEN(T$)-(M+
2)):L$=RIGHT$(T$,U1)
```

```
640 F$=F$+"    ":T$=F$+L$
650 FOR Z=1 TO 25:PRINT@M-1,"XXX";:P
RINT@M-1,"   ";:NEXT Z
660 S1=0:GOTO 380
670 SC=SC+VA:PRINT@960,"SCORE-- ";SC
;:GOTO 660
680 CLS:PRINT "TIME'S UP!  YOU SCORE
D ";SC;" POINTS!":END
690 PRINT CHR$(23);"M I C R O -
                     I N V A D E
R S"

700 PRINT STRING$(32,"*")
710 PRINT:PRINT:INPUT "DO YOU WANT I
NSTRUCTIONS (YES OR NO)";A$
720 IF A$="NO" GOTO 890
730 CLS:PRINT "YOU CAN MOVE YOURSELF
 LEFT AND RIGHT BY USING"
740 PRINT "THE APPROPRIATE ARROW KEY
S (";CHR$(93);" AND ";CHR$(94);")."
750 PRINT "PRESS THE SPACE BAR TO FI
RE A MISSLE AND ANY OTHER"
760 PRINT "KEY BESIDES THOSE ABOVE T
O STOP YOURSELF."
770 PRINT:INPUT "PRESS ENTER TO CONT
INUE";A$
780 CLS:PRINT "HERE ARE THE ALIEN'S
SCORE VALUES:"
790 PRINT CHR$(33);"------- 5 POINTS
"

800 PRINT CHR$(34);"------- 10 POINT
S"
810 PRINT CHR$(35);"------- 15 POINT
S"
820 PRINT CHR$(36);"------- 20 POINT
S"
830 PRINT CHR$(37);"------- 25 POINT
S"
840 PRINT CHR$(38);"------- 30 POINT
S"
850 PRINT "HITTING THE < OR > PARTS
OF THE TARGET SUBTRACTS"
860 PRINT "1 POINT FROM YOUR SCORE."
```

```
870 PRINT:PRINT "ALSO, WATCH OUT FOR
THE ALIEN'S MISSLES!"
880 PRINT:INPUT "PRESS ENTER TO CONT
INUE";A$:CLS
890 PRINT "ENTER YOUR SKILL LEVEL (1
-5)":INPUT "1=HARDEST  5=EASIEST ";H
2
900 H2=H2*4:CLS:RETURN
```

IGOR

Remarks

Now here's a program that will put you in your intellectual place! The "little man" inside your computer finally gets to meet you face to face in a game of strategy. Igor has a rather small and obnoxious vocabulary, but he is never at a lack for words. This is the game of twenty three matches. Each turn the player may take one, two, or three matches from the pile. The loser is the player who is forced to take the last match. Watch out, Igor is a *very* sore loser. See Fig. 6-9.

Variables

A$(X), B$(X), C$(X)—Various words in Igor's vocabulary
A(X)—Whether match #X is still in pile
N —Number of matches left in pile
J —Number of matches removed by player

Suggested Variations

1) You can personalize IGOR's vocabulary with your own favorite insults and witticisms.

2) Igor uses a very simple game strategy. You may wish to modify and improve it.

HELLO, FISH FACE, MY NAME IS IGOR AND I WANT TO THANK YOU FOR GIVING ME A CHANCE TO SHOW YOU HOW VERY FUNNY YOU REALLY ARE.

THE CONCEPT OF THIS GAME IS SIMPLE. THERE ARE 23 MATCHES ON THE TABLE. EACH TURN YOU MAY TAKE 1, 2, OR 3 MATCHES FROM THE PILE. THE PLAYER THAT TAKES THE LAST MATCH LOSES.

UNDERSTAND, DUMMY .... ? YES
GOOD! PREPARE YOURSELF FOR A
  DEFLATED EGO!
I REMOVE 2 MATCHES
O.K., GOOF THERE ARE 21 MATCHES LEFT
HOW MANY DO YOU TAKE AWAY (1, 2, OR 3) ? 1
OHHH!!! I'M SOOOO SCARED!!

Fig. 6-9. Sample run.

Program for Igor

```
10 CLEAR 200
20 CLS:DIM A(23),A$(30),B$(12),C$(10
)
30 FOR A=1 TO 23:A(A)=1:NEXT A
40 GOSUB 620
50   CLS
60   N=23
70 GOSUB 340
80 GOSUB 660:PRINT@832, STRING$(64,"
");: PRINT@ 832, "O.K., ";A$;" THERE
 ARE ";N;" MATCHES LEFT"
90 G2=25:GOSUB 910
100   PRINT@670,"
"
110 PRINT@704,STRING$(64," ");
120   PRINT@ 896, "HOW MANY DO YOU TA
KE AWAY (1, 2, OR 3)";:INPUTJ$
130 J=VAL(J$)
140 IF J=1 OR J=2 OR J=3 GOTO 160
150   PRINT@ 704,"CHEATER":FOR X=1TO
1000:NEXTX:PRINT@704,"        ":GOTO1
20
160 PRINT@832,STRING$(64," ");: N=N-
J
170   GOSUB 450
180   PRINT@896,"
"
190 H1=RND(6):ON H1 GOSUB 930,960,10
40,930,930,960
200   IF N=4 THEN Z=3:GOTO 270
210   IF N=3 THEN Z=1: GOTO 270
220   IF N=2 THEN Z=1: GOTO 270
230   IF N=23 THEN Z=2:GOTO 270
240   IF N=1 GOTO 550
250   IF N<=0 GOTO 560
260   Z=4-J
270 GOSUB 1160: PRINT@670,"I REMOVE
";Z;" MATCHES";
280 FOR V=1 TO 500:NEXT V
290   N=N-Z
300   J=Z
310   GOSUB 450
```

180

```
320   IF N=1 GOTO 560
330   GOTO 80
340   X=5
350   FOR U=1 TO 23
360   FOR Y=3 TO 8
370   SET (X,Y)
380   NEXTY
390   X=X+5
400   NEXT U
410 GOSUB 840
420   H=RND(2):IF H=1 GOSUB 840:GOTO
80
430   GOTO 200
440   RETURN
450   FOR Z=1 TO J
460   X=5
470   FOR G=1 TO 23
480   IF A(G)=0 GOTO 520
490   FOR Y=3TO8:RESET(X,Y):NEXTY
500   A(G)=0
510   GOTO 530
520   X=X+5:NEXTG
530   NEXT Z
540   RETURN
550 GOTO 1210
560 GOTO 1500
57C END
580 DATA "MOOSE BREATH","TURKEY LEGS
","MEAT LIPS","HATCHET FACE","DOG LI
PS","SALAMI HEAD","VACUUM BRAIN","SC
HMUCK","HOOK NOSE","DUMMY","FAT HEAD
","NUMBSKULL","JELLY BUTT","HUMAN TR
ASH","KNOT HEAD","FOOL","PUG NOSE","
FISH FACE","GOPHER BREATH"
590 DATA "NOODLE NOSE","SCREWBALL","
SAWDUST BRAINS","IDIOT","GOAT BREATH
","HORSE FACE","LAME BRAIN","HIDEOUS
 HUMAN","GOOF","DING-A-LING","MEAT H
EAD"
600 DATA "HOPELESSLY","HIDEOUSLY","T
ERRIBLY","INEXCUSABLY","HORRIBLY","U
NWITTINGLY","VERY","EXTREMELY","SIMP
LY","FOOLISHLY","EXPECTEDLY","PLAINL
Y"
```

```
610 DATA "STUPID","IGNORANT","IRRATI
ONAL","ILLOGICAL","USELESS","DUMB","
IDIOTIC","FUNNY","AMUSING","BRAINLES
S"
620 FOR A=1 TO 30:READ A$(A):NEXT A
630 FOR A=1 TO 12:READ B$(A):NEXT A
640 FOR A=1 TO 10:READ C$(A):NEXT A
650 GOTO 690
660 A=RND(30):A$=A$(A):RETURN
670 A=RND(12):B$=B$(A):RETURN
680 A=RND(10):C$=C$(A):RETURN
690 CLS:GOSUB 660:GOSUB 670:GOSUB 68
0
700 PRINT "HELLO, ";A$;", MY NAME IS
 IGOR AND I WANT TO THANK"
710 PRINT "YOU FOR GIVING ME A CHANC
E TO SHOW YOU HOW ";B$;" ";C$:PRINT
"YOU REALLY ARE."
720 PRINT:PRINT "THE CONCEPT OF THIS
 GAME IS SIMPLE.  THERE ARE"
730 PRINT "23 MATCHES ON THE TABLE.
 EACH TURN YOU MAY TAKE"
740 PRINT "1, 2, OR 3 MATCHES FROM T
HE PILE.  THE PLAYER THAT"
750 PRINT "TAKES THE LAST MATCH LOSE
S.
760 PRINT:GOSUB 660:PRINT "UNDERSTAN
D, ";A$;"....";:INPUT A$
770 CLS:PRINT CHR$(23);
780 IF A$="YES" OR A$="NO" GOTO 800
790 PRINT "OH.. ONE MORE THING...":P
RINT:PRINT "KEEP YOUR COMMENTS TO Y
OURSELF!":GOTO 830
800 IF A$="NO" GOTO 820
810 PRINT "GOOD! PREPARE YOURSELF FO
R A     DEFLATED EGO.":GOTO 830
820 PRINT "YOU'LL CATCH ON!"
830 FOR X=1 TO 1000:NEXT X:CLS:GOTO
50
840 FOR X=44 TO 67:SET(X,17):SET(X,2
9):NEXT X
850 FOR Y=17 TO 29:SET(44,Y):SET(67,
Y):NEXT Y
860 SET(49,20):SET(62,20)
```

```
870 FOR X=54 TO 57:SET(X,20):SET(X,2
1):SET(X,22):NEXT X
880 FOR G=537 TO 542:PRINT@G,CHR$(19
1);:NEXT G
890 PRINT @485,"<--- IGOR";
900 RETURN
910 FOR X1=1 TO G2:FOR G1=538 TO 541
:PRINT@G1,CHR$(191);:NEXT G1
920 FOR G1=538 TO 541:PRINT@G1,CHR$(
179);:NEXT G1:NEXT X1:RETURN
930 GOSUB 670:GOSUB 680
940 PRINT@ 704,"WHAT A ";B$;" ";C$;"
 MOVE!":G2=50:GOSUB 910
950 PRINT@704,STRING$(64," ");:RETUR
N
960 X=RND(5):ON X GOTO 970,980,990,1
000,1010
970 PRINT@704,"HA HA HA HA HA HA HA
HA HA HA HA HA HA HA HA HA!":GOTO 1030
980 PRINT@704,"ARK ARK ARK ARK ARK A
RK ARK ARK ARK ARK!!!";:GOTO 1030
990 PRINT@704,"CHUCKLE...SNICKER...W
HEEZE...GASP...CHORTLE";:GOTO 1030
1000 PRINT@704,"OH NO! NOT THAT! ANY
THING BUT THAT!":FOR X=1 TO 800:NEXT
 X:GOTO 970
1010 FOR X4=1 TO 5:PRINT@704,"Y O U
 M U S T   B E   K I D D I N G ! !";:F
OR Z4=1 TO 100:NEXT Z4:PRINT@704,STR
ING$(64," ");:FOR Z4=1 TO 100:NEXT Z
4:NEXT X4
1020 GOTO 990
1030 FOR X=1 TO 800:NEXT X:PRINT@704
,STRING$(64," ");:RETURN
1040 GOTO 1150
1050 FOR R4=1 TO 10:RESET(49,20):SET
(48,20):RESET(62,20):SET(63,20)
1060 RESET(48,20):SET(48,21):RESET(6
3,20):SET(63,21)
1070 RESET(48,21):SET(49,21):RESET(6
3,21):SET(62,21)
1080 RESET(49,21):SET(49,20):RESET(6
2,21):SET(62,20)
1090 NEXT R4:IF U5=1 THEN RETURN
```

```
1100 Y=16:FOR X5=1 TO 7:FOR X4=44 TO
   66 STEP 2
1110 SET(X4,Y):NEXT X4:Y=Y-1:NEXT X5
1120 FOR X5=1 TO 8:FOR X4=44 TO 66 S
TEP 2
1130 RESET(X4,Y):NEXT X4:Y=Y+1:NEXT
X5
1140 NEXT Z5:PRINT@704,STRING$(64,
" ");:RETURN
1150 PRINT@704,"O H H H I I I   I ' M
   S O O O O   S C A R E D I I";:FOR Z
5=1 TO 3:GOTO 1050
1160 PRINT@557,"IGOR'S GREAT BRAIN";
:G=621:FOR X5=1 TO 9
1170 PRINT@G, CHR$(92);" ";:G=G+2:NE
XT X5
1180 Y=30:FOR Z9=1 TO 9:FOR X=96 TO
113:SET(X,Y):NEXT X:Y=Y+1:NEXT Z9
1190 FOR H5=1 TO 50:H2=RND(32)+32:PR
INT@756,CHR$(H2);:NEXT H5
1200 FOR G5=1 TO 3:PRINT@756," ";:FO
R X1=1 TO 150:NEXT X1:PRINT@756,"*";
:FOR X1=1 TO 150:NEXT X1:NEXT G5:RET
URN
1210 CLS:GOSUB 840
1220 G=0
1230 G=G+1:ON G GOTO 1240,1260,1270,
1290,1310,1330,1360
1240 PRINT@704,"WHAT'S THIS?   ONLY O
NE MATCH LEFT?"
1250 GOSUB 1350:GOTO 1230
1260 GOTO 1250
1270 PRINT@704,"HEY-- I CAN'T LOSE!
  IT'S IMPOSSIBLE"
1280 GOTO 1250
1290 GOSUB 660:PRINT@704,"AND THAT W
OULD MAKE ME A ";A$
1300 GOTO 1250
1310 PRINT@704,"WARNING! WARNING! CI
RCUITS OVERHEATING!!"
1320 GOTO 1250
1330 FOR I=1 TO 3:U5=1:FOR P=1 TO 5:
GOSUB 1050:NEXT P:PRINT@721,"I L L O
   G I C A L I I";
```

```
1340 G2=15:GOSUB 910:PRINT@721,STRIN
G$(22," ");:NEXT I:GOTO 1230
1350 G2=20:GOSUB 910:PRINT@704,STRIN
G$(64," ");:RETURN
1360 PRINTCHR$(23):FOR I=1 TO 500:NE
XT I
1370 FORZ=1 TO 5
1380 CLS
1390 PRINT CHR$(23)
1400 FOR X=15360 TO 16383 STEP RND(7
9)
1410 POKE X,RND(94)
1420 NEXT X
1430 CLS
1440 FOR X=16383 TO 15360 STEP -RND(
79)
1450 POKE X,RND(94)
1460 NEXT X
1470 CLS:PRINT CHR$(23):FOR X=1 TO 1
50
1480 PRINT@14,"T  I  L  T   !":FO
R X=1 TO 150:NEXT X:NEXT Z
1490 CLS:PRINT@473,"I QUIT.":FOR X=1
 TO 6:PRINT:NEXT X:END
1500 CLS:GOSUB 840:PRINT@704,"YES. I
T'S TRUE. YOU PLAYED"
1510 GOSUB 670:GOSUB 680
1520 PRINT@768,"SUCH A ";B$;" ";C$;"
 GAME!":FOR X=1 TO 5:U5=1:GOSUB 1050
:NEXT X:END
```

SPACE FUNGUS VS. THE MOLDMEN

Remarks

Well, it *is* more original than Star Battle Version 2014.5! In this real-time space game, the object is simply to destroy your opponent before your opponent destroys you. PEEK keyboard reads are used so that all commands are read instantaneously. You will also find (if your worthy opponent doesn't first) that this game has a "wrap-around universe"—great for sneak attacks! Hints: try running your ship off the left or right edge of the screen. . . . Aha!!

Variables

M1   —PRINT @ position of moldmen
F1   +PRINT @ position of fungus

M2	—	Direction of moldmen
F2	—	Direction of fungus
M3,F3	—	PEEK locations for keyboard
M4,F4	—	PRINT @ positions for moldmen, fungus ships
M8,F8	—	Timers to allow ray guns to recharge
FS,MS	—	PRINT @ positions for rays
M7	—	Score of moldmen
F7	—	Score of fungus

Suggested Variations

1) You may wish to modify the delay for recharging the ray guns.

2) For goodness sake, change the title if you don't like it!

Sample Run

SPACE FUNGUS VS. THE MOLDMEN

HERE ARE THE CONTROLS FOR THE FUNGI:
YOUR VEHICLE LOOKS LIKE THIS:
(F)
PUSHING THE FOLLOWING BUTTONS WILL:
Q—TURN ROCKET COUNTER-CLOCKWISE
W—TURN ROCKET CLOCKWISE
R—FIRE ROCKETS
S—FIRE ROT RAYS
PRESS ENTER TO CONTINUE?
HEAR ARE THE CONTROLS FOR THE MOLDMEN
YOUR VEHICLE LOOKS LIKE THIS:
(M)
PUSHING THE FOLLOWING BUTTONS WILL:
LEFT ARROW —TURN ROCKET COUNTER-CLOCKWISE
RIGHT ARROW—TURN ROCKET CLOCKWISE
ENTER KEY   —FIRE ROCKETS
SPACE BAR   —FIRE SLIME RAYS
PRESS ENTER TO CONTINUE?

(M)

(F)

Program for Space Fungus vs. the MOLDMEN

```
10 CLS:PRINT "SPACE FUNGUS VS. THE M
OLDMEN":PRINT
20 CLEAR 100
30 PRINT "HERE ARE THE CONTROLS FOR
THE FUNGI:"
40 PRINT "YOUR VEHICLE LOOKS LIKE TH
IS:"
50 PRINT TAB(15),"<F>"
60 PRINT "PUSHING THE FOLLOWING BUTT
ONS WILL:"
70 PRINT "Q  ---   TURN ROCKET COUNTE
R-CLOCKWISE"
80 PRINT "W  ---   TURN ROCKET CLOCKW
ISE"
90 PRINT "R  ---   FIRE ROCKETS"
100 PRINT "S  ---   FIRE ROT RAYS"
110 PRINT:PRINT:PRINT
120 INPUT "PRESS ENTER TO CONTINUE";
A$
130 CLS
140 PRINT "HERE ARE THE CONTROLS FOR
 THE MOLDMEN:"
150 PRINT "YOUR VEHICLE LOOKS LIKE T
HIS:"
160 PRINT TAB(15),"<M>"
170 PRINT "PUSHING THE FOLLOWING BUT
TONS WILL:"
180 PRINT CHR$(93);"        --- TUR
N ROCKET COUNTER CLOCKWISE"
190 PRINT CHR$(94);"        --- TUR
N ROCKET CLOCKWISE"
200 PRINT "ENTER KEY --- FIRE ROCKET
S"
210 PRINT "SPACE BAR --- FIRE SLIME
RAYS"
220 F7=0:M7=0
230 PRINT:PRINT:PRINT
240 INPUT "PRESS ENTER TO CONTINUE";
A$
250 CLS
260 CLS:PRINT@896,STRING$(63,"*");
270 M1=RND(893):F1=RND(893):IF M1=F1
 OR M1=F1+1 OR M1=F1-1 GOTO 270
```

187

```
280 PRINT@M1-1,"<M>";:PRINT@F1-1,"<F
>";
290 M2=RND(4):F2=RND(4)
300 M3=PEEK(14340):M8=M8+1
310 IF M3=2 THEN M4=1 ELSE IF M3=128
 THEN M4=2 ELSE IF M3=4 THEN M4=3 EL
SE IF M3=8 THEN M4=4 ELSE M4=0
320 IF M4=0 GOTO 630
330 ON M4 GOTO 340,400,420,500
340 M2=M2-1:IF M2=0 THEN M2=4
350 PRINT@960,"<M>--";
360 IF M2=1 THEN PRINT CHR$(94);:GOT
O 630
370 IF M2=2 THEN PRINT CHR$(92);:GOT
O 630
380 IF M2=3 THEN PRINT CHR$(93);:GOT
O 630
390 IF M2=4 THEN PRINT CHR$(91);:GOT
O 630
400 M2=M2+1:IF M2=5 THEN M2=1
410 GOTO 350
420 IF M2=1 THEN Z=1:GOTO 460
430 IF M2=2 THEN Z=64:GOTO 460
440 IF M2=3 THEN Z=-1:GOTO 460
450 IF M2=4 THEN Z=-64:GOTO 460
460 IF M1+Z>894 OR M1+Z<1 THEN Z=0
470 PRINT@M1-1,"   ";:M1=M1+Z:PRINT@
M1-1,"<M>";
480 IF M1=F1 OR M1=F1+1 OR M1=F1+2 O
R M1=F1-1 OR M1=F1-2 THEN 970
490 GOTO 630
500 IF M8<=15 THEN 630ELSE M8=0
510 IF M2=1 THEN M5=M1+2:X=1
520 IF M2=2 THEN M5=M1:X=64
530 IF M2=3 THEN M5=M1-2:X=-1
540 IF M2=4 THEN M5=M1:X=-64
550 G=RND(40):FOR X1=1 TO G
560 IF M5+X>895 OR M5+X<0 GOTO 590
570 M5=M5+X:PRINT@M5,"+";:IF M5=F1 O
R M5=F1-1 OR M5=F1+1 GOTO 1030
580 GOTO 600
590 G=G-1
600 NEXT X1
610 X=-X:FOR X1=1 TO G
```

```
620 PRINT@M5," ";:M5=M5+X:NEXTX1
630 F3=PEEK(14400):F8=F8+1
640 IF F3=32 THEN F4=1 ELSE IF F3=64
 THEN F4=2 ELSE IF F3=1 THEN F4=3 EL
SE IF F3=128 THEN F4=4 ELSE F4=0
650 IF F4=0 GOTO 300
660 ON F4 GOTO 670,730,750,830
670 F2=F2-1:IF F2=0 THEN F2=4
680 PRINT@1005,"<F>-- ";
690 IF F2=1 THEN PRINT CHR$(94);:GOT
O 300
700 IF F2=2 THEN PRINT CHR$(92);:GOT
O 300
710 IF F2=3 THEN PRINT CHR$(93);:GOT
O 300
720 IF F2=4 THEN PRINT CHR$(91);:GOT
O 300
730 F2=F2+1:IF F2=5 THEN F2=1
740 GOTO 680
750 IF F2=1 THEN Z=1
760 IF F2=2 THEN Z=64
770 IF F2=3 THEN Z=-1
780 IF F2=4 THEN Z=-64
790 IF F1+Z>894 OR F1+Z<1 THEN Z=0
800 PRINT@F1-1,"   ";:F1=F1+Z:PRINT
@F1-1,"<F>";
810 IF M1=F1 OR M1=F1+1 OR M1=F1+2 O
R M1=F1-1 OR M1=F1-2 THEN 1000
820 GOTO 300
830 IF M8<=15 THEN 300ELSE M8=0
840 IF F2=1 THEN F5=F1+2:X=1
850 IF F2=2 THEN F5=F1:X=64
860 IF F2=3 THEN F5=F1-2:X=-1
870 IF F2=4 THEN F5=F1:X=-64
880 G=RND(40):FOR X1=1 TO G
890 IF F5+X>895 OR F5+X<0 GOTO 920
900 F5=F5+X:PRINT@F5,"+";:IF F5=M1 O
R F5=M1-1 OR F5=M1+1 GOTO 1060
910 GOTO 930
920 G=G-1
930 NEXT X1
940 X=-X:FOR X1=1 TO G
950 PRINT@F5," ";:F5=F5+X:NEXT X1
960 GOTO 300
```

```
970 R=M1:GOSUB 1090:R=F1:GOSUB 1090
980 CLS:PRINT "COLLISION CAUSED BY M
OLDMEN"
990 F7=F7+1:GOTO 1080
1000 R=F1:GOSUB 1090:R=M1:GOSUB 1090

1010 CLS:PRINT "COLLISION CAUSED BY
MOLDMEN"
1020 M7=M7+1:GOTO 1050
1030 R=F1:GOSUB 1090:FOR X=1 TO 500:
NEXT X
1040 CLS:PRINT "FUNGI SHIP DESTROYED
":M7=M7+1
1050 IF M7<5 GOTO 230ELSE GOTO 1150
1060 R=M1:GOSUB 1090:FOR X=1 TO 500:
NEXT X
1070 CLS:PRINT "MOLDMEN SHIP DESTROY
ED":F7=F7+1
1080 IF F7<5 GOTO 230ELSE GOTO 1150
1090 FOR E=1 TO 5:PRINT@R-1,CHR$(128
);:PRINT@R,CHR$(140);:PRINT@R+1,CHR$
(128);
1100 PRINT@R-1,CHR$(162);:PRINT@R,CH
R$(140);:PRINT@R+1,CHR$(145);
1110 PRINT@R-1,CHR$(153);:PRINT@R,CH
R$(128);:PRINT@R+1,CHR$(166);
1120 PRINT@R-1,CHR$(145);:PRINT@R,CH
R$(128);:PRINT@R+1,CHR$(162);
1130 PRINT@R-1,CHR$(128);:PRINT@R+1,
CHR$(128);
1140 NEXT E:RETURN
1150 INPUT "PRESS ENTER TO CONTINUE"
;A$:CLS:PRINT "FINAL SCORE:"
1160 PRINT "MOLDMEN--- ";M7
1170 PRINT "FUNGI----- ";F7
1180 END
```

SPACE RACE

Remarks

I've seen many variations of this game and all have one thing in common: they are really fun to play. Your mission is to fly your sub-light space ship into a deadly space/time warp (cliche, but suitable) and gather as much precious Trillium as you can. Watch out for the space mines and whatever you do, don't tangle with the fabric of the warp! One last note: every time you see the space/time warp change in appearance, you will notice (sooner or later) that your pathway is getting narrower. Enough said.

Variables

B, C—Boundaries of space/time warp fabric
X   —PEEK location of keyboard
LC —PRINT @ position of left side of rocket
RC —PRINT @ position of right side of rocket
D   —Direction of space/time warp pathway
A   —PRINT @ position on screen of space mines + 15360
ST —Leader starting PRINT @ position + 15360
SC —Number of times player ran into space/time warp
SD —Number of space mines hit by player
TR —Number of Trillium deposits gathered by player

Suggested Variations

1) I have seen a variation of this game that is a car race scenario. If this interests you, go to it!

Sample Run

DO YOU WANT INSTRUCTIONS (Y OR N)
YOUR MISSION IS TO FLY YOUR V-17 SUB-LIGHT ROCKET THROUGH A DEADLY SPACE/TIME WARP IN ORDER TO GATHER THE ONLY KNOWN SUPPLY OF THE PRECIOUS FUEL TRILLIUM.

HOWEVER, THE WARP HAS BEEN LADEN WITH EXPLOSIVE ANTI-MATTER MINES.
PRESS ANY KEY TO CONTINUE
THIS IS A SIMULATION BASED ON PAST MISSIONS

AS A TRAINING PROCEDURE, YOU WILL BE ALLOWED TO COLLIDE WITH THE FABRIC OF THE SPACE/TIME WARP 3 TIMES OR COLLIDE WITH A SPACE MINE 5 TIMES ANY MORE THAN THIS WILL ABORT THIS SIMULATION.

REMEMBER, THIS ONLY HAS TO HAPPEN ONCE IN REAL LIFE!
SPACE MINES LOOK LIKE THIS—0

AND TRILLIUM LOOKS LIKE THIS—#
PRESS ANY KEY TO CONTINUE
FINAL NOTES:
SOME SPACE MINES ARE 'BOGIES', THAT IS, THEY ARE
NOT ARMED. A SMART PILOT IN A DESPERATE SITUA-
TION WILL ALWAYS CHANCE COLLISION WITH A MINE
BEFORE ENTERING THE FABRIC OF THE SPACE/TIME
WARP.

ALSO, NOTICE THE PECULIAR NATURE OR THE WARP
AND STUDY. WE HAVE LOST TOO MANY PILOTS DUE TO
THESE PROPERTIES.
PRESS ANY KEY TO ENTER SIMULATION

Program for Space Race

```
10 DEFINT A-Z:CLEAR 100
20 GOTO 350
30 CLS:PRINTCHR$(23):PRINT@266,"TOUC
H RIGHT ARROW(";CHR$(94);")":PRINT@3
42,"TO STEER RIGHT":PRINT@464,"OR LE
FT ARROW(";CHR$(93);")":PRINT@534,"T
O STEER LEFT"
40 PRINT@776,"PRESS ENTER WHEN READY
"
50 A$=INKEY$:IF A$=""THENPRINT@84,"S
PACE MINER ":PRINT@84,"
":GOTO 50
60 TR=0:SC=0:SD=0:L5=133:A=16024:B=2
0:C=B:D=1:F=0:G=25:H=43:KY=14400:RI=
64:LE=32:ST=15999:PT=255:LC=165:RC=1
54:CLS
70 FOR I=0TO15:PRINTSTRING$(B,"@");T
AB(B+C)STRING$(64-B-C,"@");:NEXT
80 X=PEEK(KY):IFXANDRITHENG=G+1:GOTO
100
90 IFLEANDXTHENG=G-1
100 IFRND(8)=3THEND=-D
110 B=B+D:IFB<3THENB=3:D=-D
120 J=B+C:IFJ>60THENB=60-C:J=B+C:D=-
D
130 POKEA,H:POKEA+1,H:A=ST+G:PRINTST
RING$(B,L5);
```

```
140 T=RND(8):IF T=8 AND RND(5)=1GOTO
   160ELSEIFT=3THENPRINTSTRING$(RND(C)
   ,32);"O";TAB(J)STRING$(64-J,L5);ELSE
   PRINTTAB(J)STRING$(64-J,L5);
150 GOTO 170
160 PRINTSTRING$(RND(C),32);"#";TAB(
   J)STRING$(64-J,L5);
170 P1=PEEK(A):P2=PEEK(A+1):IF(P1=32
   )AND(P2=32)THEN180ELSEIF(P1=79) OR (
   P2=79)THEN220ELSE IF (P1=L5)OR(P2=L5
   ) THEN 200ELSE IF (P1=35)OR(P2=35)TH
   EN230ELSE 180
180 POKEA,LC:POKEA+1,RC:F=F-1:IF F<1
   THENF=40:C=C-1:L5=RND(46)+144:IFC<6T
   HEN260
190 GOTO 80

200 SC=SC+1:G=INT(C/2+B):PRINT "YOU
   RAN INTO THE WARP!"
210 FOR X5=1 TO 500:NEXT X5:FORI=101
   9TO1023:PRINTSTRING$(B,L5);TAB(B+C)S
   TRING$(64-J,L5);:NEXT:IF SC>3 GOTO 3
   40ELSE GOTO 80
220 IF RND(2)=1 GOTO 80ELSE SD=SD+1:
   PH=568+B+C/2:FORT=0TO30:PRINT@PH,"SP
   ACE MINE!";:PRINT@PH,"        ";:
   NEXT:IF SD>5 GOTO 340ELSEPRINT@960,;
   :GOTO 80
230 PRINT@LC-64,"YOU GOT IT!";:FOR X
   5=1 TO 250:NEXT X5
240 TR=TR+1:PH=568+B+C/2:FORT=0TO30:
   PRINT@PH,"GOOD JOB!";:FOR X5=1 TO 25
   :NEXT X5:PRINT@PH,"        ";:NEXT:
   PRINT@960,;:GOTO 80
250 GOTO 230
260 CLS:PRINTCHR$(23):PRINT:PRINT:PR
   INT"GAME OVER":PRINT:PRINT:PRINT"YOU
    RAN INTO THE WARP";SC;"TIMES"
270 PRINT:PRINT:PRINT"AND HIT";SD;"
   SPACE MINES"
280 PRINT "AND GATHERED ";TR*100;" L
   BS.":PRINT" OF TRILLIUM!"
290 PRINT:PRINT:PRINT"WANT TO PLAY A
   GAIN (Y OR N)?"
```

```
300 A$=INKEY$:IF (A$="Y")OR(A$="N")T
HEN 310ELSE 300
310 IF A$="Y" GOTO 350
320 END
330 END
340 CLS:PRINTCHR$(23);"SIMULATION":P
RINT"ABORTED":FOR X=1 TO 1000:NEXT X
:GOTO 260
350 CLS:PRINT"DO YOU WANT INSTRUCTIO
NS (Y OR N)"
360 A$=INKEY$:IF A$="" GOTO 360
370 IF A$="N" GOTO 40
380 PRINT "YOUR MISSION IS TO FLY YO
UR V-17 SUB-LIGHT ROCKET"
390 PRINT "THROUGH A DEADLY SPACE/TI
ME WARP IN ORDER TO GATHER"
400 PRINT "THE ONLY KNOWN SUPPLY OF
THE PRECIOUS FUEL TRILLIUM."
410 PRINT:PRINT "HOWEVER, THE WARP H
AS BEEN LADEN WITH EXPLOSIVE"
420 PRINT "ANTI-MATTER MINES."
430 PRINT:PRINT:PRINT "PRESS ANY KEY
 TO CONTINUE"
440 A$=INKEY$:IF A$="" GOTO 440
450 CLS
460 PRINT "THIS IS A SIMULATION BASE
D ON PAST MISSIONS"
470 PRINT STRING$(43,"-");
480 PRINT
490 PRINT "AS A TRAINING PROCEDURE,
YOU WILL BE ALLOWED TO"
500 PRINT "COLLIDE WITH THE FABRIC O
F THE SPACE/TIME WARP"
510 PRINT "3 TIMES OR COLLIDE WITH A
 SPACE MINE 5 TIMES"
520 PRINT "ANY MORE THAN THIS WILL A
BORT THIS SIMULATION."
530 PRINT:PRINT"REMEMBER, THIS ONLY
HAS TO HAPPEN ONCE IN REAL LIFE!"
540 PRINT:PRINT"SPACE MINES LOOK LIK
E THIS--- O"
550 PRINT "AND TRILLIUM LOOKS LIKE T
HIS--- #"
```

```
560 PRINT:PRINT:PRINT"PRESS ANY KEY
TO CONTINUE"
570 A$=INKEY$:IF A$="" GOTO 570
580 CLS
590 PRINT "FINAL NOTES:":PRINT
600 PRINT "SOME SPACE MINES ARE 'BOG
IES', THAT IS, THEY ARE"
610 PRINT "NOT ARMED.  A SMART PILOT
 IN A DESPERATE SITUATION"
620 PRINT "WILL ALWAYS CHANCE COLLIS
ION WITH A MINE BEFORE"
630 PRINT "ENTERING THE FABRIC OF TH
E SPACE/TIME WARP."
640 PRINT:PRINT"ALSO, NOTICE THE PEC
ULIAR NATURE OF THE WARP"
650 PRINT "AND STUDY.  WE HAVE LOST
TOO MANY PILOTS DUE TO"
660 PRINT "THESE PROPERTIES."
670 PRINT:PRINT:PRINT"PRESS ANY KEY
TO ENTER SIMULATION"
680 A$=INKEY$:IF A$="" GOTO 680
690 GOTO 30
```

```
HOW MAY POINTS TO WIN GAME ? 100
HOW MANY PLAYERS (MAX. 4) ? 1
PLAYER 1'S NAME ? SCOTT
WOULD YOU LIKE ME TO PLAY (YES/NO) ? ? YES


SCOTT'S TURN
PRESS ANY KEY TO THROW DART
      >

PLAYER                POINTS
SCOTT


COMPUTER
```

Fig. 6-10. Sample run.

195

DARTS

Remarks

Up to four players compete in this game of darts. The computer can also play. The game is won when a predetermined number of points has been made by one of the players. The players release the dart by pressing the space bar at the desired point in the windup. Note that just because the dart appears to hit the center of the target does not mean that it has hit a bullseye. You are only getting a side view of the target. Experimentation and practice will yield the best time to release the dart. The computer will always release the dart randomly when it plays. See Fig. 6-10.

Variables

A(X) —PRINT @ position of dart in point X of windup.
PN(X)—PRINT @ position for Player #X's name.
PL(X) —PRINT @ position for Player #X's score.
B$(X) —Player #X's name.
G — Windup position of dart.
S — Score made by throw.
R — PRINT @ position of released dart.
GA — Number of points to win game.
Y — Player's turn.

Suggested Variations

1) Add # of points during windup.

2) It would be unfair to let the computer throw a bullseye every time, but perhaps you could put in a routine to make it a very competitive player.

Program for Darts

```
10 CLS
20 CLEAR 100
30 FOR X=1 TO 8:READ A(X):NEXT X
40 DATA 449,388,326,265,269,337,403,
469
50 INPUT "HOW MANY POINTS TO WIN GAM
E ";GA
60 DATA 646,661,710,725,774,789,810,
825,902,917
70 FOR X=1 TO 5:READ PN(X),PL(X):NEX
T X
```

```
80 INPUT "HOW MANy PLAYERS (MAX. 4)"
;PL:IF PL>4 GOTO 80
90 FOR X=1 TO PL:PRINT "PLAYER ";X;"
'S NAME ";:INPUT B$(X):NEXT X
100 INPUT "WOULD YOU LIKE ME TO PLAY
 (YES/NO)? ";C$
110 IF C$="YES" THEN B$(5)="COMPUTER
"
120 Y=RND(PL+1):IF Y>PL AND C$="YES"
 THEN Y=5 ELSE Y=RND(PL)
130 GOTO 500
140 PRINT@581,"PLAYER";:PRINT@596,"P
OINTS";
150 FOR Z=1 TO 5
160 PRINT@PN(Z),B$(Z):IF B(Z)=0 GOTO
 170ELSE PRINT@PL(Z),B(Z);
170 NEXT Z
180 GOTO 520
190 G=1:X=248:FOR Z=1 TO 5:PRINT@X,C
HR$(191);:X=X+64:NEXT Z
200 G=G+1:IF G=9 THEN G=1
210 PRINT@A(G),">";
220 F=G-1:IF F=0 THEN F=8
230 PRINT@A(F)," ";
240 IF Y=5 GOTO 580ELSE A$=INKEY$
250 IF A$="" GOTO 200
260 ON G GOTO 270,270,290,290,310,33
0,310,350
270 REM ** 10 POINTS
280 GOSUB 370:S=10:GOTO 420
290 REM ** 10 OR 20 POINTS
300 GOSUB 370:S=RND(2)*10:GOTO 420
310 REM ** 30 OR 40 POINTS
320 GOSUB 370:S=(RND(2)*10)+20:GOTO
420·
330 REM ** 50 POINTS
340 GOSUB 370:S=50:GOTO 420
350 REM ** 20 OR 30 POINTS
360 GOSUB 370:S=(RND(2)*10)+10:GOTO
420
370 R=A(G)
380 PRINT@R,">";
390 R=R+1:IF R=248 OR R=312 OR R=376
 OR R=440 OR R=504 THEN RETURN
```

```
400 PRINT@R,">";:PRINT@R-1," ";
410 GOTO 390
420 PRINT @544,S;" POINTS!";
430 B(Y)=B(Y)+S
440 IF B(Y)>=GA GOTO 470
450 FOR X=1 TO 2000:NEXT X
460 GOTO 500
470 PRINT@320, B$(Y);" HAS WON THE G
AME!";
480 PRINT@PL(Y),B(Y);
490 END
500 REM ** CLS TO DISPLAY TO NEXT PL
AYER
510 CLS:GOTO 140
520 Y=Y+1:IF Y>PL AND C$="YES" AND Y
<>6 THEN Y=5:GOTO 550
530 IF Y=6 THEN Y=1:GOTO 550
540 IF Y>PL AND C$<>"YES" THEN Y=1:G
OTO 550
550 PRINT@0,STRING$(30,CHR$(128))
560 PRINT@0,B$(Y);"'S TURN";:IF B$(Y
)="COMPUTER" GOTO 570ELSEPRINT@64,"P
RESS ANY KEY TO THROW DART";
570 M1=0:U=0:GOTO 190
580 IF M1=1 GOTO 580ELSE M2=RND(50)+
20
590 U=U+1:IF U>M2 GOTO 260
600 GOTO 200
```

SAUCERS

Remarks

In this arcade style graphics shoot-em-up game, the player
tries to get as many points as possible by hitting targets with his
missiles. There is a time limit to the game which may be changed
internally. The player shoots his missiles by pressing the space
bar. See Fig. 6-11.

Variables

PL—PRINT @ position of player
T1—PRINT@ position of Target #1
T2—PRINT@ position of Target #2
T3—PRINT@ position of Target #3
T —Time units elapsed

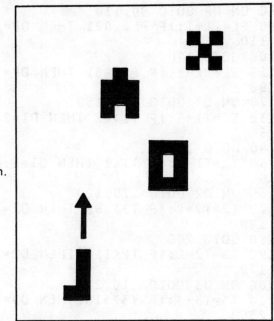

Fig. 6-11. Sample run.

DP—Direction of player
P —Point value of target hit
M —PRINT @ position of missile
Q —Status (0 if no missile fired, 1 if missile fired)
SC—Player's current score

Suggested Variations

1) A number of targets on screen each round change.
2) Give extra time to player if certain score is made.
3) Allow targets to fire missiles back at player.

Program for Saucers

```
10 CLS
20 SC=0:T=0
30 CLS:PL=RND(62)+960:T1=RND(63)+0:T
2=RND(63)+128:T3=RND(63)+256
40 DP=RND(2):D1=RND(2):D2=RND(2):D3=
RND(2)
50 T=T+1:IF T=800 GOTO 460
60 IF Q=1 GOTO 350
70 A$=INKEY$:IF A$=" " GOTO 330
```

```
80 ON DP GOTO 90,110
90 PL=PL+1:IF PL>1021 THEN DP=2:GOTO
 110
100 GOTO 120
110 PL=PL-1:IF PL<961 THEN DP=1:GOTO
 90
120 ON D1 GOTO 130,150
130 T1=T1+1:IF T1>62 THEN D1=2:GOTO
150
140 GOTO 160
150 T1=T1-1:IF T1<1 THEN D1=1:GOTO 1
30
160 ON D2 GOTO 170,190
170 T2=T2+2:IF T2>189 THEN D2=2:GOTO
 190
180 GOTO 200
190 T2=T2-2:IF T2<130 THEN D2=1:GOTO
 170
200 ON D3 GOTO 210,230
210 T3=T3+3:IF T3>316 THEN D3=2:GOTO
 230
220 GOTO 240
230 T3=T3-3:IF T3<259 THEN D3=1:GOTO
 210
240 PRINT@PL,CHR$(186);
250 IF DP=1 THEN PRINT@ PL-1," "; EL
SE PRINT@ PL+1, " ";
260 PRINT@T1,CHR$(153);CHR$(166);
270 IF D1=1 THEN PRINT@ T1-1," "; EL
SE PRINT@ T1+2, " ";
280 PRINT@T2-2," ";:PRINT@T2+2,"  "
;
290 PRINT@T2,CHR$(158);CHR$(173);
300 PRINT@T3,CHR$(183);CHR$(187);
310 PRINT@T3-3," ";:PRINT@T3+3,"  "
;
320 GOTO 50
330 Q=1
340 M=PL
350 M=M-64:PRINT@M,"↑";:PRINT@M+64,"
 ";
360 IF M=T3 OR M=T3+1 GOTO 410
370 IF M=T2 OR M=T2+1 GOTO 420
380 IF M=T1 OR M=T1+1 GOTO 430
```

200

```
390 IF M<=63 THEN Q=0:PRINT@M," ";
400 GOTO 120
410 P=10:PRINT@460,"10 POINTS!";:GOT
O 440
420 P=25:PRINT@460,"25 POINTS!";:GOT
O 440
430 P=50:PRINT@460,"50 POINTS!";
440 PRINT@M-1,"***";:FOR H=1 TO 1000
:NEXT H:SC=SC+P
450 PRINT@460,"            ";:Q=0:GOTO
 30
460 CLS
470 PRINT "TIME IS UP!  YOU SCORED "
;SC;" POINTS."
```

SAUCERS-2

Remarks

So, hotshot, you've mastered *SAUCERS* and have gained the esteemed title of B.M.I.T.C.C. (Big Man In The Computer Club). Well, here's a real test of your fine-tuned skill and savvy. In this variation of *SAUCERS*, you will be able to move your missile launcher using the right and left arrow keys. Also, using the up or down arrow simultaneously will move your launcher even faster. The up arrow key moves your launcher three spaces at a time, and the down arrow moves it five spaces at a time. Pressing neither moves you one unit at a time. Use your space bar to fire a missile, and if you can see that you're not going to hit anything, press the ENTER key to detonate it prematurely. You will also notice that the score value of the targets is reversed, and there is a new barrier added! See Fig. 6-12.

Variables

A—Reads key pressed (PEEK function)
T—Time elapsed
All other major variables unchanged

Suggested Variations

1) You may wish to extend the time limit or give bonus time for attaining a certain score.

2) You may wish to change the rate of travel of the missile launcher and targets.

3) You may wish to make the score of the targets random.

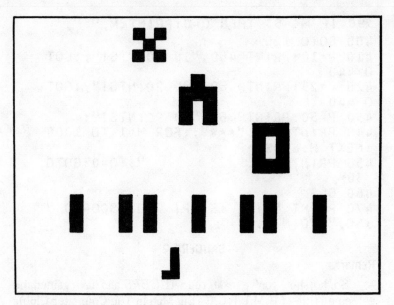

Fig. 6-12. Sample run.

Program for Saucers-2

```
10 DIM A(1023)
20 CLS
30 FOR X=576 TO 639 STEP 2:A(X)=1:NE
XT X
40 SC=0:T=0
50 CLS:PL=RND(62)+960:T1=RND(63)+0:T
2=RND(63)+128:T3=RND(63)+256
60 FOR X=576 TO 639 STEP 2:IF A(X)=1
 THEN PRINT@X,CHR$(191);
70 NEXT X
80 DP=RND(2):D1=RND(2):D2=RND(2):D3=
RND(2)
90 T=T+1:IF T=800 GOTO 580
100 IF Q=1 GOTO 450
110 A=PEEK(14400):IF A=0 GOTO 220
120 IF A=128 GOTO 430
130 IF A<>64 AND A<>72 AND A<>80 AND
 A<>32 AND A<>40 AND A<>48 GOTO 220
140 IF A=64 AND PL+1<1022 THEN G=1:G
OTO 210
```

202

```
150 IF A=72 AND PL+3<1022 THEN G=3:G
OTO 210
160 IF A=80 AND PL+5<1022 THEN G=5:G
OTO 210
170 IF A=32 AND PL-1>961 THEN G=-1:G
OTO 210
180 IF A=40 AND PL-3>961 THEN G=-3:G
OTO 210
190 IF A=48 AND PL-5>961 THEN G=-5:G
OTO 210
200 GOTO 220
210 PRINT@PL," ";:PL=PL+G:PRINT@PL,C
HR$(186);
220 ON D1 GOTO 230,250
230 T1=T1+1:IF T1>62 THEN D1=2:GOTO
250
240 GOTO 260
250 T1=T1-1:IF T1<1 THEN D1=1:GOTO 2
30
260 ON D2 GOTO 270,290
270 T2=T2+2:IF T2>189 THEN D2=2:GOTO
 290
280 GOTO 300
290 T2=T2-2:IF T2<130 THEN D2=1:GOTO
 270
300 ON D3 GOTO 310,330
310 T3=T3+3:IF T3>316 THEN D3=2:GOTO
 330
320 GOTO 340
330 T3=T3-3:IF T3<259 THEN D3=1:GOTO
 310
340 PRINT@PL,CHR$(186);
350 IF DP=1 THEN PRINT@ PL-1," "; EL
SE PRINT@ PL+1, " ";
360 PRINT@T1,CHR$(153);CHR$(166);
370 IF D1=1 THEN PRINT@ T1-1," "; EL
SE PRINT@ T1+2, " ";
380 PRINT@T2-2," ";:PRINT@T2+2,"  "
;
390 PRINT@T2,CHR$(158);CHR$(173);
400 PRINT@T3,CHR$(183);CHR$(187);
410 PRINT@T3-3," ";:PRINT@T3+3,"  "
;
420 GOTO 90
```

```
430 Q=1
440 M=PL
450 M=M-64:PRINT@M,"↑";:PRINT@M+64,"
  ";
460 IF M=T3 OR M=T3+1 GOTO 530
470 IF M=T2 OR M=T2+1 GOTO 540
480 IF M=T1 OR M=T1+1 GOTO 550
490 IF A(M)=1 THEN PRINT@M," ";:A(M)
=0:Q=0:GOTO 220
500 IF M<=63 THEN Q=0:PRINT@M," ";
510 A=PEEK(14400):IF A=1 THEN PRINT@
M," ";:Q=0:GOTO 220
520 GOTO 220
530 P=50:PRINT@460,"50 POINTS!";:GOT
O 560
540 P=25:PRINT@460,"25 POINTS!";:GOT
O 560
550 P=10:PRINT@460,"10 POINTS!";
560 PRINT@M-1,"***";:FOR H=1 TO 1000
:NEXT H:SC=SC+P
570 PRINT@460,"              ";:Q=0:GOTO
 50
580 CLS
590 PRINT "TIME IS UP!  YOU SCORED "
;SC;" POINTS."
```

CAPTURE!

Remarks

In this fast paced and often frustrating real-time game, the player tries to catch the asterisks in the least amount of time as possible. Once "captured", the target will turn into a gravestone that neither the player nor further targets will be able to pass through or over. The player may choose as many targets as he wishes (See Fig. 6-13). The player can move his symbol (X) by pressing the following keys:

    Q—MOVE UP
    A—MOVE DOWN
    L—MOVE LEFT
    ;—MOVE RIGHT
    SPACE BAR—STOP

Variables

    A(X)—Contents of PRINT@ position X
        If A(X) = 1 then it is either a border or a gravestone.

```
CAPTURE!
THE OBJECT OF THIS GAME IS TO CAPTURE THE * SYMBOL
WITH YOUR X SYMBOL IN AS LITTLE TIME AS POSSIBLE
MOVE YOUR SYMBOL USING THE FOLLOWING KEYS:
Q—UP
A—DOWN
L—LEFT
;—RIGHT
SPACE BAR—STOP

PRESS ENTER TO CONTINUE?

HOW MANY TARGETS? 1

        X


                              *
```

Fig. 6-13. Sample run.

V	—Number of targets in game
Y	—PRINT@ position of target
Y1	—# of spaces to move target
U	—Elapsed time units
G	—Number of spaces to move player
X	—PRINT@ position of player
A$	—Argument of INKEY$

Suggested Variations

1) Have more than one target on the screen at a time.
2) Give the target a strategy to avoid the player.

Program for Capture!

```
10 CLS:U=0:N=0
20 DIM A(1023)
30 GOSUB 430
40 INPUT "HOW MANY TARGETS ";V:CLS
50 I=0:FOR Q=1 TO 15:I=I+64:A(I)=1:
NEXT Q
```

205

```
60 I=63:FOR Q=1 TO 15:I=I+64:A(I)=1:
NEXT Q
70 FOR X=0 TO 127:SET(X,0):SET(X,47)
:NEXT X
80 FOR Y=0 TO 47:SET(0,Y):SET(127,Y)
:NEXT Y
90 X=RND(958):X1=X:GOSUB 380:IF X2=2
 GOTO 90
100 Y=RND(958):X1=Y:GOSUB 380:IF X2=
2 GOTO 100
110 IF X=Y GOTO 100
120 D=RND(4):IF D=1 THEN Y1=1
130 IF D=2 THEN Y1=-1
140 IF D=3 THEN Y1=64
150 IF D=4 THEN Y1=-64
160 X1=Y+Y1:GOSUB 380:IF X2=2 GOTO 1
20
170 Y2=RND(3):IF Y2=2 GOTO 120
180 X1=Y+Y1:GOSUB 380:IF X2=2 GOTO 1
20
190 Y=Y+Y1:PRINT @Y,"*";:PRINT @Y-Y1
," ";
200 IF X=Y GOTO 330
210 A$=INKEY$
220 U=U+1
230 PRINT @0,U;
240 IF A$=";" THEN G=1
250 IF A$="L" THEN G=-1
260 IF A$="Q" THEN G=-64
270 IF A$="A" THEN G=64
280 IF A$=" " THEN G=0
290 X1=X+G:GOSUB 380:IF X2=2 THEN G=
0
300 X=X+G:PRINT @X,"X";:IF G=0 GOTO
320ELSE PRINT@X-G," ";
310 IF X=Y GOTO 330
320 GOTO 170
330 FOR Z=1 TO 100:PRINT@X," ";:PRIN
T@X,"+";:NEXT Z
340 A(X)=1:N=N+1:IF N=V GOTO 360
350 GOTO 90
360 CLS:PRINT "ELAPSED TIME UNITS---
";U
370 END
```

206

```
380 X2=1
390 IF X1<63 THEN X2=2:RETURN
400 IF X1>958 THEN X2=2:RETURN
410 IF A(X1)=1 THEN X2=2:RETURN
420 RETURN
430 CLS:PRINT "CAPTURE!"
440 PRINT "THE OBJECT OF THIS GAME I
S TO CAPTURE THE * SYMBOL"
450 PRINT "WITH YOUR X SYMBOL IN AS
LITTLE TIME AS POSSIBLE"
460 PRINT "MOVE YOUR SYMBOL USING TH
E FOLLOWING KEYS:"
470 PRINT "Q-- UP"
480 PRINT "A-- DOWN"
490 PRINT "L-- LEFT"
500 PRINT ";-- RIGHT"
510 PRINT "SPACE BAR-- STOP"
520 PRINT:PRINT:INPUT "PRESS ENTER T
O CONTINUE ";A$:CLS:RETURN
```

INN-B-TWEEN

Remarks

Here is the computerized version of the popular game of Acey-Deucey. This version uses a full shuffled deck of 52 cards that is automatically reshuffled when the supply gets low. Aces must be specified high or low (a value of 1 or 14) as they are dealt. Up to 11 players can compete and the money in the pot is kept track of by the computer. No splits are recognized or allowed in this version. In play, the computer deals two cards. The player must then wager whether the next card dealt will lie numerically between the first two. If he wishes to pass his turn, he simply bets zero.

Variables

A(X)	—Numeric value of card X in the deck in sequence
B(X)	—Numeric value of card X in deck after shuffling
CARD$(X)	—Name of card X
SUIT$(X)	—Suit of card X
A$(X)	—Player X's name
Z	—Number of cards that have been dealt.
POT	—Money remaining in pot.
BET	—Amount of current player's bet
G(1)	—First card dealt
G(2)	—Second card dealt
G(3)	—Third card dealt

Suggested Variations

1) You may wish to extract this card shuffling routine for use in other computerized card games.

2) You may wish to add a routine to recognize and process splits (first two cards dealt have the same face value).

Sample Run

PLEASE WAIT . . . SHUFFLING
HOW MANY PLAYERS ? 1
PLAYER # 1'S NAME: ? SCOTT
HOW MUCH MONEY IN POT ? 5.00

SCOTT's TURN
$5 REMAINING IN POT
HERE ARE YOUR CARDS:
NINE OF HEARTS

FOUR OF CLUBS

HOW MUCH DO YOU BET ? 2.50
TEN OF CLUBS
YOU LOSE. PLEASE PUT $2.50 IN THE POT.
PRESS ENTER TO CONTINUE?
SCOTT'S TURN
$7.50 REMAINING IN POT
HERE ARE YOUR CARDS:
JACK OF DIAMONDS

THREE OF HEARTS

HOW MUCH DO YOU BET ? 7.50
EIGHT OF SPADES
YOU WIN! PLEASE TAKE $ 7.50 FROM THE POT.

POT IS EMPTY

Program for Inn-B-Tween

```
10 CLS
20 DIM A(52),B(52),CARD$(52),SUIT$(5
2),H(52)
```

```
30 GOSUB 690
40 GOTO 380
50 FOR X=1 TO 52:A(X)=X:NEXT X
60 FOR X=1 TO 52
70 Z=RND(52)
80 IF A(Z)=0 GOTO 70
90 B(X)=A(Z):A(Z)=0
100 NEXT X
110 FOR X=1 TO 52
120 K=1
130 IF B(X)<=13 GOTO 160
140 B(X)=B(X)-13:K=K+1
150 GOTO 130
160 H(X)=B(X):ON B(X) GOTO 170,180,1
90,200,210,220,230,240,250,260,270,2
80,290
170 X$="ACE":GOTO 300
180 X$="TWO":GOTO 300
190 X$="THREE":GOTO 300
200 X$="FOUR":GOTO 300
210 X$="FIVE":GOTO 300
220 X$="SIX":GOTO 300
230 X$="SEVEN":GOTO 300
240 X$="EIGHT":GOTO 300
250 X$="NINE":GOTO 300
260 X$="TEN":GOTO 300
270 X$="JACK":GOTO 300
280 X$="QUEEN":GOTO 300
290 X$="KING"
300 ON K GOTO 310,320,330,340
310 Y$="HEARTS":GOTO 350
320 Y$="DIAMONDS":GOTO 350
330 Y$="CLUBS":GOTO 350
340 Y$="SPADES"
350 CARD$(X)=X$:SUIT$(X)=Y$
360 NEXT X
370 RETURN
380 CLS:INPUT "HOW MANY PLAYERS ";G
390 FOR X=1 TO G:PRINT "PLAYER #";X;
"'S NAME: ";:INPUT A$(X)
400 NEXT X
410 INPUT "HOW MUCH MONEY IN POT ";P
OT
420 FOR L=1 TO G
```

209

```
430 CLS:PRINT A$(L);"'S TURN"
440 PRINT "$";POT;" REMAINING IN POT
"
450 PRINT "HERE ARE YOUR CARDS:"
460 PRINT CARD$(Z);" OF ";SUIT$(Z)
470 IF H(Z)=1 THEN PRINT@221,"HI OR
LO";:INPUT R$:IF R$="HI" THEN H(Z)=1
4
480 G(1)=H(Z)
490 PRINT:Z=Z+1

500 PRINT CARD$(Z);" OF ";SUIT$(Z)
510 IF H(Z)=1 THEN PRINT@349,"HI OR
LO";:INPUT R$:IF R$="HI" THEN H(Z)=1
4
520 G(2)=H(Z)
530 PRINT:INPUT "HOW MUCH DO YOU BET
 ";BET
540 IF BET>POT THEN PRINT "NOT THAT
MUCH IN THE POT":GOTO 530
550 IF BET<=0 THEN 650
560 Z=Z+1:PRINT CARD$(Z);" OF ";SUIT
$(Z)
570 G(3)=H(Z)
580 IF G(1)>G(2) GOTO 600
590 IF G(3)<G(2) AND G(3)>G(1) GOTO

630ELSE GOTO 610
600 IF G(3)<G(1) AND G(3)>G(2) GOTO
630ELSE GOTO 610
610 PRINT "YOU LOSE. PLEASE PUT $";B
ET;" IN THE POT."
620 POT=POT+BET:GOTO 650
630 PRINT "YOU WIN!  PLEASE TAKE $";
BET;" FROM THE POT."
640 POT=POT-BET:IF POT=0 GOTO 680
650 INPUT "PRESS ENTER TO CONTINUE "
;G$:Z=Z+1:IF Z>50 GOSUB 690
660 CLS:NEXT L
670 GOTO 420
680 PRINT:PRINT "POT IS EMPTY":END
690 CLS:PRINT CHR$(23);"PLEASE WAIT.
..SHUFFLING":GOSUB 50:Z=1:RETURN
```

SOCCER

Remarks

In this game, two players compete in a game of soccer. The player who has the ball tries to pass the ball to his own team members and shoot the ball past the opponent's goalie. The game ends at the score of five. The odds of a successful pass are greater for the shortest distance between the players. Likewise, the team members closest to the goal will have the best chance of making a goal when shooting. The players may pass the ball simply by typing the number of the teammate to whom he wishes to pass. He may shoot the ball by pressing the space bar. See Fig. 6-14.

Variables

A$	—First player's name
B$	—Second player's name
N	—Team member
M	—Team player #
C(M,N)	—PRINT @ positions of Team N, Player M,
B3,A3	—M and N of player in possession of ball
K	—Used to calculate odds of pass or shoot
A1	—Score of Player 1 (A$)
A2	—Score of Player 2 (B$)

Suggested Variations

1) Remove the score limit to end game and place game on a time limit.

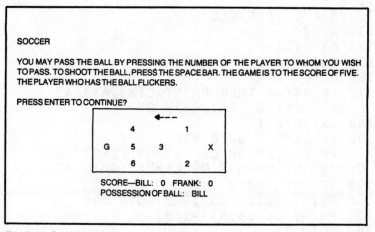

Fig. 6-14. Sample run.

2) Place time limit on amount of time player has to either pass or shoot.

3) Give the computer a game strategy so it can play against a single player.

4) Change the odds of a successful pass.

5) Change the odds of a successful shot on goal.

Program for Soccer

```
10 CLS
20 INPUT "ENTER FIRST PLAYER'S NAME"
;A$
30 INPUT "ENTER OTHER PLAYER'S NAME"
;B$
40 GOSUB 810
50 CLS
60 FOR Y=0 TO 11:SET(0,Y):SET(127,Y)
:NEXT Y
70 FOR X=0 TO 127:SET(X,0):SET(X,32)
:NEXT X
80 FOR Y=21 TO 31:SET(0,Y):SET(127,Y
):NEXT Y
90 FOR M=1 TO 2:FOR N=1 TO 7:READ C(
M,N):NEXT N,M
100 DATA 137,521,351,181,373,564,322
,182,565,352,138,330,522,381
110 PRINT @C(1,7),"G";:PRINT @C(2,7
),"G";
120 RANDOM:P=RND(2)
130 A3=7
140 A1=0:A2=0
150 GOSUB 790
160 GOSUB 250
170 IF A3<=6 THEN PRINT@C(B3,A3),A3;
 ELSE PRINT @ C(B3,A3),"G";
180 C$=INKEY$
190 IF C$=" " GOTO 420
200 IF C$="1" OR C$="2" OR C$="3" OR
 C$="4" OR C$="5" OR C$="6" GOTO 570
210 IF A3=7 GOTO 230
220 PRINT @C(B3,A3),B9;:GOTO 240
230 PRINT @C(B3,A3)-1,B9;
240 GOTO 170
```

```
250  IF P=1 THEN P=2 ELSE P=1
260  B3=P
270  ON P GOTO 280,350
280  FOR T=1 TO 6:PRINT@C(2,T)," ";:N
EXT T
290  PRINT @331," ";
300  FOR T=1 TO 6:PRINT @C(1,T),T;:NE
XT T
310  PRINT @93,"----->";
320  FOR I=896 TO 950:PRINT@I," ";:NE
XT I
330  PRINT @896,"POSSESION OF BALL: "
;A$
340  RETURN
350  FOR T=1 TO 6:PRINT @C(1,T)," ";:
NEXT T
360  FOR T=1 TO 6:PRINT @C(2,T),T;:NE
XT T
370  PRINT @374," ";
380  PRINT @ 93,"<-----";
390  FOR I=896 TO 950:PRINT @I," ";:N
EXT I
400  PRINT@896,"POSSESSION OF BALL: "
;B$
410  RETURN
420  IF A3=7 THEN K=2
430  IF A3=1 OR A3=2 THEN K=3
440  IF A3=3 THEN K=4
450  IF A3=4 OR A3=5 OR A3=6 THEN K=6
460  Z=RND(10):IF Z>K GOTO 520
470  IF B3=1 THEN A1=A1+1:ELSE A2=A2+
1
480  PRINT@ 768, "H E   S C O R E S !
 !";
490  GOSUB 790
500  IF A1=5 OR A2=5 THEN STOP
510  GOTO 740
520  Z=RND(5):IF Z=1 GOTO 550
530  PRINT @768,"GOALIE STOPS THE SHO
T!";
540  GOTO 740
550  PRINT @768,"SHOT MISSES!";
560  GOTO 740
```

```
570 K=VAL(C$)
580 G=0
590 IF A3=7 AND K=1 OR K=2 THEN G=3
600 IF A3=7 AND K=3 THEN G=2
610 IF A3=7 AND K=4 OR K=5 OR K=6 TH
EN G=1
620 IF (A3=1 OR A3=2) AND K=3 THEN G
=2
630 IF (A3=1 OR A3=2) AND (K=4 OR K=
5 OR K=6) THEN G=1
640 IF A3=3 AND (K=4 OR K=5 OR K=6)
THEN G=2
650 IF (A3=4 OR A3=5 OR A3=6) AND (K
=4 OR K=5 OR K=6) THEN G=3
660 IF G=0 GOTO 170
670 H=RND(4)
680 IF H<=G THEN A3=K ELSE GOTO 700
690 GOTO 170
700 U=RND(2):ON U GOTO 710,730
710 PRINT @768,"*** PASS INTERCEPTED
 ***";
720 GOTO 740
730 PRINT@768,"*** PASS OUT OF BOUND
S ***";
740 FOR Z=1 TO 1000:NEXT Z
750 PRINT@768,"
       ";
760 GOSUB 250
770 A3=RND(4):IF A3=4 THEN A3=7
780 GOTO 170
790 PRINT @832,"SCORE-- ";A$;": ";A1
;TAB(15)B$;": ";A2;
800 RETURN
810 CLS:PRINT "SOCCER":PRINT
820 PRINT "YOU MAY PASS THE BALL BY
PRESSING THE NUMBER"
830 PRINT "OF THE PLAYER YOU WISH TO
 PASS TO.  TO SHOOT"
840 PRINT "THE BALL, PRESS THE SPACE
 BAR.  THE GAME IS "
850 PRINT "TO THE SCORE OF FIVE."
860 PRINT "THE PLAYER WHO HAS THE BA
LL FLICKERS."
```

```
870 PRINT:INPUT "PRESS ENTER TO CONT
INUE ";A$:CLS:RETURN
```

CHRISTIAN VS. LION

Remarks

A rather brutal game in concept, but I like it just the same. You are being chased by a hungry lion as part of the festivities on a historic Saturday afternoon. The lion has been deprived of food for a week or so and is licking its lips at you. If you can avoid it long enough, the hunger-weakened animal will die from exhaustion! Also, there is a magic sling hidden somewhere in the coliseum. You will be able to see it only briefly before the lion is set loose. If you can get to the sling, you can shoot one of the three magic stones in your pocket by pressing the space bar. Alas, the magic sling doesn't have very good aim sometimes, and even a direct hit won't kill the lion everytime. This fast paced real-time game should really give you a challenge. See Fig. 6-15.

Variables

A(X) — Contents of PRINT @ position X
R,C — Row, Column in conversion subroutine
P — PRINT @ position in conversion subroutine
CH — PRINT @ position of player
L — PRINT @ position of lion
GU — PRINT @ position of sling
E1 — PRINT @ position of fired stone
K — Number of lions killed by player

CHRISTIAN VS. LION

YOU ARE THE C
THE LION IS THE L
A SLING (Y) IS HIDDEN SOMEWHERE. IT WILL BE SHOWN BRIEFLY, IF YOU GET IT YOU CAN
USE THE SPACE BAR TO SHOOT ONE OF THE THREE STONES IN YOUR POCKET. USE THE
FOUR ARROW KEYS TO MOVE YOURSELF AND AVOID THE LION.
PRESS ENTER TO BEGIN?

                          C

       Y
                                      L

       GET YOUR FINGERS READY...

Fig. 6-15. Sample run.

Suggested Variations

1) How about two lions chasing the Christian?
2) You may wish to improve the aim of the sling.

Program for Christian vs. Lion

1

```
10 CLS
20 DIM A(1087)
30 GOSUB 840
40 FOR X=0 TO 63:PRINT@X,CHR$(191);:
A(X)=-1:NEXTX
50 FOR X=832 TO 895:PRINT@X,CHR$(191
);:A(X)=-3:NEXTX
60 FOR X=0 TO 832 STEP 64:PRINT@X,CH
R$(191);:A(X)=-4:NEXTX
70 FOR X=63 TO 895 STEP 64:PRINT@X,C
HR$(191);:A(X)=-2:NEXTX
80 L2=0:V=0
90 GOTO 140
100 REM * GET R,C FROM PRINT@
110 R=INT(P/64):C=P-(64*R):RETURN
120 REM * GET PRINT@ FROM R,C
130 P=C+(64*R):RETURN
140 REM * PLACE CHRISTIAN AND LION
150 CH=RND(895):IF A(CH)<0 GOTO 150
160 L=RND(895):IF A(L)<0 GOTO 160
170 PRINT@CH,"C";:PRINT@L,"L";
180 PRINT@896,"G E T   Y O U R   F I N
   G E R S   R E A D Y . . .";
190 FOR X=1 TO 1000:NEXT X
200 PRINT@896,"
                                    ";
210 REM * LIFE OF LION AND GUN LOCAT
ION
220 LI=RND(50)+50
230 GU=RND(895):IF A(GU)<0 GOTO 230
240 FOR Z=1 TO 3
250 PRINT @GU,"Y";:FOR X=1 TO 250:NE
XT X
260 PRINT @GU," ";:FOR X=1 TO 250:NE
XT X
270 NEXT Z
```

216

```
280 PRINT@896,"G O ! ! ! !";
290 A$=INKEY$
300 IF CH=GU THEN PRINT@896,"YOU HAV
E THE SLING!";:V=1:GU=0
310 IF A$="" GOTO 380
320 A=ASC(A$)
330 IF A=91 THEN G=-64:GOTO 380
340 IF A=10 THEN G=64:GOTO 380
350 IF A=9 THEN G=1:GOTO 380
360 IF A=8 THEN G=-1:GOTO 380
370 IF A$=" " GOTO 660ELSE G=0
380 IF A(CH+G)<0 THEN PRINT@896,"OUT
 OF BOUNDS!";:FOR X=1 TO 500:NEXT X:
PRINT@896,"              ";:G=0:GOTO
 400
390 PRINT@CH," ";:CH=CH+G:PRINT@CH,"
C";
400 IF L=CH GOTO 740
410 L2=L2+1:IF L2=L1 GOTO 760
420 REM * GET R,C FROM CH
430 P=CH:GOSUB 100:X=R:Y=C
440 P=L:GOSUB 100:X1=R:Y1=C
450 IF X1=X AND Y1<Y THEN D=1:GOTO 5
30
460 IF X1>X AND Y1<Y THEN D=2:GOTO 5
30
470 IF X1>X AND Y1=Y THEN D=3:GOTO 5
30
480 IF X1>X AND Y1>Y THEN D=4:GOTO 5
30
490 IF X1=X AND Y1>Y THEN D=5:GOTO 5
30
500 IF X1<X AND Y1>Y THEN D=6:GOTO 5
30
510 IF X1<X AND Y1=Y THEN D=7:GOTO 5
30
520 IF X1<X AND Y1<Y THEN D=8
530 D=D+(RND(3)-2)
540 IF D=0 THEN D=8
550 IF D=9 THEN D=1
560 IF D>1 AND D<5 THEN X1=X1-1
570 IF D>5 THEN X1=X1+1
580 IF D>3 AND D<7 THEN Y1=Y1-1
590 IF D<3 OR D=8 THEN Y1=Y1+1
```

```
600 M=L:R=X1:C=Y1:GOSUB 120
610 L=P:IF A(L)=-1 THEN L=L+64
620 IF A(L)=-2 THEN L=L-1
630 IF A(L)=-3 THEN L=L-64
640 IF A(L)=-4 THEN L=L+1
650 PRINT@M," ";:PRINT@L,"L";:IF L=C
H GOTO 740ELSE GOTO 290
660 IF V>0 GOTO 670ELSE PRINT@896,"Y
OU DON'T HAVE THE SLING!";:GOTO 380
670 V=V+1:IF V>4 GOTO 730ELSE B=RND(
2):IF B=1 THEN J=1 ELSE J=-1
680 E1=CH+J
690 PRINT@E1,"*";:T=E1:E1=E1+J
700 PRINT@T," ";:PRINT@E1,"*";:IF E1
=L GOTO 820
710 IF A(E1)<0 THEN PRINT @E1,CHR$(1
91);:GOTO 380
720 GOTO 690
730 PRINT@896,"YOU HAVE NO MORE STON
ES!";:GOTO 380
740 PRINT @896,"HE HAS EATEN YOU!"
750 FOR X=1 TO 1000:NEXT X:CLS:GOTO
810
760 PRINT @896,"THE LION HAS DIED FR
OM EXHAUSTION!!!";
770 K=K+1
780 FOR X=1 TO 1000:NEXT X:CLS
790 INPUT "DO YOU WISH TO TAKE ON AN
OTHER (Y/N)";A$
800 IF A$="Y" THEN CLS:GOTO 40
810 PRINT "YOU DEFEATED";K;" LIONS T
ODAY!":END
820 U1=RND(2):IF U1=2 THEN 830ELSE P
RINT@896,"HOORAY! YOU GOT 'EM!!";:GO
TO 770
830 J=(RND(3)-2)*64:E1=E1+J:PRINT@L,
"L";:PRINT@E1,"*";:GOTO 710
840 PRINT "CHRISTIAN VS. LION":PRINT
:PRINT
850 PRINT "YOU ARE THE C"
860 PRINT "THE LION IS THE L"
870 PRINT "A SLING (Y) IS HIDDEN SOM
EWHERE, IT WILL BE SHOWN"
```

```
880 PRINT "BRIEFLY, IF YOU GET IT YO
U CAN USE THE SPACE BAR"
890 PRINT "TO SHOOT ONE OF THE THREE
 STONES IN YOUR POCKET."
900 PRINT "USE THE FOUR ARROW KEYS T
O MOVE YOURSELF AND"
910 PRINT "AVOID THE LION."
920 PRINT:INPUT "PRESS ENTER TO BEGI
N ";A$:CLS:RETURN
```

ECHO MEMORY GAME

Remarks

Put on your thinking cap, because this program might give you some trouble! A series of lights will flash on the screen next to their position numbers (1 through 9). You have three tries to enter the correct sequence of lights (See Fig. 6-16).

Variables

NU — Number of lights in sequence
NO — Cumulative number of lights tried by player
R — Number of rounds
C(X) — Light # in sequence position X
A(X) — PRINT @ position for light #X
MI — Number of incorrect entries per round
U — Number of correct sequences entered

Suggested Variations

1) You may wish to display the lights for a shorter length of time. How about a skill factor from one to ten?

ECHO MEMORY GAME

A SERIES OF LIGHTS WILL BE FLASHED. YOU MUST REPEAT THE LIGHTS IN THEIR PROPER ORDER.
YOU WILL HAVE THREE TRIES TO GET IT RIGHT. THEN THE COMPUTER WILL TELL YOU THE CORRECT SEQUENCE.
HOW MANY ROUNDS WOULD YOU LIKE TO PLAY? 1
ROUND # 1
HOW MANY LIGHTS? 1
HERE IS THE SEQUENCE...   7   8   9
                                 4   5   6
                                 1   2   3

                                         ▮

Fig. 6-16. Sample run.

2) Alright, I won't dwell on this but there is a way to enter a very long string of memorized numbers (phone number, social security, etc.) and have the computer play this sequence only when you have asked for that exact number of lights. Let me tell you how this can impress your friends...

Program for Echo Memory Game

```
10 DIM A(10),C(25)
20 CLS:PRINT "E C H O   M E M O R Y
   G A M E":PRINT:PRINT
30 PRINT "A SERIES OF LIGHTS WILL BE
   FLASHED. YOU MUST REPEAT THE LIGHTS
   IN THEIR PROPER ORDER."
40 PRINT "YOU HAVE THREE TRIES TO GE
T IT RIGHT.  THEN THE COMPUTER WILL
   TELL YOU THE CORRECT SEQUENCE"
50 FOR K=1 TO 9:READ A(K):NEXT K
60 DATA 649,659,669,457,467,477,265,
275,285
70 INPUT "HOW MANY ROUNDS WOULD YOU
LIKE TO PLAY ";R
80 FOR R1=1 TO R:CLS:MI=0:PRINT "ROU
ND #";R1
90 INPUT "HOW MANY LIGHTS ";NU
100 NO=NO+NU
110 CLS:FOR Q=1 TO 9:PRINT@A(Q)-65,Q
;:NEXT Q
120 PRINT@0,"HERE IS THE SEQUENCE...
";:FOR Z=1 TO 500:NEXT Z
130 FOR K=1 TO NU:H=RND(9)
140 C(K)=H:PRINT@A(H),CHR$(191);:FOR
 X5=1 TO 250:NEXT X5:PRINT@A(H)," ";

150 NEXT K
160 PRINT @832,"NOW ENTER THE NUMBER
S IN SEQUENCE"
170 FOR X=1 TO NU
180 A$=INKEY$:IF A$="" THEN 180ELSE
W=VAL(A$)
190 PRINT@A(W),CHR$(191);:FOR X5=1 T
O 250:NEXT X5:PRINT@A(W)," ";
200 IF W<>C(X) THEN 210ELSE NEXT X:G
OTO 290
```

```
210 PRINT@64,"********* W R O N G! *
********";:FOR Z=1 TO 500:NEXT Z:PRI
NT@64,"
  ";:MI=MI+1:IF MI=3 THEN 220ELSE 170

220 PRINT@832,"T H E   C O R R E C T
  S E Q U E N C E   W A S :";
230 FOR K=1 TO NU
240 PRINT@A(C(K)),CHR$(191):FOR X5=1
  TO 250:NEXT X5:PRINT@A(C(K))," ";
250 NEXT K:NEXT R1
260 CLS:PRINT "YOU GOT";U;" OUT OF";
R1-1;" SEQUENCES RIGHT!"
270 PRINT "FOR A COMPOSITE SCORE OF
";U*NO;" SKILL POINTS";
280 END
290 PRINT@832,"          A B S O L U T
  E L Y   R I G H T ! ! "
300 FOR X=1 TO 500:NEXT X
310 U=U+1:INPUT"PRESS ENTER TO CONTI
NUE";A$:NEXT R1:GOTO 260
```

POOL

Remarks

In this program you will try to bank your cue ball off the wall on the top of the screen down into the pocket at the lower right corner of the screen. Sound simple? Wait until you've tried a couple rounds! You are allowed only to bank the ball off of the top wall. Use the right and left arrow keys to position the unlit spot on the top wall where you wish the cue ball to bank. Press the space bar to shoot the ball. The ball will be graphically plotted as it travels. This program makes use of a routine to plot a line given only one point and a decimal slope. See Fig. 6-17.

Variables

K,Y   —X and Y coordinates of ball when shot
B   —Y intercept of line formed by ball
SLOPE—Slope of line formed by ball
R   —Number of rounds to be played

Suggested Variations

1) Place other "losing" pockets on the screen and allow the ball to continue banking until it goes into a pocket.

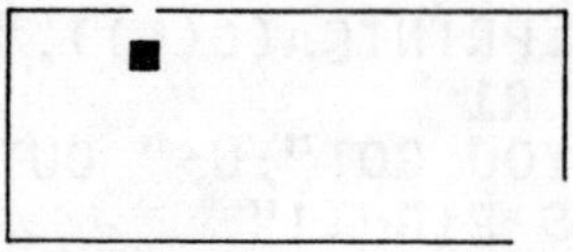

Fig. 6-17. Sample run.

Program for Pool

```
10 P1=0
20 CLS
30 GOSUB 640
40 FOR H=1 TO R
50 GOTO 270
60 IF X2=X1 GOTO 200
70 SLOPE=(Y2-Y1)/(X2-X1)
80 B=Y1-SLOPE*X1
90 REM *LINE EQUATION IS    Y=SLOPE*X
+B
100 IF X2<X1 GOTO 130
110 Z1=1:FOR K=X1 TO X2
120 IF Z1=1 GOTO 140
130 FOR K=X1 TO X2 STEP -1
140 Y=SLOPE*K+B
150 Y=Y+.5:Y=INT(Y)
160 SET(K,Y)
170 NEXT K
180 A$=INKEY$:IF A$="" GOTO 180
190 RETURN
200 IF Y2<Y1 GOTO 230
210 Z1=1:FOR K=Y2 TO Y1 STEP -1
220 IF Z1=1 GOTO 240
230 FOR K=Y1 TO Y2 STEP -1
240 SET(X1,K)
```

222

```
250 NEXT K
260 GOTO 180
270 CLS:FOR X=0 TO 127:SET(X,0):SET(
X,47):NEXT X
280 FOR Y=0 TO 47:SET(0,Y):SET(127,Y
):NEXT Y
290 X1=RND(85):Y1=RND(35)+12:IF POIN
T(X1,Y1)=-1 GOTO 290
300 FOR X=1 TO 100:SET(X1,Y1):RESET(
X1,Y1):NEXT X
310 FOR Y=44 TO 47:RESET(127,Y):NEXT
 Y
320 FOR X=121 TO 127:RESET(X,47):NEX
T X
330 PRINT @960,"ROUND #";H;
340 SET(X1,Y1)
350 X2=X1+1:Y2=0
360 RESET(X2,Y2)
370 P=PEEK(14400)
380 IF P=64 AND X2<126 THEN SET(X2,Y
2):X2=X2+1:RESET(X2,Y2)
390 IF P=32 AND X2>X1+1 THEN SET(X2,
Y2):X2=X2-1:RESET(X2,Y2)
400 IF P=128 GOTO 420
410 GOTO 370
420 GOSUB 60
430 X=X2
440 SLOPE=-SLOPE
450 B=0-SLOPE*X
460 FOR Z=X TO 126
470 Y=SLOPE*Z+B
480 Y=Y+.5:Y=INT(Y)
490 IF Y>=47 GOTO 520
500 SET(Z,Y)
510 NEXT Z
520 IF Y>47 GOTO 610ELSE IF POINT (Z
,Y)=-1 GOTO 590
530 PRINT@0,"YOU GOT IT!";
540 P1=P1+1
550 FOR X=1 TO 1000:NEXT X
560 NEXT H
570 CLS:PRINT "OUT OF ";R;" ROUNDS Y
OU MADE ";P1;" SHOTS."
580 END
```

```
590 PRINT@0, "YOU MISSED!";
600 GOTO 550
610 Y=47:X=Y/(M+B)
620 X=X+.5:X=INT(X):SET(X,Y)
630 GOTO 520
640 CLS:PRINTCHR$(23);"POOL GAME"
650 INPUT "INSTRUCTIONS (YES/NO) ";A
$
660 IF A$="NO" OR A$="N" THEN CLS:GO
TO 750
670 CLS:PRINT "THE OBJECT OF THIS GA
ME IS SIMPLY TO PUT THE"
680 PRINT "POOL BALL IN THE LOWER RI
GHT POCKET."
690 PRINT "YOU MUST BANK THE BALL OF
F OF THE TOP CUSHION AT"
700 PRINT "A POINT WHERE YOU SPECIFY
."
710 PRINT "USE THE RIGHT AND LEFT AR
ROW KEYS TO POSITION"
720 PRINT "YOUR BANKING SPOT AND PRE
SS THE SPACE BAR TO"
730 PRINT "PUT THE BALL IN MOTION"
740 PRINT
750 INPUT "HOW MANY ROUNDS DO YOU WI
SH TO PLAY ";R
760 RETURN
```

TIC-TAC-TOE

Remarks

An old computer classic finally comes to your very own living room! Unless you have intentionally changed this program to be "stupid", I don't believe you'll be able to muster anything better than a draw against this mechanical genius. Look over the program logic and I think you'll be amazed at how simple it really is (see Fig. 6-18). Deceptively simple...

Variables

N,L   —Whose turn (1=human   2=computer)
SUM —Value of symbols in row being examined
A,B,C—Each of the squares in the row being examined
A(X) —Contents of square X

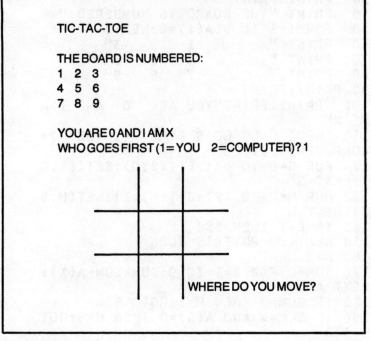

TIC-TAC-TOE

THE BOARD IS NUMBERED:
1 2 3
4 5 6
7 8 9

YOU ARE 0 AND I AM X
WHO GOES FIRST (1=YOU   2=COMPUTER)? 1

WHERE DO YOU MOVE?

Fig. 6-18. Sample run.

M — Player's or computer's move (place symbol in square #M)

R,S — X,Y coordinates to draw symbol on screen

Suggested Variations

1) You may wish to add a "dummy factor" to this program to allow the human player to win every once in a while.

2) If you really look into the logic of this program, you will see that the computer looks to see if you have two symbols and an empty square (a winning threat), before anything else. You may wish to change this to have the computer check to see if it has a winning move first, then looking to see if the human needs blocking.

Program for Tic-Tac-Toe

```
10   X=0:Y=0:Z=0
20   CLS:PRINT:PRINT"TIC-TAC-TOE":PRI
NT
```

225

```
30    PRINT:PRINT
40    PRINT "THE BOARD IS NUMBERED:"
50    FOR I=1 TO 9:A(I)=0:NEXTI
60    PRINT "        1   2   3"
70    PRINT "        4   5   6"
80    PRINT "        7   8   9"
90   PRINT:PRINT
100    PRINT:PRINT"YOU ARE  O  AND I A
M  X"
110  INPUT "WHO GOES FIRST (1=YOU  2=
COMPUTER)";L:CLS
120 FOR G=0 TO 41:SET(42,G):SET(84,G
):NEXT G
130 FOR H=0 TO 127:SET(H,13):SET(H,2
6):NEXT H
140 IF L=1 THEN 380
150 REM *COMPUTER'S TURN
160 N=2
170 SUM=0:FOR X=1 TO 9:SUM=SUM+A(X):
NEXT X
180 IF SUM=0 THEN M=5:GOTO 370
190 IF SUM=4 AND A(5)=0 THEN M=5:GOT
O 370
200 IF SUM=4 AND A(1)=0 THEN M=1:GOT
O 370
210 RESTORE
220 FOR X=1 TO 8:READ A,B,C:SUM=A(A)
+A(B)+A(C):IF SUM=8 GOTO 250ELSE NEX
T X
230 RESTORE:FOR X=1 TO 8:READ A,B,C:
SUM=A(A)+A(B)+A(C):IF SUM=20 THEN 25
0ELSE NEXT X
240 GOTO 280
250 IF A(A)=0 THEN M=A:GOTO 370
260 IF A(B)=0 THEN M=B:GOTO 370
270 M=C:GOTO 370
280 RESTORE:FOR X=1 TO 8:READ A,B,C:
SUM=A+B+C:IF SUM=10:GOTO 340
290 NEXT X
300 RESTORE:FOR X=1 TO 8:READ A,B,C:
SUM=A+B+C:IF SUM=0 GOTO 340
310 NEXT X
320 C=RND(9):IF A(C)=0 THEN M=C:GOTO
 370
```

226

```
330 GOTO 320
340 IF A(A)=0 THEN M=A:GOTO 370
350 IF A(B)=0 THEN M=B:GOTO 370
360 M=C:GOTO 370
370 A(M)=10:PRINT@896,"THE COMPUTER
MOVES TO:";:GOTO 430
380 REM* HUMAN'S TURN
390 N=1
400 PRINT@896,"WHERE DO YOU MOVE";:I
NPUT M
410 IF M>9 OR A(M)<>0 THEN PRINT@896
,STRING$(30," ");:GOTO 400
420 A(M)=4
430 FOR M1=1 TO 9
440   IF M=1 THEN R=15:S=1
450   IF M=2 THEN R=56:S=1
460   IF M=3 THEN R=98:S=1
470   IF M=4 THEN R=15:S=14
480   IF M=5 THEN R=56:S=14
490   IF M=6 THEN R=98:S=14
500   IF M=7 THEN R=15:S=27
510   IF M=8 THEN R=56:S=27
520   IF M=9 THEN R=98:S=27
530   IF A(M)=0 GOTO 560
540   GOTO 560
550 NEXT M1
560   IF N=1 GOTO 640
570   E=R:F=S:FOR Q=1 TO 12
580   SET (E,F):E=E+1:F=F+1
590   NEXT Q
600   E=R+10:F=S:FOR Q=1 TO 12
610   SET (E,F):E=E-1:F=F+1
620   NEXT Q
630 GOTO 780
640   E=R:F=S:FOR Q=1 TO 11
650   SET(E,F):E=E+1
660   NEXT Q
670   FOR Q=1 TO 11
680   SET(E,F):F=F+1
690   NEXT Q
700   FOR Q=1 TO 11
710   SET(E,F):E=E-1
720   NEXT Q
730   FOR Q=1 TO 11
```

```
740    SET(E,F):F=F-1
750    NEXT Q
760 GOTO 780
770 DATA 1,2,3,4,5,6,7,8,9,1,4,7,2,5
,8,3,6,9,1,5,9,3,5,7
780 RESTORE:FOR X=1 TO 8:READ A,B,C:
SUM=A(A)+A(B)+A(C)
790 IF SUM=12 THEN 860:REM* HUMAN WI
NS
800 IF SUM=30 THEN 890:REM* COMPUTER
 WINS
810 NEXT X
820 FOR X=1 TO 9:IF A(X)=0 GOTO 830E
LSE NEXT X:GOTO 920:REM* DRAW
830 PRINT@896,STRING$(30," ");
840 IF N=2 THEN N=1:GOTO 380
850 N=2:GOTO 150
860 PRINT@896,STRING$(30," ");
870 PRINT@896,"YOU WIN!!"
880 GOTO 940
890 PRINT@896,STRING$(30," ");
900 PRINT@896,"YOU LOSE!!"
910 GOTO 940
920 PRINT@896,STRING$(30," ");
930 PRINT@896,"IT'S A DRAW!!";
940 FOR X=1 TO 1000:NEXT X
950 CLS:INPUT "ANOTHER GAME (YES/NO)
";A$
960 IF A$="Y" OR A$="YES" THEN 10
970 END
```

HORSE

Remarks

Here's a game that even has financial potential! I actually field-tested this program as a money making booth for an organization at a local carnival, offering small prizes to the winners. Needless to say (or I wouldn't mention it), we made big bucks in our spare time. The game is entirely self-contained from start to finish. The horses will run the race randomly, with no favorites. One final note: if you press the M key instead of the space bar to start a race, one of the horses will die at random during the race! Be careful: people tend to be suspicious of this sort of thing.

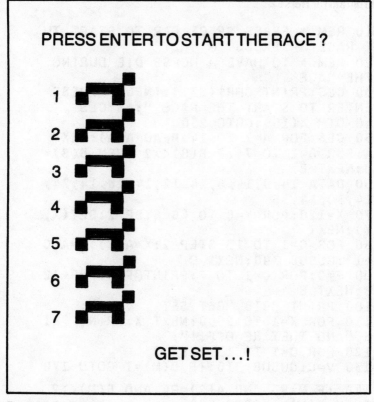

Fig. 6-19. Sample run.

Variables

A(X) — Contains X position of horse #X— A(X+1) is the Y
position of horse #X

C — Whether current horse moves or not

B(M)— Whether horse #M is dead or not

W — Whether current horse advances

M — Winning horse at end of race

Suggested Variations

1) You might wish to shorten the length of the track. I had it
this long purely for the dramatic value.

2) Given the routine for "killing" a horse, you might want to
have them doing all sorts of crazy things during the race. I'll leave
this to your imagination.

229

Program for Horse

```
10 REM * PRESS SPACE BAR TO START TH
E RACE OR PRESS 'M' KEY
20 REM * TO HAVE A HORSE DIE DURING
THE RACE
30 CLS:PRINT CHR$(23);:INPUT "PRESS
ENTER TO START THE RACE ";A$:CLS
40 DIM A(15):GOTO 250
50 CLS:FOR A=1 TO 14:READ A(A):NEXT
A:FOR B=1 TO 7:IF B(B)<>2 THEN B(B)=
0:NEXT B
60 DATA 14,0,14,6,14,12,14,18,14,24,
14,30,14,36
70 X=120:FOR Y=0 TO 40 STEP 2:SET(X,
Y):NEXT Y
80 FOR C=1 TO 13 STEP 2:X=A(C):Y=A(C
+1):GOSUB 390:NEXT C
90 F=0:FOR C=1 TO 7:PRINT@F,C:F=F+12
8:NEXT C
100 PRINT @916,"GET SET . . .!";
110 FOR X=1 TO 2500:NEXT X:PRINT @91
6,"AND THEY'RE OFF!!";
120 FOR C=1 TO 13 STEP 2
130 V=C:GOSUB 310:IF B(M)=1 GOTO 170

140 IF M=R3 AND A(C)=R4 AND B(M)<>2
THEN B(M)=1:GOTO 520
150 IF B(M)=1 GOTO 170
160 W=RND(2):IF W=2 THEN A(C)=A(C)+3

170 NEXT C
180 FOR V=1 TO 13 STEP 2:GOSUB 310:X
=A(V):Y=A(V+1):IF B(M)=1 GOTO 190ELS
E GOSUB 390
190 NEXT V
200 GOTO 120
210 FOR R=60 TO 828 STEP 64:PRINT@R,
"*";:NEXT R
220 PRINT@916,"THE RACE IS OVER!!!";
:FOR X=1 TO 1000:NEXT X
230 FOR X=1 TO 1000:NEXT X
240 CLS:FOR P=1 TO 250:NEXT P
250 CLS:PRINT CHR$(23);"W I N N E R
:":PRINT "H O R S E  # ";M
```

```
260 RESTORE
270 E$=INKEY$
280 IF E$=" " THEN CLEAR:DIM A(15):G
OTO 50
290 IF E$="M" THEN CLEAR:DIM A(15):G
OTO 470
300 FOR P=1 TO 250:NEXT P:GOTO 240
310 IF V=1 THEN M=1
320 IF V=3 THEN M=2
330 IF V=5 THEN M=3
340 IF V=7 THEN M=4
350 IF V=9 THEN M=5
360 IF V=11 THEN M=6
370 IF V=13 THEN M=7
380 RETURN
390 SET(X,Y):SET(X-1,Y)
400 FOR Z=X-7 TO X-1:SET(Z,Y+1):NEXT
 Z
410 SET(X-8,Y+2):SET(X-1,Y+2)
420 RESET(X-3,Y):RESET(X-4,Y)
430 RESET(X-8,Y+1):RESET(X-9,Y+1):RE
SET(X-10,Y+1)
440 RESET(X-4,Y+2)
450 IF X>=120 GOSUB 310:GOTO 210
460 RETURN
470 R3=RND(7):R4=RND(50)+14
480 R=14
490 IF R4=R GOTO 510
500 R=R+3:IF R>70 GOTO 470ELSE GOTO
490
510 GOTO 50
520 X=A(C):Y=A(C+1)
530 RESET(X,Y):RESET(X-1,Y)
540 FOR B5=X-8 TO X:RESET(B5,Y+1):NE
XT B5
550 FOR B5=X-9 TO X:RESET(B5,Y+2):NE
XT B5
560 SET(X-2,Y+1):SET(X-9,Y+1)
570 FOR G=X-8 TO X-2:SET(G,Y+2):NEXT
 G
580 SET(X,Y+3):SET(X-1,Y+3)
590 GOTO 150
```

Appendix A
Internal Codes for BASIC Keywords

KEYWORD	DECIMAL CODE	HEX CODE
FOR	129	81
RESET	130	82
SET	131	83
CLS	132	84
CMD	133	85
RANDOM	134	86
NEXT	135	87
DATA	136	88
INPUT	137	89
DIM	138	8A
READ	139	8B
LET	140	8C
GOTO	141	8D
RUN	142	8E
IF	143	8F
RESTORE	144	90
GOSUB	145	91
RETURN	146	92
REM	147	93
STOP	148	94
ELSE	149	95
TRON	150	96
TROFF	151	97

KEYWORD	DECIMAL CODE	HEX CODE
DEFSTR	152	98
DEFINT	153	99
DEFSNG	154	9A
DEFDBL	155	9B
LINE	156	9C
EDIT	157	9D
ERROR	158	9E
RESUME	159	9F
OUT	160	AO
ON	161	A1
OPEN	162	A2
FIELD	163	A3
GET	164	A4
PUT	165	A5
CLOSE	166	A6
LOAD	167	A7
MERGE	168	A8
NAME	169	A9
KILL	170	AA
LSET	171	AB
RSET	172	AC
SAVE	173	AD
SYSTEM	174	AE
LPRINT	175	AF
DEF	176	BO
POKE	177	B1
PRINT	178	B2
CONT	179	B3
LIST	180	B4
LLIST	181	B5
DELETE	182	B6
AUTO	183	B7
CLEAR	184	B8
CLOAD	185	B9
CSAVE	186	BA
NEW	187	BB
TAB	188	BC
TO	189	BD
FN	190	BE
USING	191	BF
VARPTR	192	CO

KEYWORD	DECIMAL CODE	HEX CODE
USR	193	C1
ERL	194	C2
ERR	195	C3
STRING$	196	C4
INSTR	197	C5
POINT	198	C6
TIME$	199	C7
MEM	200	C8
INKEY$	201	C9
THEN	202	CA
NOT	203	CB
STEP	204	CC
+	205	CD
–	206	CE
*	207	CF
/	208	DO
↑	209	D1
AND	210	D2
OR	211	D3
>	212	D4
=	213	D5
<	214	D6
SGN	215	D7
INT	216	D8
ABS	217	D9
FRE	218	DA
INP	219	DB
POS	220	DC
SQR	221	DD
RND	222	DE
LOG	223	DF
EXP	224	EO
COS	225	E1
SIN	226	E2
TAN	227	E3
ATN	228	E4
PEEK	229	E5
CVI	230	E6
CVS	231	E7
CVD	232	E8
EOF	233	E9

KEYWORD	DECIMAL CODE	HEX CODE
LOC	234	EA
LOF	235	EB
MKI$	236	EC
MKS$	237	ED
MKD$	238	EE
CINT	239	EF
CSNG	240	FO
CDBL	241	F1
FIX	242	F2
LEN	243	F3
STR$	244	F4
VAL	245	F5
ASC	246	F6
CHR$	247	F7
LEFT$	248	F8
RIGHT$	249	F9
MID$	250	FA

Appendix B
ASCII Codes

DEC. CODE	HEX CODE	MEANING
0-7	00-07	None
8	08	Backspace and erase current character
9	09	None
10	0A	Line feed with carriage return
11	OB	Move carriage to top of form
12	OC	Move carriage to top of form
13	OD	Line feed with carriage return
14	OE	Turns on cursor
15	OF	Turns off cursor
16-22	10-16	None
23	17	Converts video display to 32 characters/line mode
24	18	Backspace cursor
25	19	Advance cursor forward
26	1A	Downward linefeed
27	1B	Upward linefeed
28	1C	Return cursor to home position, converts video display to 64 character/ line mode

DEC. CODE	HEX CODE	MEANING
29	1D	Move cursor to beginning of line
30	1E	Erase to end of current line
31	1F	Clear to the end of the frame
32	20	Space
33	21	!
34	22	"
35	23	#
36	24	$
37	25	%
38	26	&
39	27	'
40	28	(
41	29	)
42	2A	*
43	2B	+
44	2C	,
45	2D	-
46	2E	.
47	2F	/
48	30	0
49	31	1
50	32	2
51	33	3
52	34	4
53	35	5
54	36	6
55	37	7
56	38	8
57	39	9
58	3A	:
59	3B	;
60	3C	<
61	3D	=
62	3E	>
63	3F	?
64	40	@
65	41	A
66	42	B

DEC. CODE	HEX CODE	MEANING
67	43	C
68	44	D
69	45	E
70	46	F
71	47	G
72	48	H
73	49	I
74	4A	J
75	4B	K
76	4C	L
77	4D	M
78	4E	N
79	4F	O
80	50	P
81	51	Q
82	52	R
83	53	S
84	54	T
85	55	U
86	56	V
87	57	W
88	58	X
89	59	Y
90	5A	Z
91	5B	Up arrow
92	5C	Down arrow
93	5D	Left arrow
94	5E	Right arrow
95	5F	-(underline cursor)
96	60	@
97	61	a
98	62	b
99	63	c
100	64	d
101	65	e
102	66	f
103	67	g
104	68	h
105	69	i
106	6A	j
107	6B	k

DEC. CODE	HEX CODE	MEANING
108	6C	l
109	6D	m
110	6E	n
111	6F	o
112	70	p
113	71	q
114	72	r
115	73	s
116	74	t
117	75	u
118	76	v
119	77	u
120	78	v
121	79	w
122	7A	x
123	7B	y
124	7C	z

DEC. CODE	HEX CODE	MEANING
192	C0	Tab 0 spaces
193	C1	Tab 1 space
194	C2	Tab 2 spaces
195	C3	Tab 3 spaces
196	C4	Tab 4 spaces
197	C5	Tab 5 spaces
198	C6	Tab 6 spaces
199	C7	Tab 7 spaces
200	C8	Tab 8 spaces
201	C9	Tab 9 spaces
202	CA	Tab 10 spaces
203	CB	Tab 11 spaces
204	CC	Tab 12 spaces
205	CD	Tab 13 spaces
206	CE	Tab 14 spaces
207	CF	Tab 15 spaces
208	D0	Tab 16 spaces
209	D1	Tab 17 spaces
210	D2	Tab 18 spaces
211	D3	Tab 19 spaces
212	D4	Tab 20 spaces
213	D5	Tab 21 spaces
214	D6	Tab 22 spaces

DEC. CODE	HEX CODE	MEANING
215	D7	Tab 23 spaces
216	D8	Tab 24 spaces
217	D9	Tab 25 spaces
218	DA	Tab 26 spaces
219	DB	Tab 27 spaces
220	DC	Tab 28 spaces
221	DD	Tab 29 spaces
222	DE	Tab 30 spaces
223	DF	Tab 31 spaces
224	EO	Tab 32 spaces
225	E1	Tab 33 spaces
226	E2	Tab 34 spaces
227	E3	Tab 35 spaces
228	E4	Tab 36 spaces
229	E5	Tab 37 spaces
230	E6	Tab 38 spaces
231	E7	Tab 39 spaces
232	E8	Tab 40 spaces
233	E9	Tab 41 spaces
234	EA	Tab 42 spaces
235	EB	Tab 43 spaces
236	EC	Tab 44 spaces
237	ED	Tab 45 spaces
238	EE	Tab 46 spaces
239	EF	Tab 47 spaces
240	FO	Tab 48 spaces
241	F1	Tab 49 spaces
242	F2	Tab 50 spaces
243	F3	Tab 51 spaces
244	F4	Tab 52 spaces
245	F5	Tab 53 spaces
246	F6	Tab 54 spaces
247	F7	Tab 55 spaces
248	F8	Tab 56 spaces
249	F9	Tab 57 spaces
250	FA	Tab 58 spaces
251	FB	Tab 59 spaces
252	FC	Tab 60 spaces
253	FD	Tab 61 spaces
254	FE	Tab 62 spaces
255	FF	Tab 63 spaces

Appendix C
Numeric Base Equivalents

DECIMAL	BINARY	HEXADECIMAL	OCTAL
0	00000000	00	000
1	00000001	01	001
2	00000010	02	002
3	00000011	03	003
4	00000100	04	004
5	00000101	05	005
6	00000110	06	006
7	00000111	07	007
8	00001000	08	010
9	00001001	09	011
10	00001010	0A	012
11	00001011	0B	013
12	00001100	0C	014
13	00001101	0D	015
14	00001110	0E	016
15	00001111	0F	017
16	00010000	10	020
17	00010001	11	021
18	00010010	12	022
19	00010011	13	023
20	00010100	14	024
21	00010101	15	025
22	00010110	16	026

DECIMAL	BINARY	HEXADECIMAL	OCTAL
23	00010111	17	027
24	00011000	18	030
25	00011001	19	031
26	00011010	1A	032
27	00011011	1B	033
28	00011100	1C	034
29	00011101	1D	035
30	00011110	1E	036
31	00011111	1F	037
32	00100000	20	040
33	00100001	21	041
34	00100010	22	042
35	00100011	23	043
36	00100100	24	044
37	00100101	25	045
38	00100110	26	046
39	00100111	27	047
40	00101000	28	050
41	00101001	29	051
42	00101010	2A	052
43	00101011	2B	053
44	00101100	2C	054
45	00101101	2D	055
46	00101110	2E	056
47	00101111	2F	057
48	00110000	30	060
49	00110001	31	061
50	00110010	32	062
51	00110011	33	063
52	00110100	34	064
53	00110101	35	065
54	00110110	36	066
55	00110111	37	067
56	00111000	38	070
57	00111001	39	071
58	00111010	3A	072
59	00111011	3B	073
60	00111100	3C	074
61	00111101	3D	075
62	00111110	3E	076
63	00111111	3F	077

DECIMAL	BINARY	HEXADECIMAL	OCTAL
64	01000000	40	100
65	01000001	41	101
66	01000010	42	102
67	01000011	43	103
68	01000100	44	104
69	01000101	45	105
70	01000110	46	106
71	01000111	47	107
72	01001000	48	110
73	01001001	49	111
74	01001010	4A	112
75	01001011	4B	113
76	01001100	4C	114
77	01001101	4D	115
78	01001110	4E	116
79	01001111	4F	117
80	01010000	50	120
81	01010001	51	121
82	01010010	52	122
83	01010011	53	123
84	01010100	54	124
85	01010101	55	125
86	01010110	56	126
87	01010111	57	127
88	01011000	58	130
89	01011001	59	131
90	01011010	5A	132
91	01011011	5B	133
92	01011100	5C	134
93	01011101	5D	135
94	01011110	5E	136
95	01011111	5F	137
96	01100000	60	140
97	01100001	61	141
98	01100010	62	142
99	01100011	63	143
100	01100100	64	144
101	01100101	65	145
102	01100110	66	146
103	01100111	67	147
104	01101000	68	150

DECIMAL	BINARY	HEXADECIMAL	OCTAL
105	01101001	69	151
106	01101010	6A	152
107	01101011	6B	153
108	01101100	6C	154
109	01101101	6D	155
110	01101110	6E	156
111	01101111	6F	157
112	01110000	70	160
113	01110001	71	161
114	01110010	72	162
115	01110011	73	163
116	01110100	74	164
117	01110101	75	165
118	01110110	76	166
119	01110111	77	167
120	01111000	78	170
121	01111001	79	171
122	01111010	7A	172
123	01111011	7B	173
124	01111100	7C	174
125	01111101	7D	175
126	01111110	7E	176
127	01111111	7F	177
128	10000000	80	200
129	10000001	81	201
130	10000010	82	202
I31	10000011	83	203
132	10000100	84	204
133	10000101	85	205
134	10000110	86	206
135	10000111	87	207
136	10001000	88	210
137	10001001	89	211
138	10001010	8A	212
139	10001011	8B	213
140	10001100	8C	214
141	10001101	8D	215
142	10001110	8E	216
143	10001111	8F	217
144	10010000	90	220
145	10010001	91	221

DECIMAL	BINARY	HEXADECIMAL	OCTAL
146	10010010	92	222
147	10010011	93	223
148	10010100	94	224
149	10010101	95	225
150	10010110	96	226
151	10010111	97	227
152	10011000	98	230
153	10011001	99	231
154	10011010	9A	232
155	10011011	9B	233
156	10011100	9C	234
157	10011101	9D	235
158	10011110	9E	236
159	10011111	9F	237
160	10100000	A0	240
161	10100001	A1	241
162	10100010	A2	242
163	10100011	A3	243
164	10100100	A4	244
165	10100101	A5	245
166	10100110	A6	246
167	10100111	A7	247
168	10101000	A8	250
169	10101001	A9	251
170	10101010	AA	252
171	10101011	AB	253
172	10101100	AC	254
173	10101101	AD	255
174	10101110	AE	256
175	10101111	AF	257
176	10110000	BO	260
177	10110001	B1	261
178	10110010	B2	262
179	10110011	B3	263
180	10110100	B4	264
181	10110101	B5	265
182	10110110	B6	266
183	10110111	B7	267
184	10111000	B8	270
185	10111001	B9	271
186	10111010	BA	272

DECIMAL	BINARY	HEXADECIMAL	OCTAL
187	10111011	BB	273
188	10111100	BC	274
189	10111101	BD	275
190	10111110	BE	276
191	10111111	BF	277
192	11000000	C0	300
193	11000001	C1	301
194	11000010	C2	302
195	11000011	C3	303
196	11000100	C4	304
197	11000101	C5	305
198	11000110	C6	306
199	11000111	C7	307
200	11001000	C8	310
201	11001001	C9	311
202	11001010	CA	312
203	11001011	CB	313
204	11001100	CC	314
205	11001101	CD	315
206	11001110	CE	316
207	11001111	CF	317
208	11010000	D0	320
209	11010001	D1	321
210	11010010	D2	322
211	11010011	D3	323
212	11010100	D4	324
213	11010101	D5	325
214	11010110	D6	326
215	11010111	D7	327
216	11011000	D8	330
217	11011001	D9	331
218	11011010	DA	332
219	11011011	DB	333
220	11011100	DC	334
221	11011101	DD	335
222	11011110	DE	336
223	11011111	DF	337
224	11100000	E0	340
225	11100001	E1	341
226	11100010	E2	342
227	11100011	E3	343

DECIMAL	BINARY	HEXADECIMAL	OCTAL
228	11100100	E4	344
229	11100101	E5	345
230	11100110	E6	346
231	11100111	E7	347
232	11101000	E8	350
233	11101001	E9	351
234	11101010	EA	352
235	11101011	EB	353
236	11101100	EC	354
237	11101101	ED	355
238	11101110	EE	356
239	11101111	EF	357
240	11110000	F0	360
241	11110001	F1	361
242	11110010	F2	362
243	11110011	F3	363
244	11110100	F4	364
245	11110101	F5	365
246	11110110	F6	366
247	11110111	F7	367
248	11111000	F8	370
249	11111001	F9	371
250	11111010	FA	372
251	11111011	FB	373
252	11111100	FC	374
253	11111101	FD	375
254	11111110	FE	376
255	11111111	FF	377

Appendix D
Illegal Level II BASIC Variable Names

@	ABS	AND	ASC
ATN	AUTO	CDBL	CHR$
CINT	CLEAR	CLOCK	CLOSE
CLS	CMD	CONT	COS
CSNG	CVD	CVI	CVS
DATA	DEFDBL	DEFFN	DEFINT
DEFSNG	DEFUSR	DEFSTR	DELETE
DIM	EDIT	ELSE	END
EOF	ERL	ERR	ERROR
EXP	FIELD	FIX	FN
FOR	FORMAT	FRE	FREE
GET	GOSUB	GOTO	IF
INKEY$	INP	INPUT	INSTR
INT	KILL	LEFT$	LET
LSET	LEN	LINE	LIST
LOAD	LOC	LOF	LOG
MEM	MERGE	MID$	MKD$
MKI$	MKS$	NAME	NEW
NEXT	NOT	ON	OPEN
OR	OUT	PEEK	POINT
POKE	POS	POSN	PRINT
PUT	RANDOM	READ	REM
RENAME	RESET	RESTORE	RESUME
RETURN	RIGHT$	RND	RSET
SAVE	SET	SGN	SIN
SQR	STEP	STOP	STRING$
STR$	TAB	TAN	THEN
TIME$	TO	TROFF	TRON
USING	USR	VAL	VARPTR
VERIFY			

Index